'Starting from a revisited concept of the Florida 'creative class', the book analyses location preferences of creative industries workers and highly qualified human resources in Europe (or North Europe) for urban development and spatial planning in large European cities.' — *Francesco Capone, PhD, University of Florence, Italy.*

'This book presents a fascinating collection of empirical insights into the residential preferences of knowledge workers and the role of amenities for their locational choices. It thereby fosters an empirically grounded debate on agglomeration advantages in knowledge societies.' — *Prof. Dr. Ilse Helbrecht, Humboldt University, Germany.*

'Over the past decades, scholars have forcefully debated whether skilled workers are attracted to cities because of job opportunities or amenities. This landmark book marks the latest developments in research on skills and cities, with a special emphasis on stated and revealed locational preferences of highly-educated workers and their implications for urban development. This impressive volume contains a large amount of empirical chapters by prominent scholars in the field, and provides an excellent and balanced view on one of the hottest and highly-debated topics in urban and economic geography in the last decades.' — *Ron Boschma, Utrecht University, the Netherlands; Lund University, Sweden.*

Skills and Cities

Creative industries have become fundamental in signalling the economic well-being of cities and urban regions. Workers who are attracted to the sector tend to have strong preferences when it comes to the neighbourhoods they want to live in, with factors such as job availability and urban amenities playing a large part in their decision.

Skills and Cities analyses these factors and looks at the implications for urban and regional policy across a range of European cities. Drawing conclusions from the Netherlands and Scandinavian cities Copenhagen and Helsinki, this book sheds new light on the debate about the importance of jobs and urban amenities for attracting high-skilled employees. This edited collection brings together international literature and individual residential experiences from different cities, presenting policy simulations and highlighting the differences between urban and suburban groups. Subsequent chapters discuss the location preference and settlement process of international migrants and students in an attempt to understand what it is that attracts highly skilled workers to a particular area. This book concludes by expertly drawing together the key issues surrounding the residential behaviour of highly educated workers and students.

This collection will be of interest to researchers and policy makers in urban planning, as well as postgraduate students researching housing preferences.

Sako Musterd is Professor of Urban Geography at the Centre for Urban Studies of the University of Amsterdam, the Netherlands.

Marco Bontje is Assistant Professor at the Centre for Urban Studies of the University of Amsterdam, the Netherlands.

Jan Rouwendal is Professor at the Department of Spatial Economics of VU University of Amsterdam, the Netherlands.

Regions and Cities

Series Editor in Chief
Susan M. Christopherson, *Cornell University, USA*

Editors
Maryann Feldman, *University of Georgia, USA*
Gernot Grabher, *HafenCity University Hamburg, Germany*
Ron Martin, *University of Cambridge, UK*
Martin Perry, *Massey University, New Zealand*
Kieran P. Donaghy, *Cornell University, USA*

In today's globalised, knowledge-driven and networked world, regions and cities have assumed heightened significance as the interconnected nodes of economic, social and cultural production, and as sites of new modes of economic and territorial governance and policy experimentation. This book series brings together incisive and critically engaged international and interdisciplinary research on this resurgence of regions and cities, and should be of interest to geographers, economists, sociologists, political scientists and cultural scholars, as well as to policy-makers involved in regional and urban development.

For more information on the Regional Studies Association visit www.regional studies.org

There is a **30% discount** available to RSA members on books in the *Regions and Cities series*, and other subject related Taylor and Francis books and e-books including Routledge titles. To order just e-mail alex.robinson@tandf.co.uk, or phone on +44 (0) 20 7017 6924 and declare your RSA membership. You can also visit www.routledge.com and use the discount code: **RSA0901**

Skills and Cities

Implications of location preferences
of highly educated workers for spatial
development of metropolitan areas

**Edited by Sako Musterd, Marco Bontje
and Jan Rouwendal**

LONDON AND NEW YORK

First published 2016 by Routledge

2 Park Square, Milton Park, Abingdon, Oxfordshire OX14 4RN

52 Vanderbilt Avenue, New York, NY 10017

Routledge is an imprint of the Taylor & Francis Group, an informa business

First issued in paperback 2019

British Library Cataloguing in Publication Data
A catalogue record for this book is available from the British Library

Library of Congress Cataloging in Publication Data
Names: Musterd, Sako, editor. | Bontje, Marco Arjan, editor. |
    Rouwendal, Jan, 1959- editor.
Title: Skills and cities : implications of location preferences of highly educated
    workers for spatial development of metropolitan areas / edited by Sako
    Musterd, Marco Bontje and Jan Rouwendal.
Description: Abingdon, Oxon ; New York, NY : Routledge, 2016. |
    Includes bibliographical references and index.
Identifiers: LCCN 2015039746| ISBN 9781138812239 (hardback : alk. paper) |
    ISBN 9781315748924 (ebook : alk. paper)
Subjects: LCSH: Urban economics. | Space in economics. | Skilled labor. |
    Intellectual capital. | Creative industries. | Industrial location.
Classification: LCC HT321 .S5645 2016 | DDC 330.9173/2—dc23
LC record available at http://lccn.loc.gov/2015039746

ISBN: 978-1-138-81223-9 (hbk)
ISBN: 978-0-367-87090-4 (pbk)

Typeset in Times New Roman
by Swales & Willis Ltd, Exeter, Devon, UK

Contents

Figures

Tables

Contributors

Marco Bontje, Department of Geography, Planning and International Development Studies, Centre for Urban Studies, Section Urban Geography, University of Amsterdam.

Willem R. Boterman, Department of Geography, Planning and International Development Studies, Centre for Urban Studies, Section Urban Geography, University of Amsterdam.

Jasper Dekkers, Department of Spatial Economics and Spatial Information Laboratory, Faculty of Economics and Business Administration, VU University, Amsterdam.

Mark Van Duijn, Department of Economic Geography, Faculty of Spatial Sciences, University of Groningen.

Or Levkovich, Department of Spatial Economics, Faculty of Economics and Business Administration, VU University, Amsterdam.

Jan Möhlmann, Department of Spatial Economics, Faculty of Economics and Business Administration, VU University, Amsterdam; and CPB, Netherlands Bureau for Economic Policy Analysis, The Hague.

Ismir Mulalic, Department of Transport, DTU, Technical University of Denmark, Lyngby, Denmark.

Sako Musterd, Department of Geography, Planning and International Development Studies, Centre for Urban Studies, Section Urban Geography, University of Amsterdam.

Jan Rouwendal, Department of Spatial Economics, Faculty of Economics and Business Administration, VU University, Amsterdam.

Carla Sá, Department of Economics and NIPE, Universidade do Minho, Braga, Portugal.

Bart Sleutjes, Department of Geography, Planning and International Development Studies, Centre for Urban Studies, Section Urban Geography, University of Amsterdam; and NIDI, Netherlands Interdisciplinary Demographic Institute, The Hague.

Acknowledgements

This book is based on a research project called Higher Educated Location Preferences (HELP) that was part of a larger research programme, Urban Regions in the Delta (URD). This programme was embedded in an even broader 'knowledge initiative' called Connecting Sustainable Cities (in Dutch: VERDUS), which aims to bridge the gap between scientists and urban professionals. The Dutch research council (NWO), Platform 31, and several Dutch government ministries were involved as the main funding institutions. We are grateful for their willingness to support the research underlying this volume. We also wish to thank several other organisations that co-funded our research or otherwise provided much support. These were: the Netherlands Environmental Assessment Agency (PBL), the Municipality of Amsterdam, and the Universities of Helsinki and Copenhagen. We also much appreciated the comments and support provided by the members of the Advisory Board of the research project and of other societal partners in the project.

Members of the Advisory Board

Kees Dignum	Dienst Wonen, Zorg en Samenleven gemeente Amsterdam
Kirsty Gilsing	Samenwerkingsverband Regio Eindhoven
Julian Jansen	Dienst Ruimtelijke Ordening, gemeente Amsterdam
Jan Klinkenberg	Platform 31/URD/VERDUS
Menno Moen	Sector Gebiedsontwikkeling, Gemeente Eindhoven
Linco Nieuwenhuyzen	Brainport Development
Eva Olde Monnikhof	Amsterdam Economic Board
Otto Raspe	Planbureau voor de Leefomgeving
Risto Rautava	City Board, City of Helsinki (Chair)
Ossi Savolainen	Uusimaa Region
Jeroen Slot	Dienst Onderzoek en Statistiek, gemeente Amsterdam
Paul Tholenaars	Woonbedrijf Eindhoven

Other societal partners

Sjoerd Roodenburg	NUFFIC
David van Traa	Expat Center Amsterdam
Ilona Vierveijzer	Dienst Onderzoek en Statistiek, gemeente Amsterdam
Martijn van Vliet	Dienst Economische Zaken, gemeente Amsterdam
Rijk van Walsem	Netwerk Kennissteden

Sako Musterd, Marco Bontje and Jan Rouwendal

Amsterdam, October 2015

Part I

1 Skills and cities

An introductory framework

Sako Musterd, Marco Bontje and Jan Rouwendal

Skills and cities

Interest in the residential preferences of those who are qualified for and economically active in creative industries and knowledge-intensive industries has recently been increasing. The human capital of these workers is seen as an important economic asset for cities and urban regions. Knowledge of their households' locational preferences may enable the development of policy instruments by means of which a labour force with the right skills for today's urban economies can be attracted to or retained in specific places. Since qualified labour is, next to capital and land, one of the key conditions for establishing economic activity, knowledge about locational preferences seems to open up new possibilities for place-based economic policies. However, what looks like a simple logic in reality turns out to be much more complicated and causing much debate in which polarized ideas are competing for attention. A key issue in that debate is the 'order of things'. One idea is that it is essential to attract qualified labour in the first place, the logic being that when a city succeeds in doing that, economic activity will follow. Here the key question is: how can qualified *labour* be attracted? A second idea is that it is essential to attract and develop firms that will subsequently offer job opportunities, leading to the attraction of employees. The question then is: how can these *firms* be attracted?

As will become clear in this volume, such views are closely related to each other and insights from both perspectives could be of mutual benefit. However, some academics and practitioners opt for only one interpretation and advocate a single view that is then 'sold' as a package aimed at 'saving the city'. In one of the favourite packages the assumption is that today's cities are in fact consumer cities rather than producer cities. These cities will be attractive to people who are active in creative and knowledge-intensive industries; that is, if certain conditions are met. The logical next step is to ensure that the required conditions will be met. In the eyes of the believer, this implies that a city should have the right set of amenities, with attractive public space, a wide range of services, green spaces, strong institutions for higher education, cultural amenities, a good climate and a well-functioning and attractive housing market. This will help to attract a qualified labour force and will be the key to a flourishing and growing local urban economy (Clark *et al.* 2002; Florida 2002, 2004). Supporters of the importance of amenities and consumer-city ideas do not all stress the same sorts of amenities as being relevant; although they do seem to agree that the availability of good facilities for higher education is essential. It is our observation that the matter of higher education receives wide support because it is also seen as a classic means to ensure that enough highly skilled labour can be attracted to a city that as yet has no intervention from firms. Moreover, firms may consider the presence of higher education institutions before they make decisions about location. However, advocates of the consumer city do not promote the other conditions or amenities in the same way. Glaeser *et al.* (2001) and Glaeser and Gotlieb (2006) present their views on the importance of amenities in a balanced way and see a good package of amenities in general as an opportunity for trade-off with labour costs related to jobs. They also explicitly refer to climate conditions as essential amenities; Florida stresses factors like 'openness to diversity' and 'tolerance', while Clark *et al.* focus on cultural amenities, in particular.

Unsurprisingly, the above-mentioned perspective has also given rise to significant criticism and debate. An essential element of the debate is the question whether cities, even those that are known for their superb quality of life and a great set of amenities and urban qualities in general, will be able to attract the creative and knowledge workers on that basis and will subsequently be able to attract or develop economic activity. An alternative approach that seems to receive substantial support from academics states that cities should first have economic activity and firms, in place. These firms will attract employees because they offer jobs that fit them, which is a vital condition for employees to settle somewhere. In a paper that reports a detailed empirical study of migrating engineers, and where the aim was to investigate to what extent these engineers were driven by amenities or by other factors, Scott (2010) concludes that 'at least for the case of engineers, migrants of working age are drawn primarily to locations whose economic structure and job opportunities correspond closely to their particular professional expertise, and that amenities have virtually no impact on these relationships' (p. 60). On the basis of a large-scale comparative research project in thirteen European urban regions, in which reasons for settling in a specific place were investigated for those who eventually became employed in creative and knowledge-intensive industries, the researchers came to a similar conclusion. While they explicitly included a wide range of amenity variables in their research, next to employment and personal network-related variables, the results of various surveys and in-depth interviews showed that availability of jobs was a far more important factor than the broad array of amenities; in fact, amenities were hardly mentioned as a factor. If job opportunities were not the reason to move, personal networks and the presence of institutions for higher education were mentioned as important. Other amenities played a secondary role, at best, in the decision to settle somewhere (see Musterd and Murie 2010). Further support for the view that job opportunities have priority in choice-of-location behaviour is provided by Storper and Manville (2006), Hansen and Niedomysl (2009), Storper and Scott (2009), and others. From this perspective it is thus more important to understand the conditions under which firms settle somewhere or expand. These firms may see value in the presence of good amenities precisely because this may play a role as a trade-off factor in relation to, for example, wages. However, in the urban economic literature the most frequently mentioned reason for firms to settle somewhere remains agglomeration advantages. In this volume, however, we will not focus on the reasons why firms settle or expand in specific urban regions; rather, we will focus on the employees and self-employed, whom, for reasons of convenience, we will call 'workers'.

The reason for proceeding in this way is not that we think that locational preferences of workers are the single driving forces of urban development. In fact we sympathize with many arguments that have been put forward by those who criticize that view. However, we do not want to treat the arguments in an 'either-or' fashion. Skilled workers choosing a residential location do, of course, look first for the availability of suitable jobs in the vicinity, and in many cases decide to move only after such a job has been found. But that does not imply that amenities do not play a role in their decision making. Apart from the type of job and the associated wage offered by a local employer, they will also take into account the quality of local amenities and the price of housing, and although the job characteristics weigh heavily, it seems unlikely that the attractiveness of the amenities plays no role at all. This point of view is incorporated in the model developed by Roback (1982), which takes into account that workers attach value to job characteristics, house prices and local amenities. Better amenities make it easier to attract workers to a city, but workers will come only if enough jobs are available. Hence unemployment will not rise, but relative wages will adjust. Lower wages stimulate labour demand. The Roback model is static, but it is easy to imagine an extension in which greater numbers of employed people will stimulate endogenous urban amenities, like shops, theatres and music halls, and the model allows for more exploration of agglomeration economies, which contribute to further urban growth.

Aim and focus of the book

The main aim of this volume is to address the stated and revealed residential preferences of workers in creative and knowledge-intensive industries and to estimate what the impact of these preferences is on urban and regional development. A related aim is to develop scenarios of the possible implications of our investigations for local and regional spatial development and housing market strategies.

A detailed analysis of the residential preferences of 'creative knowledge workers' might easily be seen as an effort to provide knowledge that can be used to develop a one-sided urban policy to invest in housing market conditions. Such housing conditions might facilitate the attraction of an appropriately qualified labour force. We hope it is clear from the discussion in the previous section that this is not our objective. But we certainly think that it is useful to investigate workers' preferences for urban amenities. By explicitly paying attention to stated and revealed preferences (actual residential behaviour) we aim to contribute to a balanced view of the importance of labour demand (job) and supply (amenities) considerations. In the stated preference studies we are able to measure a wide range of factors that are likely to have had an impact on residential behaviour or may have an impact on future behaviour, and we can also show what the position is in terms of factors related to work or amenities.

It is clearly important to know where different categories of 'creative knowledge workers' settle, and how that relates to the supply of housing and residential environments and workers' stated preferences. Although this may be of secondary importance, as the availability of jobs will usually come first in decision-making on residential location, labour demand and supply in the urban economy develop in interaction with each other and current labour-market outcomes play a role in the next rounds of economic dynamics. There should be enough suitable residential opportunities to sustain a qualified labour force in the urban economic region, which then will be an important factor for firms' decision-making on where to settle, where to develop, and where to expand. If housing conditions are bad over an extended period of time, this may have an impact on firms' behaviour and, subsequently, on job availability, and thus on the influx of qualified employees. That is an important reason to elaborate on the residential preferences and behaviour of various categories of people who are active in creative industries and knowledge-intensive industries.

Another important reason is that the residential factor may indeed not be the most important incentive for moving to a certain urban region, but still it is an essential condition. It may even be a key condition in the ultimate decision to settle in a certain municipality or neighbourhood *within* the region. For that decision, the availability of specific dwellings, the quality of the environment, the social composition of the area, and other amenities, take centre stage. Therefore, in this volume we will also pay attention to that internal differentiation. The residential factor may also turn out to be very important as a reason for households *to stay* in the places where they have settled. While demonstrating awareness that jobs are key to moving to a certain place, we will also include the physical and social structure, the residential climate, and other factors, such as 'personal networks', in the analysis. Even though they may play a more modest role initially, they may become more important factors in the longer term.

A final reason for paying ample attention to the residential preferences of 'creative knowledge workers' relates to the differences between the 'old' and 'new' labour force. The professional composition of the labour force has changed rapidly, due to economic restructuring and global change. This has happened along with changes in households, in terms of types, labour-market participation and incomes. This change in the professional composition of the labour force also may have changed the residential preferences structure. The housing stock and the set of residential milieus normally do not change that rapidly, however. This may have created a situation of imbalance between housing demand and housing supply. As said, a lasting imbalance in the housing market may have serious negative impacts on the urban economy.

Theoretical considerations

The focus of this study is on highly skilled or highly educated workers. In our globalizing world people with high levels of education, knowledge and skills are important assets in enabling cities to maintain and perhaps even strengthen their position in an increasingly competitive economic environment. Lucas (1988) argued that differences in development are related to differences in human capital and the associated external effects and, referring to the work of Jacobs (1969), he suggested that these would be realized especially in cities. Rauch (1993) found that differences in wages and rents between cities were strongly correlated with the average levels of education. According to his estimates, an additional year of average education of a Standard Statistical Metropolitan Area could be expected to increase total factor productivity by 2.8% (Rauch, 1993, 398). Later work has usually found smaller effects. For instance, in a carefully designed study Moretti (2004) finds an impact of 0.6 to 1.2%. He develops a theoretical framework in which low- and high-skilled labour are substitutes. The conventional supply–demand analysis then predicts that an increase in the proportion of higher-educated workers will decrease their relative wage, unless this effect is counteracted by a sufficiently large external effect. The empirical results confirm that an increase in the proportion of higher-educated workers has the largest impact on the wages of the lower-educated, but that the net effect on the wages of the higher-educated is still positive. The evidence thus clearly points in the direction of substantial external effects and although the literature has not converged to a particular number, there seems little doubt that human capital is an important driver of the level of productivity of all workers in an urban area as well as its growth.

These results provide an important underpinning for the current interest of many local governments in policies that aim to attract highly skilled workers, or to prevent their departure. In current advanced economies knowledge production is rightly regarded as essential, and education and specialized skills are seen as key conditions for maintaining or improving an urban economy's competitive position. With the demise of labour-intensive manufacturing production in advanced economies, the new growth sectors in the economy are to be found in creative industries and in high-tech industries, with spin-offs in services in law, finance, insurance, health and care; these are all strongly linked to education and knowledge. On top of this, there is a stable demand for consumer services such as restaurants, bars, cleaning, and transport. Highly skilled and well-educated workers embody the human capital which is regarded as the crucial input for urban economic development (Lucas 1988; Glaeser and Saiz 2003). Issues related to economic activity in creative and knowledge-intensive industries, also presented as the 'cognitive-cultural economy' (Scott 2008, p. 2014), are receiving special attention, since these sectors are not only generally regarded as leading in today's advanced economies but are also clearly overrepresented in the larger urban areas. One reason is that large and diversified urban labour markets have important advantages for households with two highly educated adults (the so-called 'power couples'), who often have specialized skills (Costa and Kahn 2000). Another is that the higher-educated usually have stronger preferences for urban amenities such as cultural heritage (e.g. Van Duijn and Rouwendal 2013). Beyond that, it is well known that preferences for housing and residential environments are closely related to one's education, income and lifestyle. All this suggests that locational preferences are relevant to the attractiveness of urban areas for the highly skilled, and a main purpose of this volume is to deepen out insight into this issue.

There is a close connection between the highly skilled and the creative sectors that are currently regarded by many as the main drivers of (urban) growth. One difficulty with this point of view is that it is not easy to determine what exactly the creative and knowledge-intensive sectors are and how the creative jobs can be distinguished from others in which highly skilled workers are employed. In many cases it is therefore a relatively safe strategy to focus on the group of highly skilled workers as a whole. However, we should not close our eyes to the signals that the residential behaviour and residential ambitions of those who are working in creative industries or in knowledge-intensive industries may differ both from each other and from those of the employment categories that previously domi-nated the urban scene. This is a matter not just of the higher incomes of some of those employed in the mentioned sectors, but also of different lifestyles that may characterize them. In a study of the residential locations of employees who were employed in the city of Amsterdam, Musterd (2006) found that, typically, those who were employed in the information, communication and technological sec-tors, in the financial sector, and in the (natural) sciences tended to live in suburban environments, whereas those who were employed in creative sectors, such as the media, (creative parts of) advertising, architecture and social sciences tended to live in more urban locations. These revealed preferences were associated with the concentrations of employment in the sectors mentioned. To the extent that employees in creative industries also have more creative or cultural capital, the cosmopolitan and distinguishing characteristics of inner-city living may play a role in explaining the urban orientation (Bridge 2006). Frenkel *et al.* (2013) focused on workers employed in high-tech and financial services industries in Tel Aviv and found that the price of dwellings and distances and commuting times were most important. Cultural amenities were of secondary importance. At the same time we should not forget that socio-economic and demographic factors are also likely to continue to have a strong impact on residential choice.

Preferences and behaviour with respect to the residential location of highly edu-cated workers (both national and international employees) in creative industries and in knowledge-intensive industries will be the main focus of our analyses in this volume. However, we will also pay explicit attention to international migrants, including international students. The reason for including international students is that today's urban economies are increasingly international. International students generally move to a specific city not for a job, but because they can find the right and good-quality courses that they are interested in, and perhaps also because they perceive that city to be an interesting place to be, at least for a while. International students therefore have other reasons than those of workers to settle somewhere. Once they have decided to go to a certain place they may become attached to that place, and this will increase the probability of their becoming future contributors to the local economy.

However, also in the case of the labour market, a distinction between 'natives' and 'international migrants' seems to be relevant. An international orientation of the economy is likely to help firms to stay relevant. This is evident from firms' habit of strengthening their links to global pools of creative knowledge in order to remain competitive. International migrants not only can complement but also augment existing skills and knowledge in the workforce. The international migration of highly skilled people serves a variety of purposes in the economy. It can fill short-term labour gaps or be used to address long-term skills shortages and help in the gradual development of a skilled labour force.

The availability of jobs is also a key condition for attracting international migrants, and existing relations with people already present in the city appear to be of crucial importance too (Pethe *et al.* 2010). For highly skilled international migrants, as for others, that the city has something to offer in terms of amenities, how the housing market is structured, and how it functions, seem to be relevant factors in order to *retain* these workers. This is important for demand-led international migrants (who moved to the city because there was a job or because they were sent to the place), but perhaps it is even more important for so-called supply-led migrants, such as the already mentioned international student population or other migrants, including students from within the country, who came to the city for other reasons than to work. When they develop a relationship to the city and when they enter the labour market, they begin to demand suitable environments and dwelling types that fit their profiles. These demands are not necessarily similar to those of comparable categories of non-migrants.

In any case, we can observe that an increasing proportion of the population of important cities nowadays have their roots elsewhere, and a large proportion of those with roots elsewhere come from relatively affluent countries. In a city like Amsterdam, in 2014, some 16% of the population originated from a so-called 'Western' country with an advanced economy. This tells a story about internationalization and globalization processes. These 'immigrants' are seen as vital to the urban economy. They are expected to express residential preferences and residential behaviour that differ from those of the 'natives', if only because some of them will not be intending to stay for a long time. Their specific residential orientation is visible in their predominant location choice, which seems to be especially 'urban'. Many seem to prefer a location in the inner city and some directly adjacent neighbourhoods. However, we should not forget that the category 'immigrated from a "Western" country' is rather heterogeneous and that the general picture perhaps requires some refinement. The category includes those who are staying for only a short period of time. They will likely prefer accommodation that fits this condition and it is to be expected that this will imply a focus on rental housing in an urban setting. International students are part of the well-skilled immigrants category. Many of them will stay for several years, and perhaps longer. So far, knowledge about the specific residential orientations of various categories of creative knowledge workers is rather limited. This is an important reason for us to dig deeper into the residential steps they take, from the moment they arrive in the chosen 'port of entry', but also including experiences in later stages of their careers.

In this volume, the residential preferences of higher-skilled employees in creative and knowledge intensive-industries and international students are studied on the basis of stated and revealed preferences. The advantage of the combination of stated and revealed preference research is that the information from stated preferences research can also be used in revealed preference models when building models for different scenarios of future behaviour. In some chapters of this volume the behaviour of workers will be integrated in more general models for choice of household location in an urbanized area.

In order to study to what extent the preferences can be realized in actual urban areas, we finally have to move from the level of the individual to that of the city. Most cities have been in existence for a very long time already, and past land use decisions have important consequences for the present and future. The pattern of the streets, the location of residential and work areas, the presence of cultural heritage and of natural amenities are all important for the possibilities to improve life in and the liveability of cities. In order to deal with these issues, models have been built that give stylized descriptions of the phenomena one would like to address. This route will also be followed in this study, and the models that will be constructed focus on the way preferences with regard to residential location translate into the distribution of a heterogeneous population over a designated urban area. The preferences of the individual actors are the driving force of the model. The housing market constraints, which will always be there, imply that choices have to be made. Past decisions about land use, prices or other allocation mechanisms (rationing in the rental housing market, and land use restrictions in the land market) direct these choices, and also the allocation of workers over the urban area. An important feature of the sorting models that will be employed is that they focus on the structural relationships: preferences, budget constraints, land use patterns and amenities. This gives such models a substantial advantage over conventional hedonic models. These hedonic models focus on house prices in a particular market equilibrium. These prices will probably be sensitive to policy measures such as the creation of more open space or the change of a brownfield site into a new residential area, which makes such models less suitable for policy analysis because some of the parameters can be expected to take on different values as a consequence of policy changes. Structural models avoid this complication by their concentration on parameters that are invariant to policy changes, and determine policy-relevant variables like the willingness to pay for urban amenities on the basis of these structural parameters. The models can be used to study the consequences of urban and land use policies like transforming brownfield sites to high-density residential areas, or the preservation of open space close to cities by decentralizing residential development to growth centres.

We will base our empirical analyses on research that has mainly been carried out in the Netherlands, in particular in the metropolitan regions of Amsterdam and Eindhoven, two of the key economic areas of the country. These regions have different profiles and are different in size, but both have substantial employment in creative industries as well as in high-tech industries and in internationally oriented industries, yet these industries operate in very different contexts. For the stated preference studies we explicitly highlighted the opinions of employees in selected creative industries and in the most leading high-tech industries, and for the latter especially we investigated the preferences of highly skilled (international) employees in large and leading firms – more specifically, Shell Technology Centre in Amsterdam and ASML in the Eindhoven region. We believe that the experiences of employees in these firms will provide more generalizable outcomes that can also be applied in other more-or-less similar contexts. To test this assertion we also gathered information for the cities of Copenhagen and Helsinki, mainly so as to reflect on the generalizability of the knowledge obtained in the Dutch settings.

Data and methods

Our insights are based on several unique data sources. Longitudinal register data at individual level for the entire population, including demographic, cultural, socio-economic and housing data, aimed at discovering *revealed* preferences – have been made available by Statistics Netherlands. In addition, a large-scale targeted survey was developed among highly skilled employees in creative and knowledge-intensive industries, aimed at discovering *stated* preferences. Various Geographical Information System (GIS) data have been used as well, aimed at visualization and scenario building for urban planning. The volume is based on a large-scale research project called The Higher Educated Location Preferences (HELP) but, as already stated, it aims to provide more general insights beyond the selected empirical contexts.

In some of the modelling scenarios we explicitly combined the insights gained from stated preferences research with the revealed preferences. More precisely, scenarios of the revealed preferences were modelled on the basis of assumptions that could be derived from the stated preferences part of the project. We believe this has helped us to come up with more realistic scenarios of expected actual residential behaviour.

Questions, and the content of the book

The issues addressed above resulted in the formulation of eight research questions. These will be addressed in the chapters that follow. The questions are:

1   What is the literature telling us about the stated and revealed preferences of workers in creative and knowledge-intensive industries?
2   What are the stated preferences of 'natives' and 'international migrants' working in creative and knowledge-intensive industries in the urban regions of Amsterdam and Eindhoven?
3   What can sorting models, based on revealed preferences that include housing and neighbourhood characteristics, accessibility of employment, consumer amenities, and budget constraints, tell us about the most likely future spatial distribution of household types?
4   How can the sorting models be related to policy-oriented economic development scenarios and prognoses of population development that describe current and future land use in the Netherlands on different scales?

5   What are the determinants of international mobility of students in higher education and what is the position of the Amsterdam metropolitan area in this process?

6   To what extent do foreign international students stay in the Netherlands, and in particular in the Amsterdam metropolitan area, after completing their studies?

7   What drives the location choices of international migrants within the Netherlands and to what extent do they differ from those of (domestic) Dutch workers?

8   What drives the location choices of international migrants within the Amsterdam metropolitan area and to what extent do they differ from those of (domestic) Dutch workers?

The volume in divided into four parts. The first part consists of the introductory chapters, comprising this chapter, a literature review chapter, and a chapter in which the most important case studies are introduced and set within a wider framework. Part II deals with the highly skilled workers in creative and knowledge-intensive industries in general, mostly dominated by 'native' employees, while Part III the attention focuses on the preferences and behaviour of international migrants who have entered jobs in creative and knowledge-intensive industries, and of international students. Both parts are briefly introduced in Chapters 4 and 8, respectively. Part IV contains a short concluding chapter.

The introduction in this chapter is supplemented by a literature review in Chapter 2, the aim of which is to present an overview of the international literature on stated and revealed preferences and the impact of job availability, amenities and other factors on residential mobility preferences. Studies from the US figure prominently amongst this literature and provide a useful background and a basis on which to investigate the strengths and weaknesses of assets and processes in European cities that are explored in European literature. Particular attention will be paid to the role of historical and cultural amenities that are prominent in European urban policy.

In Chapter 3 the focus is on existing knowledge with regard to the stated and revealed preference for residential locations and housing situations in the two most important Dutch cases that form the basis of the empirical research in this volume: the metropolitan areas of Amsterdam and Eindhoven. Since we believe that this knowledge will also have meaning for other contexts, albeit not unconditional, it was decided to compare the state-of-the-art in the two main cases with knowledge about structures and processes in the metropolitan areas of Copenhagen and Helsinki – cases that present significant similarities to, respectively, Amsterdam and Eindhoven. Each of these cities has flourished in the 1990s and early 2000s. In all of these cities human capital is acknowledged as an important factor for the local economy, and a crucial question is what considerations have helped to attach 'creative knowledge workers' to the respective cities. The information gathered for the four cases, and coming from various sources, is complemented with information obtained through interviews with key persons.

In Chapter 5, the first substantial chapter of Part II (following the introduction in Chapter 4), the stated preferences of highly educated workers and their households are dealt with. The focus is on the urban regions of Amsterdam and Eindhoven. The chapter starts with a brief discussion of the 'creative class' concept and its relevance to residential preference, together with related criticism and contradictions. Attention is paid to empirical findings about the factors that are relevant for attracting knowledge workers to a city or region, and factors that help in retaining them. The chapter also provides new knowledge about the extent to which the residential choice of creative-knowledge workers is determined by limitations in the available supply of dwellings and residential social environments. Finally, in this chapter the focus is on differences in terms of residential orientations between those who are employed in creative industries and those who are connected to high-tech industries, in various locations.

Chapter 6 aims to understand the locational revealed preferences of highly educated workers in Amsterdam and Eindhoven, and for comparison also in Copenhagen. The strengths and weaknesses of different models for similar research tasks are discussed; this will provide a more in-depth review of sorting models and their applicability to the locational preferences research that was undertaken. A detailed description of the data used in the research is also presented. This is essential, since the strengths and limitations of the data determine the possibilities for comparison and reference between cities and countries. Finally, models created in order to understand the locational preferences of highly educated workers in Amsterdam, Eindhoven and Copenhagen are described in detail.

In Chapter 7 the authors describe how the models that represent the findings of our research into the location preferences of highly educated workers can be integrated into strategic urban development processes and applied as policy. The first part of this chapter relates the models to the so-called Land Use Scanner, a grid-based, policy-oriented GIS that describes current land use in the Netherlands as well as potential future land use under various socio-economic scenarios. In particular it discusses the purpose and suitability of land use models as tools for downscaling national policy scenarios to local land use patterns, and the process of incorporating results from models into the GIS system. The second part of the chapter discusses the potential applications of the combined sorting and Land Use Scanner models for a welfare-maximizing policy scenario; for the study of governance issues by distinguishing different policy makers, each with their own set of instruments; for the study of the interaction between welfare and governance measures; and to study all of the above, throughout different time periods using '4D' GIS to determine appropriate policy-intervention time-frames.

In Part III international migrants and students take centre stage, starting with an introduction in Chapter 8. Chapter 9 presents research findings that address the stated preferences of highly educated international migrants. It focuses exclusively on the city of Amsterdam. The chapter identifies the growth of transnational highly skilled migrants in world cities that occurs alongside the internationalization of economies, and relates the case of Amsterdam to the social science and economic literature of residential preferences. It includes a discussion of the growth of transnational highly skilled migrants in Amsterdam and the spatial concentration patterns for the Amsterdam region. These patterns are contrasted with assertions in the literature from the US and Europe regarding the particular residential preferences of international workers. The chapter also outlines how the empirical research has attempted to fill existing gaps in knowledge.

The determinants of mobility for international students in the Netherlands are dealt with in Chapter 10. The chapter also investigates to what extent these students stay in the host country after completing their studies. More precisely, the role and importance of international students in forming highly skilled labour pools are discussed, as well as the role of regional and urban amenities in this process. The chapter builds on the results of research to identify the key determinants of international student mobility. The focus is on the Amsterdam metropolitan area. Attention is also given to indicators for university quality and for the quality of life in destination locations, disaggregated as far as possible into specific amenities that are relevant to students. Key determinants for international students' decisions to return to their home country or to stay in the Netherlands also receive attention.

The following two chapters, 11 and 12, address the revealed preference or location choices of highly educated foreign workers. Chapter 11 aims to discuss the importance of urban amenities in the location choices of highly educated foreign workers, with reference to a case study of the Netherlands and the Amsterdam metropolitan region. The chapter discusses the potentially different location choices of highly educated international workers in the Netherlands, as compared to those of their domestic counterparts, and investigates what drives the location choices of foreign workers within the Netherlands and within the Amsterdam metropolitan areas, and to what extent they differ from those of (domestic) Dutch workers.

Chapter 12, while also addressing the revealed preference of international migrants, focuses on the settlement process of international migrants in creative and knowledge-intensive industries, over time. The chapter presents findings on the actual settlement and mobility behaviour of new international migrants at two moments in time: first, upon their entry into the urban regions of Amsterdam and Eindhoven, and second, during the next or later steps of their housing careers in the metropolitan regions. In particular, the chapter discusses the types of residential milieu that belong to the 'ports of entry' in which highly skilled international migrants from different countries settle when first arriving from abroad in the Amsterdam region; the patterns of their subsequent moves in terms of residential milieu and housing characteristics; and what factors drive international migrants to certain neighbourhoods and locations in the wider metropolitan area.

In Part IV, in Chapter 13, the most important findings of the book are briefly summarized and evaluated, while new avenues for research are also identified.

References

Bridge, G 2006, It's not just a question of taste: gentrification, the neighbourhood and cultural capital. *Environment and Planning A* 38(10), 1965–1978.

Clark, TN, Lloyd, R, Wong, KK and Jain, P 2002, Amenities drive urban growth. *Journal of Urban Affairs* 24(5), 493–515.

Costa, DL and Kahn, M 2000, Power couples: changes in the locational choice of the college educated, 1940–1990. *Quarterly Journal of Economics* 115, 1287–1315.

Florida, R 2002, *The rise of the creative class*. New York: Basic Books.

Florida, R 2004, *Cities and the creative class*. London: Routledge.

Frenkel, A, Bendit, E and Kaplan, S 2013, Residential location choice of knowledge workers: the role of amenities, workplace and lifestyle. *Cities* 35, 33–41.

Glaeser, E and Gotlieb, J 2006, Urban resurgence and the consumer city. *Urban Studies* 43, 1275–1299.

Glaeser, E and Saiz, A 2003, *The rise of the skilled city*. Working paper 10191. http://www.nber.org/papers/w10191. Cambridge, MA: National Bureau of Economic Research.

Glaeser, E, Kolko, J and Saiz, A 2001, Consumer city. *Journal of Economic Geography* 1, 27–50.

Hansen, HK and Niedomysl, T 2009, Migration and the creative class: evidence from Sweden. *Journal of economic geography* 9(2), 191–206.

Jacobs, J 1969, *The economy of cities*. New York: Random House.

Lucas, RE 1988, On the mechanics of economic development. *Journal of Monetary Economics* 22, 3–42.

Moretti, E 2004, Estimating the social return to higher education: evidence from longitudinal and repeated cross-sectional data. *Journal of Econometrics* 121(1–2), 175–212.

Musterd, S 2006, Segregation, urban space and the resurgent city. *Urban Studies* 43(8), 1325–1340.

Musterd, S and Murie, A (eds) 2010, *Making competitive cities*. Chichester: Wiley-Blackwell.

Pethe, H, Hafner, S and Lawton, P 2010, Transnational migrants in the creative knowledge industries: Amsterdam, Barcelona, Dublin and Munich. In: S. Musterd and A. Murie (eds) *Making competitive cities*, 163–190. Chichester: Wiley-Blackwell.

Rauch, JE 1993, Productivity gains from geographic concentration of human capital: evidence from the cities. *Journal of Urban Economics* 34, 380–400.

Roback, J 1982, Wages, rents and the quality of life. *Journal of Political Economy* 90, 1257–1278.

Scott, AJ 2008, *Social economy of the metropolis: cognitive-cultural capitalism and the global resurgence of cities*. Oxford: Oxford University Press.

Scott, AJ 2010, Jobs or amenities? Destination choices of migrant engineers in the USA. *Papers in Regional Science* 89(1), 43–63.

Storper, M and Manville, M 2006, Behaviour, preferences and cities: urban theory and urban resurgence. *Urban Studies* 43(8), 1247–1274.

Storper M and Scott, AJ 2009, Rethinking human capital, creativity and urban growth. *Journal of Economic Geography* 9, 147–167.

Van Duijn, M and Rouwendal, J 2013, Cultural heritage and the location choice of Dutch households in a residential sorting model. *Journal of Economic Geography* 13, 473–500.

2 Housing and amenities as attracting factors for cities and their regions

A literature review

Bart Sleutjes

Introduction

This chapter places the research analysed in this volume in the context of an academic and policy debate on (creative) knowledge cities and the attraction of knowledge workers. Through a literature review, existing literature on the emergence of resurgent or knowledge cities, the spatial preferences and choices of different groups of knowledge workers and the importance that amenities and other 'soft' location factors play therein is summarized.

Before turning to the residential preferences, it is important to first describe the economic context in which increasing attention to knowledge workers and their residential preferences has evolved: the spatially unequal transition from a Fordist capital-intensive to a post-Fordist knowledge-intensive economy. The transition towards this 'new economy' is illustrated by three major shifts: a shift in geographic scale from cities to polycentric urban regions, a shift in economic specialisation from manufacturing to services, and a shift in the composition of the labour force from blue-collar workers to high-skilled labour (Phelps and Ozawa 2003). Because of the increasing focus on skills and qualifications, the new economy is also referred to as the 'knowledge economy' (Van Winden 2010). Rather than physical assets and natural resources, the quality and size of the knowledge base or human capital of cities and urban regions co-determines their economic potential and competitiveness. Facilitating and retaining skilled workers in creative and knowledge-intensive industries ('creative knowledge workers') is therefore an important part of their competition strategies (Bontje and Musterd 2009). The knowledge economy is a way out of a path-dependent development trajectory dominated by manufacturing, but is also seen as a way to escape from the recession and to become less vulnerable to economic downturns (Romein and Trip 2011).

There are many possible interpretations of the term 'knowledge worker', most of them relating to people's educational background. According to Horwitz, Heng and Quazi (2003), knowledge workers 'have a high level of skills/education, with technological literacy, high cognitive power and abstract reasoning. This includes the ability to observe, synthesise and interpret data, and to communicate new perspectives and insights to lead to more effective decisions, processes and solutions for the organisation. The knowledge creation process is part of the organisation's competitive strategy, characterized by information/knowledge sharing and team collaboration to produce more effective actions and solutions' (p. 31). However, others suggest that it is more important to focus on what people actually do, rather than what they studied in the past. Being active in a 'creative class occupation', covering almost all creative or highly skilled professions, is considered a better measure of human capital than the level of education (Mellander and Florida 2006). In his study on the rise of the creative class, Florida (2002) divided this class into two subgroups based on occupation. First, the 'super creative core', consisting of persons occupied with computers, mathematics, architecture, arts, science and education. Second, 'creative professionals', which include workers in management, businesses, finance and legal issues, healthcare and high-end sales. Florida's (2002) subdivisions still cover a large number of different occupations and individuals, some of which can hardly be considered creative. Krätke (2010) suggested a division into two main groups: the 'scientifically and technologically creative occupations' and the 'dealer class', consisting of high-ranking professionals in finance, real estate, management and consultancy. In his view, the dealer class should not be counted among the creative class. Kotkin (2000) proposed a dichotomy of 'bohemians' and 'nerds'. The first category largely overlaps with workers in creative industries, and the latter category with workers in technical professions such as high-tech or information and communications technology (ICT). However, other studies suggest that this division is still insufficient to illustrate the diversity within the creative class (Kooijman and Romein 2007). According to Atzema (2007), the creative class in the Netherlands is primarily an ideal type and consists for a large part of 'ordinary working people' who all possess some – though not all – of the characteristics of the creative class.

Creative knowledge workers are assumed to be highly mobile, based on evidence from the US. But also in Europe, the possibility to move to a different country or even to another continent becomes increasingly relevant. In the knowledge economy, many jobs are highly specialized and found in only a limited number of locations per country, most often in the largest urban centres. International competition for knowledge-intensive companies and their workers makes it important to know what sets cities apart from their competitors and how the profile can be strengthened through the policy agenda. In this respect, suitable employment is the most likely attracting factor for creative knowledge workers, but amenities may nonetheless play an important secondary role, or even a crucial role if two cities offer the same employment opportunities. Besides, urban attractiveness, including amenities and housing, may be important for retaining knowledge workers once they have made a choice of a certain region.

Most studies on the role of urban attractiveness in location choice are based on experiences from the US, and the few studies dealing with the European context give a more nuanced view on its relevance. In particular, the European context differs considerably from that of the US in terms of cultural and institutional barriers (e.g., language, tax systems) and levels of commuting tolerance. Consequently,

workers in Europe generally relocate across smaller distances than their counterparts in the US, have fewer cities to choose from and have lower mobility rates
(Martin-Brelot *et al.* 2010). In this chapter, we aim to get a clear overview of the
factors that are mentioned in the literature as determining why creative knowledge
workers make a choice for a specific locality and the factors that steer the intra-
regional residential orientations of those who have settled in a certain region. At
the interregional level reasons for the settling of creative knowledge workers are
mainly related to job availability. At the intra-regional level, the role of amenities
in attracting the workers to a certain residential milieu may be more important.

The next section presents some more background on the emergence of the
knowledge economy and its uneven spatial distribution. In the third section,
we briefly summarize the academic discussion on which factors determine the
location choices of knowledge workers, distinguishing between hard and soft
conditions. The fourth section deals with the sorting of different categories of
knowledge workers within regions. The review focuses on both the dominant
US-based literature and a number of recent European empirical studies.

The emergence of the knowledge economy and the urban turn in policy making

The knowledge economy has reinforced the role of cities and their metropolitan regions, and local aspects have become more important as determinants of
economic success (Musterd and Murie 2010). Despite the rapid development
of ICT and a substantial decrease in transportation costs, economic development
in modern economies is increasingly concentrated in metropolitan areas. Creative
knowledge workers and their interactions with similar and other workers play an
important role in the functioning of these urban economies. According to Florida
(2010), a 'chain reverse' from a supply- to a demand-driven model of consumption has taken place in which perceived status and 'experiences' play an important
role, and these are more often found in cities. The 'symbolic value' of cities and
places has become an important factor of urban competitiveness, and the cultural capital of specific locations is exploited for economic benefits (Zukin 1995).
However, there is little consensus in the literature on the relevance of these factors. Since 2010 several European studies have shown evidence for the enduring
importance of employment opportunities and have shown little belief in attracting
talents directly through amenities or consumption. Still, these aspects may be relevant for retaining talent (Musterd and Murie 2010).

In the EU, urban agglomerations and metropolitan regions are considered the
engines of economic development and hubs for European integration in the global
economy (Krätke 2007). In cities, knowledge processes start and flourish, and
networks (social capital) and place-specific qualities (geographical capital) are
brought together (Helbrecht 2004). Because of economies of scale, cities combine
large and specialised labour markets with markets for luxury consumer goods
and amenities (Van Winden 2010). It is argued that in an era of globalisation,
cities with strong creative and knowledge-intensive sectors, such as high-tech

production, business and financial services, media and cultural industries, have the most favourable conditions (Scott 2006). According to Amin and Thrift (2007), cities' cultural assets provide 'the services demanded by scientific, technical and professional communities; the cultural buzz that attracts artistic and creative communities; the trust, reciprocity and ties that characterize knowledge-intensive work; the varied urban ecology that sparks new opportunity; and the infrastructure required by the industries and institutions that make up the knowledge economy' (p. 151).

The renewed importance of metropolitan areas is reflected by an 'urban turn' in the European spatial policy agenda, initiated by the European Union's Lisbon Agenda 2000, which stated the ambition for Europe to become 'the most competitive and dynamic global knowledge economy by 2010'. Rather than egalitarian policies, the comparative advantages of a small number of promising urban regions were to be strengthened through targeted investments. Consequently, EU member states increased investments in knowledge, education and research and development (R&D), in order to raise productivity and create economic growth. A growing number of European cities started marketing themselves internationally as knowledge cities, while using 'branding' techniques to create distinctiveness. The cooperation between city governments, regional universities and the business sector, the 'Triple Helix', was stimulated and supported through subsidies and networking events, with the aim of reducing the chances of firm relocation. The role of universities is recognised by urban planners because of their supposed effect on the regeneration of urban areas, their central role in new, mixed-knowledge districts and the economic significance of the student population as both potential creative knowledge workers and consumers: the 'economisation of higher education' (Van Winden 2010). The Peaks in the Delta (PiD) programme in the Netherlands (2004) is a good example of the urban turn in policy making. Whereas Dutch economic policy had previously focused mainly on reducing regional inequalities and relocating public sector institutions to peripheral regions, the PiD policy increased spending on a small number of strong economic hubs: the North Wing of the Randstad (including Amsterdam), the port of Rotterdam (Mainport Rotterdam) and the high technology hub of Southeast Brabant (Brainport Eindhoven) (Geerdink *et al.* 2010; Van Winden 2010).

Both in Europe and the in US, knowledge-intensive economic activities show a selective pattern of concentration. Cities with a strong formal knowledge base and cities specialised in advanced services, creative industries or innovative manufacturing sectors stand out as the most successful knowledge cities (Van Winden, Van den Berg and Pol 2007; Krätke 2007). However, a large number of cities have not been able to successfully adapt to the new economy and are still struggling to escape a development path dominated by declining industries, high unemployment and low scores on quality of life. In particular, cities with a strong legacy of relatively uniform manufacturing, such as the steel industry in the German Ruhr area (Grabher 1993) and the well-known example of the car manufacturing industry in Detroit (Klepper 2002; Galster 2012), face difficulties in developing a knowledge-based service economy and attracting creative knowledge workers.

Several studies have presented typologies of cities based on their knowledge potential. Cities that have successfully managed to attract new and growing activities and to offer attractive and vibrant living environments are referred to as 'resurgent cities' (Musterd 2006). Glaeser, Kolko and Saiz (2001) distinguished between 'resurgent dense cities', which have successfully adapted their economies to the post-industrial service sector, 'older dense cities' with small opportunities for growth and a traditional manufacturing profile without political functions, and 'edge cities', characterised by decentralised employment, lower density and high levels of car dependence (Glaeser, Kolko and Saiz 2001). In the European context, cities such as Amsterdam, Paris and Barcelona are good examples of resurgent dense cities, while the Ruhr Area, Liverpool and Manchester are examples of the second type. Edge cities are not very common in the European context, however. Van Winden, Van den Berg and Pol (2007) presented a more detailed typology in their comparative study on European cities. The typology is based on cities' scores on a listed number of 'structural characteristics' of the knowledge economy. The 'knowledge base' of cities consists of universities, polytechnics and other public and private R&D activities. The 'industrial structure' is made up of the city-region's economic base, its degree of economic specialisation and the innovation capacity of local firms. In this respect, a diversified economy offers advantages, since it makes cities less vulnerable in rapidly changing economic circumstances and may lead to incubations and innovations. 'Urban amenities and quality of life' determine a city-region's attractiveness as a place to live. Finally, 'accessibility' is crucial for a city-region's ability to acquire, create, disseminate and use knowledge effectively (Van Winden, Van den Berg and Pol 2007). Six types of metropolitan areas that have successfully or unsuccessfully adapted to the new economy were distinguished. 'Stars' score high on almost all structural and progress indicators. 'Metropoles in transition' are generally characterised by lower scores on quality-of-life indicators and are struggling with a legacy of declining sectors and lower performance rates. 'Knowledge pearls' is the allocated label for smaller cities with a high score on virtually all criteria while being located near a large urban agglomeration. 'Star niche players' are specialised cities in terms of their knowledge and economic bases, perform well in terms of progress indicators and have excellent cooperation between business, university and local government. 'Niche players in transition' are characterised by some degree of specialisation and have high-quality knowledge institutes, but are still dealing with a legacy of declining industries and are often not well endowed in terms of quality of life. Finally, 'intellectuals' have a strong university but lack a knowledge-intensive business sector (Van Winden, Van den Berg and Pol 2007).

What attracts talents? A discussion on the assumed role of soft conditions

A main component of European 'knowledge city policies' is a strong focus on 'soft conditions'. The underlying assumption is that the supposedly highly mobile group of creative knowledge workers is attracted and retained not only by employment opportunities but also by a good 'people's climate'. Creative knowledge workers are supposedly attracted by urban environments with low levels of segregation, high levels of tolerance and cultural diversity and a rich supply of cultural, historical and leisure amenities (Florida 2002). Therefore, public investments in local quality of life are often justified for their supposed economic impacts (Musterd and Murie 2010).

However, the literature is divided when it comes to the aspects that are important for the attraction of both skilled employment and creative knowledge workers. In classic location theory, economic or 'hard' factors (such as job availability) are the main determinants of location choice (Musterd and Murie 2010). However, the majority of literature within classic location theory deals with the location behaviour of firms, rather than human capital (Storper 1997), and the most important aspects determining the economic quality of a location for a firm are infrastructure, accessibility, connections, the availability of affordable (office) space, labour availability, wage policies and tax arrangements (Sassen 2002; Musterd and Kovács 2013).

Other theories focus on social aspects. Some theories stress the importance of social capital and personal networks for making location choices (Grabher 2002; 2004). The location choices of firms can be explained by networks that were established in the past, whereas location choices of individuals are generally, next to job opportunities, steered by existing personal relationships and personal life trajectories (Musterd and Murie 2010). Besides the strand focusing on networks and social capital, several streams of thought within the literature focus directly on personal preferences that attract people, rather than companies, to a city-region. Although there is disagreement within the literature on the specific dominant attracting factors, they all emphasise the quality of the living environment as one of the drivers of location choice for skilled individuals (Storper and Scott 2009).

Florida's (2002) 'Creative Class Theory' dominated urban economic and cultural policies in the 2000s. This theory suggests that economic growth is spurred not only by individuals' level of education but also by creativity, resulting from social interaction, authenticity and identity. Talented and creative people supposedly congregate together in metropolitan areas because of tolerance and diversity, which are therefore regarded as the keys to economic success. Companies locate in large cities with large concentrations of talented people and gather competitive advantage. The ability to rapidly mobilise talent from such large talent pools is regarded as an important source of competitive advantage. Inspired by Jacobs (1961), Florida considers cities to be the ultimate location for innovative industries, since heterogeneity drives creativity and innovations (Florida 2002; Helbrecht 2004). Universities play an important role as hub institutions of the talent-driven creative economy and the supply of amenities is strongly correlated with the distribution of human capital (Mellander and Florida 2006).

Wojan, Lambert and McGranahan (2007) found a correlation between a surplus of 'bohemians' and regional growth of other sub-groups of the creative class, suggesting that creative people attract more creative people. An underlying assumption in this field of work is that people do not follow jobs, but instead jobs follow people. The policy implications derived from these studies therefore have a large emphasis on the development of cities' soft conditions (Scott 2006).

According to the 'consumer city' approach, human capital or the availability of skilled workers steers economic growth, and amenities (divided into climatic aspects and consumer goods) play an important role in the attraction of these workers (Glaeser, Kolko and Saiz 2001). Climatic and cultural amenities, respectively, explain the success of Sunbelt cities in the South of the US and consumer cities in the North with respect to attracting human capital (Glaeser 2004). Glaeser and his colleagues stressed that the success and failure of big cities depends largely on consumption, rather than production. After a period of urban decline, cities recovered after the 1980s and again appeared to become attractive places to live for the middle classes. This urban resurgence may (at least in the US) be explained by rapidly declining crime rates, but also by rising incomes and education levels, which increased the demand for urban amenities such as museums, restaurants and music concerts (Glaeser and Gottlieb 2006). Metropolitan areas with a rich variety of amenities and consumer goods, such as theatres and restaurants, are more likely to attract residents with middle and higher incomes. In addition, the aesthetics of the built environment, the quality of public services and liveability play important roles in the attraction of skilled workers to a metropolitan region and the sorting of this group within that region. Furthermore, it is important that workers can move around the city quickly and easily, increasing the range of services and jobs that are within reach. Cities with high scores on these aspects have performed better in terms of economic growth since the 1980s than cities with less favourable conditions (Glaeser, Kolko and Saiz 2001; Glaeser 2004).

Similar to the consumer city approach, the strand dominated by Clark and his colleagues considers urban amenities as the principal drivers of urban growth and competitiveness (Clark *et al.* 2002). Cities are seen as 'entertainment machines', and those cities with the most and highest-quality urban amenities would be most likely to attract human capital. The definition of 'amenities' used by Clark includes aspects ranging from attractive residential milieus to shopping centres, cultural facilities, restaurants and facilities for sports and recreation (Jacobs 1961; Clark *et al.* 2002). Yigitcanlar, Baum and Horton (2007) concluded, in line with Florida and Clark, that urban amenities are among the dominant attracting factors for knowledge workers. In their view, the knowledge worker is a 'radically new type of worker' (p. 7) who is highly mobile, has a considerable disposal income and prefers cities and regions with thick labour markets and a retail rich environment. Where people settle, either between or within regions, was supposedly mainly steered by their leisure-time activities. In this respect, quality of life, social equality and urban diversity are seen as important attracting factors, next to access to more basic amenities such as childcare, healthcare and higher-quality education. According to Yigitcanlar, Baum and Horton's study, knowledge workers tend to look for smaller dwellings, because of their generally smaller households. It does not become clear, however, how these preferences change after family enlargement.

The work of Currid (2007; 2009) on the 'Warhol economy' is also supportive to some degree of the amenity-based strands and emphasises the importance of the arts and cultural amenities as a meaningful part of urban, regional or national economies. Apart from creating distinctiveness, the arts sector contributes to networking potential, since people like to gather in cultural clusters. A more recent paper by Van Duijn and Rouwendal (2013) indicated that cultural heritage plays an important role in city attractiveness, especially for highly educated workers, who, relative to other types of households, are more often prepared to pay more for housing in a municipality if it is close to a high concentration of cultural heritage.

However, all three approaches within the people-based perspective have been criticised as well. The work of Florida, Glaeser and Clark is often criticised for neglecting, or at least under-estimating or not mentioning, the importance of employment opportunities, whereas the role of soft conditions is regarded to be over-estimated. Their studies also failed to distinguish between necessary and sufficient conditions under which skilled and creative workers will settle or remain in particular areas. Storper and Scott (2009) argued that growth crises in regions result from a lack of jobs, rather than a lacking inflow of people, and that highly educated people are less mobile than is often presumed. Knowledge workers have invested heavily in acquiring know-how, skills and qualifications, and are therefore unlikely to move to places that lack sufficient employment opportunities. According to Scott (2006), the economic networks and production system within a region have a larger impact on the attraction of talent than do the social and cultural atmosphere. In the European context, 'hard' location factors such as job opportunities are the most important factors in attracting native and international knowledge migrants to European regions, while natural and cultural amenities are of secondary, though still significant, importance (Miguelez and Moreno 2014). Marlet and Van Woerkens (2005; 2007) found that for the Dutch creative class, job opportunities are the most important attracting factors of cities. Aesthetic features such as nature and historic buildings, as well as 'traditional' amenities like culture and cafés, are considered attractive but cannot be seen apart from employment opportunities. Hansen and Niedomysl (2009) concluded that for making relocation decisions, employment (main reason for 26 per cent) and social reasons (24 per cent) are the most decisive factors, whereas soft conditions play only a secondary role: half of their sample considered cultural and entertainment facilities (very) unimportant, but for 20 per cent it was an important aspect. Their study found that work was regarded as much more important by high-educated workers than by low-educated workers, whereas the valuation of soft factors did not differ strongly between the two groups. Cultural and entertainment facilities are more often considered as a migration reason by older migrants, especially by retired people (Hansen and Niedomysl 2009). In similar studies, Niedomysl (2010) and Niedomysl and Hansen (2010) suggested that amenities should be considered as preferences, rather than needs or demands. These aspects are relevant mainly when other factors – such as jobs and affordable housing – are equal in different potential destinations. In short, soft conditions can be seen as necessary, but not the most important and certainly not sufficient conditions for attracting creative knowledge workers.

Other studies argue that the role of creativity is over-estimated. For example, Markusen's (2006) in-depth study on artists doubted the relationship between high-tech industry and arts. In fact, high-tech centres such as Silicon Valley have relatively few artists whereas most artistic cities are neither the largest nor the fastest-growing cities. Borén and Young (2013) concluded after their study on artists' location preferences in the Stockholm region that even for these highly creative workers, work opportunities and professional networks are at least as important as city attractiveness for choosing to migrate to a city-region. A US-based study found that workers, particularly those with high levels of education, are principally drawn to locations where jobs are to be found, whereas soft factors (e.g., climatic amenities) appear to be more relevant for retirees than for workers (Chen and Rosenthal 2008). The quality of Florida's empirical evidence, his broad definition of the creative class and his subjective and hard-to-measure quality-of-place indicators have also been criticised in many studies (e.g., Musterd and Ostendorf 2004; Storper and Manville 2006; Kooijman and Romein 2007). In particular, the fact that the creative class is considered one homogenous group with uniform residential preferences has been subject to fierce debate. Servillo, Atkinson and Russo (2012) suggested that the role that environmental, physical and social attributes play in the attractiveness of a city-region is different for specific groups within the creative class.

Also the social consequences of the related policy implications are the topic of fierce debate. One point of critique is the strong focus on the middle and upper classes, while the importance of low-skilled employment is neglected. The policies related to the creative class theory are believed to result in increasing social polarisation (Peck 2005; Markusen 2006; Bontje and Musterd 2009). Scott (2008) pointed to a strong divide between the 'surface glitter' of the new economy and its amenities and the 'underlying squalor' that accompanies it, including crime and violence, increasing social polarisation, social conflicts and informal-economy jobs. In particular, policies aiming at attracting the creative class may lead to strong competition between municipalities in the same region to attract the so-called 'economically sustainable population' and, simultaneously, the displacement of the socially and economically marginalised population (Andersen, Lund Hansen and Clark 2001; Larsen and Lund Hansen 2008) and a mismatch between cities' strategies and the 'economic reality' (Peck 2005). McGuigan (2009) associated Florida's discourse with class interests rather than cultural policy, and referred to it as an 'articulation of neoliberal economics with cool culture' (p. 298).

Furthermore, the applicability of Florida's concepts for urban policies is much debated, since it was argued that creative cities cannot be created out of thin air (Hall 2004), and creative-city policies depend on a complex interplay of housing, working and leisure agendas by different departments (Kooijman and Romein 2007). Servillo, Atkinson and Russo (2012) and Borén and Young (2013) argued that there is no one-size-fits-all policy for creating knowledge cities. Rather, each city-region has its own unique features that distinguish it from other cities and regions, and focusing on these particularities and historic development paths is a more likely road to success than copying best practices in other cities (Pratt 2008; Musterd and Kovács 2013). In fact, if each city-region adopts the same policy measures and focuses on the same features and amenities, this will ultimately increase uniformity and result in the loss of unique characteristics and competitive advantage (Peck 2012).

Finally, all three approaches are criticised for being too strongly US-centred, while their usefulness in the European context is questioned. Cultural and institutional differences, such as different languages, tax systems and labour market rules, form a significant barrier to (transnational) migration within Europe (Andersen and Lorenzen 2005; Martin-Brelot *et al*. 2010). Furthermore, Europe is different from the US in terms of a smaller number of cities to move between and subsequent more modest inter-city competition at the national level (Hansen and Niedomysl 2009), lower commuter tolerance (Martin-Brelot *et al*. 2010), smaller income differences between creative knowledge workers and the rest of the population (Andersen and Lorenzen 2005), combined with higher levels of income redistribution through welfare systems (Esping-Andersen 1990), and, finally, a more polycentric form of urban development (Kooijman and Romein 2007).

Thus, the main factors in attracting talents to a certain region are employment and personal considerations, while amenities seem to play a secondary role. However, once the choice of a certain region has been made, the offer of amenities may influence the intra-regional sorting of skilled workers within this region. Moreover, it can be argued that for specific types of knowledge workers, amenities and other soft conditions may be more important than for others. Here, demographic and lifestyle aspects, as well as occupation, may come into play. In the next section, we will therefore turn to the residential preferences of creative knowledge workers, while acknowledging the large diversity within this group of workers.

The sorting of creative knowledge workers within city-regions

Several European empirical studies on creative knowledge workers, albeit they are defined differently in each study, outlined large differences in residential preferences between different sub-groups of the creative class. The most notable conclusion from these studies is that the creative class as one uniform group is non-existent. A 2013 empirical study on Dublin's creative class has shown that residential preferences of the creative class – using the broad definition including workers in creative and knowledge-intensive industries – are highly diverse. Half of Dublin's creative workers live in the inner city, whereas 29 per cent live in the city outskirts and another 20 per cent in the periphery (Lawton, Murphy and Redmond 2013).

In particular, household and lifestyle characteristics are important drivers of location choice. In their empirical study on knowledge workers in Scandinavian countries, Andersen *et al*. (2010) concluded that metropolitan areas are not more or less attractive for knowledge workers than suburban areas but, rather, attract different groups of knowledge workers, and also for different reasons. Both metropolitan areas and smaller urban, suburban or rural centres attract workers especially because of job opportunities, but retain workers for different reasons. Whereas in metropolitan areas cultural amenities are important retention factors, smaller centres retain people especially because of 'social soft conditions', such as quietness, space and social cohesion. In line with this, workers with families are relatively often attracted to smaller centres, while younger workers more often prefer central urban locations (Andersen *et al.* 2010).

Also Lawton, Murphy and Redmond (2013) found a relationship between demographic aspects and residential preferences. Based on their Dublin case study, the younger age cohorts (under 35) relatively often prefer central urban milieus, whereas preferences for the urban periphery are largely consistent across different age cohorts. Events in the personal life cycle, especially becoming parents, are highly important for making location decisions as well. Similar findings were presented in studies from Scandinavia (Andersen *et al.* 2010), Israel (Frenkel, Bendit and Kaplan 2013) and Australia (Verdich 2010): younger knowledge workers – especially singles or couples without children – prefer inner city districts with large concentrations of (cultural) amenities, while older and 'settled' knowledge workers more often prefer suburban residential milieus. Relocation decisions are influenced by a complex set of push and pull factors, and the importance attached to each factor shifts during the life cycle. Hansen and Niedomysl (2009) studied which factors are considered important for the migration decisions of the creative class in Sweden. They distinguished between workers with high and low levels of education and between different age groups, and found only marginal differences in migration activities between low- and high-educated workers. Only the group of people up to 25 years, including many students, tends to move relatively often towards regions with high degrees of quality of life. After entering the job market, many move away from the larger cities and also toward lower-ranking regions. Thus, migration to places with a high-ranking 'living climate' takes place *before* people become part of the creative class, whereas people move in the opposite direction *after* entering the creative class. In their study on the residential preferences of knowledge migrants in the Netherlands, Beckers and Boschman (2013) found that although this group has a relatively strong orientation towards central urban milieus and upmarket neighbourhoods, these preferences change over time. Once individuals start living together or start a family, quieter neighbourhoods become more popular and proximity to school outweighs proximity to work. Apart from life-cycle events, activity patterns outside working hours also play a decisive role in the sorting of creative knowledge workers within a city-region. An empirical study from Israel showed that culture-oriented and sport-oriented activity patterns increase the tendency to reside in the metropolitan core, whereas a home-oriented activity pattern increases the propensity to reside in the outer suburbs and the metropolitan fringe (Bendit, Frenkel and Kaplan 2011). Finally, an earlier study on the residential preferences of Dutch ICT workers showed that within this group, the choice for residential locations differs between lifestyle groups and is often related to differences in household situation. About one quarter of all ICT workers prefer a location in or near the city centre, while the rest – generally older and settled workers – prefer a suburban or exurban location (Van Oort, Weterings and Verlinde 2003).

A number of studies have looked into differences in residential preferences between different occupational sub-groups within the workforce. A twofold relationship between the urban environment and specific forms of employment was observed. On the one hand, specific economic activities have become more urban, and many of the workers in these sectors prefer living close to work and therefore increasingly settle in (inner) cities (Kloosterman 2004). On the other hand, workers in 'new economy' sectors such as advertising and design form a new middle class with a different taste and different residential preferences than the 'traditional' middle class (Butler 1997). The process of gentrification, or the transformation of specific urban neighbourhoods into areas attractive for the middle classes, is linked to the changing occupational profiles of these areas (Zukin 1987; Ley 2003). According to Butler and Robson (2003), the residential behaviour of the middle classes is the result of a trade-off between the fields of consumption, education, housing and employment, which in turn is influenced by the (financial) resources and the composition of their households, and likely by residential background and social networks as well (Boterman 2013).

Previous empirical evidence indicates that residential preferences of the creative class as a whole do not differ much from the choice characteristics of the general population, but a clearer picture emerges when looking more specifically at job categories. Most notably, whereas workers in creative industries show a highly urban residential pattern, the residential preferences of workers in other, less creative, knowledge-intensive occupations are more similar to those of the general public (Lawton, Murphy and Redmond 2013). These findings are in line with an earlier empirical study on different categories of knowledge workers in Amsterdam. Workers in creative occupations had the strongest urban orientation: of all architects employed in Amsterdam, 71 per cent lived within the city, whereas this was the case for only 17 per cent of all the ICT workers working in Amsterdam. Other sectors of which employees predominantly have urban residential preferences are the public sector (60 per cent), advertising (52 per cent) and the social sciences and law faculties of polytechnics and universities (around 50 per cent) (Musterd 2002). Helbrecht (1998) and De Wijs-Mulkens (1999) found similar results in their studies, which differentiated between the residential preferences of occupational and educational groups.

Kotkin (2000) stated, based on a study of high-tech workers in the US, that technical workers have residential preferences that differ strongly from those of the highly urban oriented workers in creative industries. Instead of dense urban areas, they generally prefer safe, suburban communities, which he refers to as 'nerdistans'. A study by Van Oort, Weterings and Verlinde (2003) on Dutch ICT workers provided a more nuanced view and found that their residential preferences do not differ much from those of highly skilled workers in general. Their study found that ICT workers have a high 'commuting tolerance': good accessibility to the workplace was considered more important than proximity. When choosing a residential area, the characteristics of the house, the neighbourhood and the availability of facilities are taken into consideration (Van Oort, Weterings and Verlinde 2003).

Urban centres appear to be relatively more popular for workers in creative industries (Markusen 2006), likely because of a stronger preference for living near cultural amenities and meeting places that enable them to live near 'the scene', or the relative importance of symbolic values for creative workers (Smit 2012). However, this claim is challenged, since other studies have found no convincing evidence of creative workers having stronger urban preferences (Borén and Young 2013).

Differences between the residential preferences of native and international knowledge migrants have not received much attention in the literature. Still, a number of regionally focused studies have been conducted on the group of (highly skilled) international migrants, but without making a direct comparison to native workers. Chapter 9 will elaborate in more detail on some of these studies dealing with international migrants in the Amsterdam and Eindhoven regions.

Conclusion

The literature review shows that there is large disagreement with respect to the main factors determining the choice for a location. A common theme in the empirical and theoretical studies on the location choices of creative knowledge workers in the European context is the ongoing importance of employment opportunities for attracting skilled workers to a certain region, whereas soft conditions play a secondary role in the decision-making process. Furthermore, the 'creative class' can by no means be considered as one homogeneous group. Residential preferences are to a large extent driven by demographic factors, and also differ between different occupational groups.

In wrapping up the main findings from the literature review, a number of overall conclusions stand out. First, *the* knowledge worker does not exist. While urban policies often target the presumed homogenous 'creative class', this group can be subdivided into several subgroups that differ largely in terms of both income and housing preferences. Many studies have shown that workers in creative industries generally express the housing preferences that were presented by Florida (2002), for highly urban and diverse districts, although their results may be biased, since precisely these studies included only people already living in central urban districts. However, other studies have found that highly educated professional workers in business services or technical sectors have housing preferences that do not differ much from those of the general population and that many of them also tend to live in suburban areas.

A second overall conclusion from the existing literature is that work and career opportunities are dominant factors in determining the attractiveness of a region for knowledge workers, although amenities are by no means unimportant. People move to a region because they can find jobs there. Talent does not attract companies, but companies attract talent. Previous studies argue that soft conditions such as amenities play a secondary role for individuals or households who are making location choices. They are not the primary attractors, but become important once a job has been found, as people expect a good-quality living environment. In the case of two regions having a similar job offer, then a rich amenity structure and, especially, an attractive housing stock may make one region more attractive than the other. Again, the diversity within the knowledge worker group should be considered here, since for some sub-groups amenities and other soft conditions may be at least equally important. Therefore, the chapters in this volume build further on the idea that both sets of factors play an important, but different, role in attracting skilled workers to cities.

Third, while employment is the main attractor at the regional level, the choice of a certain location *within* this region is steered mainly by demographic factors and lifestyle. In general young workers and people with a 'bohemian' lifestyle appear to prefer living in highly urban districts, whereas older and settled workers with families more often prefer suburban or even rural residential locations. The highly urban residential preferences that are prominent in the work of Florida (2002), Glaeser, Kolko and Saiz (2001) and Clark *et al.* (2002) appear to be applicable especially to particular sub-sections of the highly diverse creative class: workers in creative industries, and especially the younger ones among them. The preferences of knowledge workers in other professions, working with more analytical knowledge, are more diverse.

Although the literature review has depicted a dominant role for employment opportunities, one preliminary policy implication is that policies aiming at attracting or retaining knowledge workers should focus both on employment opportunities and on housing and amenities. With respect to employment, the influence of regional policy makers is limited, since labour market regulation is organised at the national level in most countries. Amenities and other soft conditions can be influenced by regional policies, however. These amenities *combined with* employment opportunities may play a significant role for the attraction of workers. If economic conditions are equal in two regions, people are likely to choose the region with the best set of living conditions, and housing in particular, albeit in a trade-off relation to the level of wages to be earned. Soft conditions may play a significant role for a minority of relocating workers and may help to *retain* rather than attract workers at the regional level. Furthermore, especially depending on life-cycle phase and lifestyle, they influence the residential sorting of creative knowledge workers *within* regions. Thus, soft conditions seem to be necessary but not sufficient to attract knowledge workers. Rather, the most successful outcomes can be expected from cross-sector policies at the regional level that integrate work, housing and amenities.

References

Amin, A and Thrift, N 2007, Cultural-economy and cities. *Progress in Human Geography* 31(2), 143–161.

Andersen, KV and Lorenzen, M 2005, *The geography of the Danish creative class; a mapping and analysis*, Frederiksberg: Copenhagen Business School.

Andersen, KV, Bugge, MM, Hansen, HK, Isaksen, A and Raunio, M 2010, One size fits all? Applying the creative class thesis onto a Nordic context. *European Planning Studies* 18(10), 1591–1609.

Atzema, O 2007, Over de creatieve klasse [About the creative class] *ROM Magazine*, 17 July, 20–27.

Beckers, P and Boschman, S 2013, *A place called home: residential choices of highly skilled migrants in the Netherlands and the role of local amenities*, Paper presented at the 7th International Conference of Population Geographies (ICPG) in Groningen, the Netherlands, 25–28 June 2013.

Bendit, E, Frenkel, A and Kaplan, S 2011, *Residential location choice of knowledge workers in a 'Startup Metropolis': the role of amenities, workplace and lifestyle*, Paper presented at the 51st European Congress of the Regional Science Association International, 30 August–3 September 2011, Barcelona.

Bontje, M and Musterd, S 2009, Creative industries, creative class and competitiveness: expert opinions critically appraised. *Geoforum* 40, 843–852.

Borén, T and Young, C 2013, The migration dynamics of the "creative class": evidence from a study of artists in Stockholm, Sweden. *Annals of the Association of American Geographers* 103(1), 195–210.

Boterman, WR 2013, Dealing with diversity: middle-class family households and the issue of 'Black' and 'White' schools in Amsterdam. *Urban Studies*, 50(6), 1130–1147.

Butler, T 1997, *Gentrification and the middle classes*, Aldershot: Ashgate.

Butler, T and Robson, G 2003, *London calling: the middle classes and the re-making of inner London*, London: Berg Publishers.

Chen, Y and Rosenthal, SS 2008, Local amenities and life-cycle migration: do people move for jobs or fun? *Journal of Urban Economics* 64(3), 519–537.

Clark, TN, Lloyd, R, Wong, KK and Jain, P 2002, Amenities drive urban growth. *Journal of Urban Affairs* 24(5), 493–515.

Currid, E 2007, *The Warhol economy*, Princeton, NJ: Princeton University Press.

Currid, E 2009, Bohemia as subculture; 'Bohemia' as industry: art, culture, and economic development. *Journal of Planning Literature* 23(4), 368–382.

De Wijs-Mulkens, E 1999, *Wonen op stand. Lifestyles en landschappen van de culturele en economische elite [Living in respectable areas. Lifestyles and landscapes of the cultural and economic elite]*, Amsterdam: Spinhuis.

Esping-Andersen, G 1990, *Three worlds of welfare capitalism*, Cambridge, UK: Polity Press.

Florida, R 2002, *The rise of the creative class and how it's transforming work, leisure, community and everyday life*, New York: Basic Books.

Florida, R 2010, *The great reset: How new ways of living and working drive post-crash prosperity,* New York: Harper.

Frenkel, A, Bendit, E and Kaplan, S 2013, The linkage between the lifestyle of knowledge-workers and their intra-metropolitan residential choice: a clustering approach based on self-organizing maps. *Computers, Environment and Urban Systems* 39, 151–169.

Galster, G 2012, *Driving Detroit: The quest for respect in the motor city*, Philadelphia: University of Pennsylvania Press.

Geerdink, M, Krauss, P, Krebbekx, J, Van der Mark, R, Soentken, M and Van der Wilt, M 2010, *Pieken in de Delta; Evaluatie subsidieregeling [Peaks in the Delta; evaluation of the subsidy regulation]*, Utrecht: Berenschot.

Glaeser, EL 2004, *Review of Richard Florida's 'The rise of the creative class'*, (http://post. economics.harvard.edu/faculty/glaeser/papers/ Review_Florida.pdf)

Glaeser, EL and Gottlieb, JD 2006, *Urban resurgence and the consumer city*, Discussion Paper Number 2109, Cambridge, MA: Harvard Institute of Economic Research, Harvard University.

Glaeser, EL, Kolko, J and Saiz, A 2001, Consumer city. *Journal of Economic Geography* 1, 27–50.

Grabher, G 1993, The Weakness of strong ties: the lock-in of regional development in the Ruhr area. In: G Grabher (ed.) *The embedded firm: on the socioeconomics of industrial networks*, 255–277. London: Routledge.

Grabher, G 2002, Cool projects, boring institutions: temporary collaboration. Social context. *Regional Studies* 36(3), 205–214.

Grabher, G 2004, Learning in projects, remembering in networks? Communality, sociality, and connectivity in project ecologies. *European Urban and Regional Studies* 11(2), 103–123.

Hall, P 2004, Creativity, culture, knowledge and the city. *Built Environment* 30(3), 256–258.

Hansen, HK and Niedomysl, T 2009 Migration of the creative class: evidence from Sweden. *Journal of Economic Geography* 9(2), 191–206.

Helbrecht, I 1998, *The creative metropolis; services, symbols and spaces*, Paper presented at the yearly conference for the association of Canadastudies, Grainau.

Helbrecht, I 2004, Bare Geographies in knowledge societies – creative cities as text and piece of art: two eyes, one vision. *Built Environment* 30(3), 194–203.

Horwitz, FM, Heng, CT and Quazi, HA 2003, Finders, keepers? Attracting, motivating and retaining knowledge workers. *Human Resource Management Journal* 13(4), 23–44.

Jacobs, J 1961, *The death and life of great American cities*, New York: Random House.

Klepper, S 2002, The capabilities of new firms and the evolution of the US automobile industry. *Industrial and Corporate Change* 11(4), 645–666.

Kloosterman, RC 2004, Recent employment trend in the cultural industries in Amsterdam, Rotterdam, The Hague and Utrecht: a first exploration. *Tijdschrift voor Economische en Sociale Geografie* 95(2), 243–252.

Kooijman, D and Romein, A 2007, *The limited potential of the creative city concept: policy practices in four Dutch cities*, Draft based on a presentation and paper at the 'Regions in Focus' conference in Lisbon, April 2007.

Kotkin, J 2000, *The new geography: how the digital revolution is reshaping the American landscape*, New York: Random House.

Krätke, S 2007, Metropolisation of the European economic territory as a consequence of increasing specialisation of urban agglomerations in the knowledge economy. *European Planning Studies* 15(1), 1–27.

Krätke, S 2010, 'Creative cities' and the rise of the dealer class: a critique of Richard Florida's approach to urban theory. *International Journal of Urban and Regional Research* DOI: 10.1111/j.1468-2427.2010.00939.x

Larsen, HG and Lund Hansen, A 2008, Gentrification – gentle or traumatic? Urban renewal policies and socioeconomic transformations in Copenhagen. *Urban Studies* 45(12), 2429–2448.

Lawton, P, Murphy, E and Redmond, D 2013, Residential preferences of the 'creative class'? *Cities* 31(2), 47–56.

Ley, D 2003, Artists, aestheticisation and the field of gentrification. *Urban Studies* 40(12), 2527–2544.

Lund Hansen, A, Andersen, HT and Clark, E 2001, Creative Copenhagen: globalization, urban governance and social change. *European Planning Studies* 9(7), 851–869.

Markusen, A 2006, Urban development and the politics of a creative class: evidence from a study of artists. *Environment and Planning A* 38, 1921–1940.

Marlet, G and Van Woerkens, C 2005, *Tolerance, aesthetics, amenities or jobs? Dutch city attraction to the creative class*, Tjalling C. Koopmans Research Institute, Utrecht School of Economics Utrecht University, Discussion Paper Series no. 05-33.

Marlet, G and Van Woerkens, C 2007, The Dutch creative class and how it fosters urban employment growth. *Urban Studies* 44(13), 2605–2626.

Martin-Brelot, H, Grossetti, M, Eckert, D, Gritsai, O and Kovácz, Z 2010, The spatial mobility of the 'creative class': a European perspective. *International Journal of Urban and Regional Research* 34(4), 854–870.

McGuigan, J 2009, Doing a Florida thing: the creative class thesis and cultural policy. *International Journal of Cultural Policy* 15(3), 291–300.

Mellander, C and Florida, R 2006, *The creative class or human capital? Explaining regional development in Sweden*, CESIS, Electronic Working Paper Series No. 79. Available at: http://www.infra.kth.se/cesis/documents/WP79.pdf.

Miguelez, E and Moreno, R 2014, What attracts knowledge workers: the role of space and social networks. *Journal of Regional Science* 54(1), 33–60.

Musterd, S 2002, *De Nieuwe Amsterdamse Kernvoorraad; Woonmilieus in de Creatieve Culturele Kennisstad*, Bestuursdienst, Gemeente Amsterdam, Amsterdam.

Musterd, S 2006, Segregation, urban space and the resurgent city. *Urban Studies* 43(8), 1325–1340.

Musterd, S and Kovács, Z (eds) 2013, *Place-making and policies for competitive cities*, Chichester: Wiley-Blackwell.

Musterd, S and Murie, A (eds) 2010, *Making competitive cities*, Chichester: Wiley-Blackwell.

Musterd, S and Ostendorf, W 2004, Creative cultural knowledge cities: perspectives and planning strategies. *Built Environment* 30(3), 189–193.

Niedomysl, T 2010, Towards a conceptual framework of place attractiveness: a migration perspective. *Geografiska Annaler: Series B, Human Geography* 92(1), 97–109.

Niedomysl, T and Hansen, HK 2010, What matters more for the decision to move: jobs versus amenities. *Environment and Planning A* 42, 1636–1649.

Peck, J 2005, Struggling with the creative class. *International Journal of Urban and Regional Research* 29(4), 740–770.

Peck, J 2012, Recreative city: Amsterdam, vehicular ideas and the adaptive spaces of creativity policy. *International Journal of Urban and Regional Research* 36(3), 462–485.

Phelps, NA and Ozawa, T 2003, Contrasts in agglomeration: proto-industrial, industrial and postindustrial forms compared. *Progress in Human Geography* 27(5), 583–604.

Pratt, AC 2008, Creative cities: the cultural industries and the creative class. *Geografiska Annaler B* 90(2), 107–117.

Romein, A and Trip, JJ 2011, *Economic downturn: a threat for creative city policy or a blessing in disguise?* Paper presented at the RSA Annual International Conference 2011 Regional development and policy – challenges, choices and recipients, Newcastle upon Tyne, 17–20 April, 1–13.

Sassen, S 2002, *Global networks, linked cities*, New York: Routledge.

Scott, AJ 2006, Creative cities: conceptual issues and policy questions. *Journal of Urban Affairs* 28(1), 1–17.

Scott, AJ 2008, *Social economy of the metropolis*, Oxford: Oxford University Press.

Servillo, L, Atkinson, R and Russo, AP 2012, Territorial attractiveness in EU urban and spatial policy: a critical review and future research agenda. *European Urban and Regional Studies* 19(4), 349–365.

Smit, AJ 2012, *Spatial quality of cultural production districts*, Enschede: Ipskamp.

Storper, M 1997, *The regional world: territorial development in a global economy*, New York: Guilford Press.

Storper, M and Manville, M 2006, Behaviour, preferences and cities: urban theory and urban resurgence. *Urban Studies* 43(8), 1247–1274.

Storper, M and Scott, AJ 2009, Rethinking human capital, creativity and urban growth. *Journal of Economic Geography* (9), 147–167.

Van Duijn, M and Rouwendal, J 2013, Cultural heritage and the location choice of Dutch households in a residential sorting model. *Journal of Economic Geography* 13, 473–500.

Van Oort, F, Weterings, A and Verlinde, H 2003, Residential amenities of knowledge workers and the location of ICT-firms in the Netherlands. *Tijdschrift voor economische en sociale geografie* 94(4), 516–523.

Van Winden, W 2010, Knowledge and the European city. *Tijdschrift voor Economische en Sociale Geografie* 101(1), 100–106.

Van Winden, W, Van den Berg, L and Pol, P 2007, European cities in the knowledge economy: towards a typology. *Urban Studies* 44(3), 525–549.

Verdich, M 2010, Creative migration? The attraction and retention of the 'creative class' in Launceston, Tasmania. *Australian Geographer* 41(1), 129–140.

Wojan, TR, Lambert, DM and McGranahan, DA 2007, Emoting with their feet: Bohemian attraction to creative milieu. *Journal of Economic Geography* 7, 711–736.

Yigitcanlar, T, Baum, S and Horton, S 2007, Attracting and retaining knowledge workers in knowledge cities. *Journal of Knowledge Management* 11(5), 6–17.

Zukin, S 1987, Gentrification: culture and capital in the urban core. *Annual Review of Sociology* 13, 129–147.

Zukin, S 1995, *The culture of cities*, Oxford: Blackwell.

3 Residential sorting of creative knowledge workers in four European knowledge cities

Bart Sleutjes

Introduction

Following the previous chapter's discussion of the main insights from the academic literature on residential preferences of creative knowledge workers, this chapter illustrates how different city regions have coped with attracting and retaining creative knowledge workers to their regions. Based on region-specific literature and the results of a series of qualitative interviews with regional stakeholders, the main strengths and weaknesses of the Amsterdam and Eindhoven regions, the main research areas in this volume, will be described. What were their experiences with respect to the attraction of (international) creative knowledge workers? In order to place these cities in a broader perspective, an international comparison was made with two cities with a more or less comparable economic profile and climate. Copenhagen, a relatively diverse urban economy, and Helsinki, a high-tech pole, were chosen as comparative case studies. These four city regions will be briefly introduced in this section, while the second section addresses their specific strengths and weaknesses with respect to hard and soft location factors. The third and fourth sections of the chapter describe the sorting of creative knowledge workers in, respectively, the Dutch cities and the Nordic cities. The concluding section chapter wraps up the findings from the four case studies and describes the main similarities and differences between the Dutch and Nordic cities.

The choice for these four city-regions was based on their similarities. In all four city-regions, human capital is an important driver of the local economy and natural amenities do not play an important role. In addition, all four cities have flourished in the 1990s and early 2000s. However, Eindhoven differs from the other three cities in a number of ways. Apart from being smaller in size, it is the only one of the four cities without a capital function and it has no waterfront development. However, Eindhoven's important position in terms of economic output, certainly in terms of the knowledge economy, justifies its inclusion. The findings are derived from existing literature on the regions' strengths and weaknesses as knowledge cities, from their current economic profiles and – when available – from findings of previous studies on the residential preferences of creative knowledge workers in the respective city-regions. These findings are based on 23 expert interviews with, in total, 31 stakeholders in the four cities. These experts were employed at local or regional government or governance institutions and at universities (see Sleutjes 2013 for a more detailed description of these four cities, their economic development and the concentration of creative knowledge workers within them).

Amsterdam, with over 800,000 inhabitants in 2012, is the largest Dutch city (O+S 2012). The Amsterdam metropolitan region, Metropoolregio Amsterdam (hereafter MRA), has over 2.3 million inhabitants and the region is part of the largest urban conurbation in the Netherlands, the Randstad (approximately 7 million inhabitants). Although it is also the Dutch capital, the government seat is in The Hague. Still, Amsterdam is regarded as the most important city in the Netherlands in terms of culture and is also the main hub for the financial and business services sectors.

The city of Eindhoven is located in the south-eastern part of the country, in the province of North Brabant, near the Belgian border. With around 220,000 inhabitants in 2011, it is the fifth-largest Dutch city and the major city of the country's second urban network, Brabantstad, which also includes the cities of Breda, Tilburg, 's-Hertogenbosch and Helmond. The Eindhoven region is part of the functional city-region Eindhoven Metropolitan Region (*previously Samenwerkingsverband Regio Eindhoven, or SRE*), consisting of 21 municipalities, with Eindhoven and Helmond being the main urban cores. The Metropolitan Region has approximately 750,000 inhabitants.

Copenhagen is Scandinavia's second-largest metropolitan area after Stockholm. The municipality of Copenhagen has a population of 550,000, whereas the Capital Region (*Region Hovedstaden*) has approximately 1.7 million inhabitants, or 30 per cent of the country's total population (Website Region Hovedstaden). Copenhagen is also part of the Øresund region, a cross-border Danish–Swedish double city-region, linking the Copenhagen and Malmö regions via the Øresund bridge. The Øresund region has 3.7 million inhabitants, including 1.2 million people living in the south-western part of Sweden (Skåne). The Øresund region is sometimes considered as a single urban knowledge area (Hospers 2003), although its functionality has also been contested. Being the only metropolis in Denmark, Copenhagen can be seen as a primate city that is dominant in terms of economic, political and cultural functions.

Helsinki is the capital and largest city of Finland. Early 2013, the city of Helsinki had over 600,000 inhabitants, but 1.4 million people live in the wider metropolitan region, Helsinki Metropolitan Area (HMA). Apart from Helsinki, the HMA includes two large municipalities, Espoo (257,000 inhabitants) and Vantaa (205,000 inhabitants), and the smaller municipality of Kauniainen (almost 9,000 inhabitants). Although relatively small from a European perspective, the HMA is the only international-sized agglomeration in Finland, accommodating 20 per cent of Finland's total population and one third of all economic activity (City of Helsinki Urban Facts 2013).

Hard and soft conditions in the four city-regions

Based on local literature and in-depth interviews, what are the main strengths and weaknesses of the four city-regions with respect to attracting creative knowledge workers? This section summarizes these strengths and weaknesses, subdivided into four categories: the economic profile and institutional context, space and infrastructure, soft conditions and the housing market.

The economic profile and institutional context

A large strand of literature indicated that employment and education opportunities are the most important 'hard' factors for location decisions (see Chapter 2). In this respect, all four city-regions have a favourable profile, especially due to the presence of a highly skilled labour force and strong higher education institutions. The two Dutch cities, Amsterdam and Eindhoven, have different labour market profiles but both are among the economic 'mainports' of the Netherlands. The economic profile of Amsterdam is highly diverse and its main economic clusters include financial and business services, ICT and a broad range of cultural industries. This heterogeneity makes the city-region attractive for a large and diverse group of workers and less vulnerable to economic crises. If one sector collapses, the regional economy can rely on others. Amsterdam seems to cherish this diversity as its main economic strength. However, apart from the positive aspects of diversity, some of the interviewees criticized the lack of economic profiling. This makes it difficult to 'brand' the region in order to attract very specific types of knowledge workers, such as technical knowledge workers.

Eindhoven's economic profile is much more specialized. The regional economy is dominated by the high-tech sector, and within this sector it is the main regional cluster in the Netherlands. Amsterdam has a strong beta cluster as well (e.g., ICT companies of various sizes and the Shell laboratory), yet Eindhoven offers jobs that are unique within the Netherlands. The economy is dominated by a few clusters of large companies (e.g. Philips, ASML) and their spin-offs, as well as a technical university. Eindhoven also has a growing creative industries cluster, the major part of which consists of activities related to design. The region also has clusters related to the automotive and food industries. Despite the economic crisis of 2008, Eindhoven achieved economic growth. However, the city-region has some problems related to its limited scale. Both the city-region and its university are too small to ensure sufficient critical mass and, even more important, there is a shortage of qualified labour to fill job vacancies. Although this problem is being tackled at the national level through the encouragement of studying beta disciplines, Eindhoven, at least in the short term, is highly dependent on the inflow of international creative knowledge workers. Through a 'triple helix' structure[1] (Brainport Development) and a branding strategy, the public sector, regional business sector and education institutes actively look for foreign talent in targeted countries.

Helsinki's economic profile can best be compared to Eindhoven's because of the dominant IT sector, of which it is one of Europe's main clusters. However, as the city is the capital of Finland, the public sector is also an important source of employment. Helsinki has long been dominated by the ICT sector, and mobile telecommunication (Nokia) in particular. This has made Helsinki's economy vulnerable to economic shocks and, since 2010, job losses at Nokia have led to increasing unemployment. However, Nokia's demise did not turn out to be all bad news, since it also paved the way for other sectors to flourish. The rise of the gaming sector and high-potential start-ups, which are actively stimulated and assisted through partnerships between municipalities and universities, are the main examples. Helsinki has some difficulty in attracting international creative knowledge workers because of its peripheral location within Europe, its cold climate and language barriers.

Copenhagen occupies a position somewhere in between, since the region's economic profile is not as homogeneous as Helsinki's and Eindhoven's, but also not as diverse as that of Amsterdam. The region excels in medical technology and life tech. Copenhagen functions as a magnet for Danish talent but – like Helsinki – is struggling to attract sufficient international creative knowledge workers. Restrictive immigration policies at the national level conflict with the needs of the regional business sector, which largely depends on international talent.

A similarity between all four city-regions is the strong growth in cultural industries over the past years, although the profiling with respect to specific sub-sectors of the creative industries is different in the four regions. Eindhoven has a clear specialization in activities related to design but also has a strong advertising sector. Amsterdam has a wide range of creative industries, but compared to other city-regions in the Netherlands is particularly strong in the arts and media sectors. Helsinki has a particularly strong position in design, architecture and, more recently, video gaming. Copenhagen, like Amsterdam, has a highly diverse profile concerning its creative industries, and the city-region is especially known as a hub for design, fashion, architecture and video and film industries.

A large difference between Amsterdam and the other three cities concerns clustering policies. Whereas Amsterdam emphasizes its diversity and focuses its policy making on seven clusters, Eindhoven, Copenhagen and Helsinki have strong and more sector-specific cluster policies and a number of large multinationals that attract both native and international creative knowledge workers.

Eindhoven (Brainport Development) and Helsinki are very strong in terms of public-private partnerships and examples for other city-regions; Copenhagen (e.g. Medicon Valley) and Amsterdam also have public-private partnerships in the regional economic domain. Both Copenhagen and Helsinki have problems related to regional governance. Rather than cooperating, municipalities in the region are in competition for high income-tax payers. Although the Øresund Committee is aiming for an integrated cross-border labour market, there remains strong competition between municipalities and universities on the Danish and the Swedish sides of the Sound. In the Netherlands, this is less of an issue, since taxes are determined at the national level.

Space and infrastructure

In terms of infrastructure, Amsterdam's main strength is Schiphol Airport, Europe's fourth-largest airport, which ensures Amsterdam's global connectivity and is also an important economic hub. Amsterdam has some problems with shortage of space and resulting high prices for housing and business real estate, as well as high levels of congestion. Copenhagen and Helsinki are both known for their excellent public transport systems and low levels of congestion. Both cities have an international airport that ranks among the world's top 20. The Dutch cities and Copenhagen are also known for their high-standard bicycle infrastructure. Copenhagen's active efforts to become bicycle friendly have led to the use of the term 'Copenhagenization' when referring to bicycle infrastructure planning. Although Eindhoven has a peripheral location from a Dutch perspective, it is located not too far from larger European cities, to which it has good highway connections. Local experts also mentioned that the distance to Amsterdam (1.5 hours by train) is not long when viewed from an international perspective. Being the fifth city of the Netherlands, Eindhoven has a much smaller airport than the other three case study cities, but it offers connections to a number of European destinations. Helsinki has an issue related to it geographical location. Its peripheral location within Europe is generally seen as a disadvantage, but in the interviews its good (train) connections with Russia were also considered an opportunity.

Soft conditions

Concerning the regional soft conditions, the four city-regions are very different from one another. In the two Nordic cities, low crime levels and the easy way of living ('everything works') were mentioned as strengths. These aspects also apply to a large degree to the Netherlands, but were not specifically mentioned as strengths distinguishing the two Dutch city-regions from their competitors. In terms of image and social climate, Amsterdam and Eindhoven are in contrast to Copenhagen and Helsinki. Both Dutch cities have a large international population and an image of tolerance toward people coming from outside, although this image has been contested at the national level, at least since 2002, with the rising popularity of populist political parties with anti-immigration agendas. Copenhagen and Helsinki are mainly magnets for native rather than international talents, which, according to the interviewees, is partly due to a less open social climate that makes it more difficult to attract and, especially, retain internationals. Just like the Netherlands, Denmark and Finland have also seen a (recent) rise of right-wing populist parties aiming at limiting immigration.

With respect to historic amenities and authenticity, Amsterdam has a strong profile via the historic inner city with its unique morphology, including the canal belt. Copenhagen's inner city is no older than the eighteenth century, due to a number of fires that destroyed most of the medieval city, but many buildings have been rebuilt and the historic street pattern with its many narrow streets has been preserved. With increasing gentrification and the re-entry of families with children into the inner city and its surrounding neighbourhoods in both Amsterdam and Copenhagen, some critics assert that part of the lively and authentic character of the cities is diminishing. Some of the interviewees in Amsterdam mentioned strict regulations in, for example, the catering sector as bottlenecks for creativity.

Eindhoven and Helsinki seem to have more problems with their image, although they are not insurmountable, according to the interviewees. Eindhoven does not have a historic inner city and is known as a 'large village' rather than a vibrant city. Still, recent developments in and around the inner city have resulted in the transformation of industrial heritage sites into residential and commercial destinations, as well as the addition of innovative architecture. Also a few large cultural events, such as the Dutch Design Week and the Glow light festival, contribute to Eindhoven's urban exposure. Although Helsinki has a number of historic buildings in the inner city, the city lacks the image of a vibrant metropolis. However, in particular, the stimulation of grassroots activities in the field of social cohesion and culture by the city government since about 2011 was mentioned by the interviewees as a positive development.

Regarding cultural amenities, Amsterdam, Copenhagen and Helsinki have a strong advantage because of their capital status. Eindhoven, compared to the other three regions, is less well endowed with cultural amenities, although for a city of 200,000 its offer is above average. Even more important than having a diverse cultural offer is the accessibility of this cultural offer. This is related both to short travel distances and low congestion within the region (Copenhagen) and to other cities outside the region (Eindhoven), and also to the barriers to visiting cultural amenities. For example, in Copenhagen, the small and accessible cultural venues and initiatives (street-level culture) in particular were highly valued because creative knowledge workers prefer to have immediate access to them.

Housing market

Housing is problematic in all four metropolitan areas, especially in the core cities. In terms of the housing market, Amsterdam, Copenhagen and Helsinki show some similarities. All three cities are characterized by high population density and a housing stock that consists mainly of smaller rented dwellings, many of which are apartments. All cities have a large but decreasing social rented sector, and expensive private rented and owner-occupied sectors.

In Amsterdam, Copenhagen and Helsinki high rents and exploding housing prices made certain central parts of the city almost inaccessible for newcomers with lower incomes. Especially in Amsterdam and Copenhagen, these developments are the result of state-led gentrification. For example, the spatial and housing policies of the municipality of Amsterdam are targeted at making the inner parts of the city more attractive for middle- and higher-income households and families. These policies include increasing the proportion of owner-occupied dwellings at the expensive of social rented dwellings and the cleaning up of public space in once run-down and relatively poor inner-city districts. These developments have been a topic of academic debate for years, since they are assumed to make parts of the city inaccessible for lower-income groups and also lead to displacement by higher-income groups and family gentrifiers (Van Gent 2013; Boterman and Van Gent 2014). Similar developments have taken place in some central parts of Copenhagen (Lund Hansen, Andersen and Clark 2001; Larsen and Lund Hansen 2008).

Eindhoven is the least urbanized of the four city-regions in this study but, according to the interviewees, its housing stock, dominated by single-family dwellings in a green environment, is one of the main strengths of the region, especially when combined with the relative affordability of dwellings as compared to the Randstad region. However, the city still lacks affordable rented apartments outside the social sector, which, according to some of the literature are the type of dwellings that are often demanded by younger (single) creative knowledge workers.

Residential patterns of creative knowledge workers in the Amsterdam and Eindhoven regions

Different categories of creative knowledge workers have distinct residential orientations. Based on the region-specific literature and interviews with regional experts in the main study areas of this book, the MRA and the Eindhoven Metropolitan Region, we are able to draw some pictures of the concentrations.

Concentrations of creative knowledge workers in the MRA

Figure 3.1 shows the location of the districts and projects that were mentioned most in the literature as creative hotspots or popular residential districts for (international) creative knowledge workers. Previous research on the residential preferences of creative knowledge workers in Amsterdam has shown that both within the region and within the core city several areas of concentration of creative knowledge workers exist. There is an overlap of workspaces for creative industries and residential spaces for their workers (Bontje, Musterd and Pelzer 2011). As was shown in Chapter 2, an earlier empirical case study on (international) creative knowledge workers in Amsterdam showed that residential preferences are different between occupation categories, with those in the creative professions preferring the most centrally located districts (Musterd 2002).

The most popular destinations for architects were Grachtengordel-Zuid (southern canal belt) and the Jordaan district in the city centre and the 'islands' of the Eastern Harbour District. Artists also expressed a preference for the districts within the A10 ring road in Amsterdam, especially the inner city and the nineteenth-century districts. Workers in the media sector were strongly represented both in the central districts of Amsterdam and in the suburbs of Hilversum and Bussum, which are located close to the main media cluster of the Netherlands. In contrast, knowledge workers within the financial sector expressed a strong preference for suburban locations and were often found in Almere, Maarssen, Bussum, Heemstede and Waterland. However, media workers also lived in newly constructed areas within the ring road, such as De Omval, near Amstel Station in the eastern part of the city. Also, among the students studying in Amsterdam, those studying alpha and gamma sciences (media and creativity, social sciences)

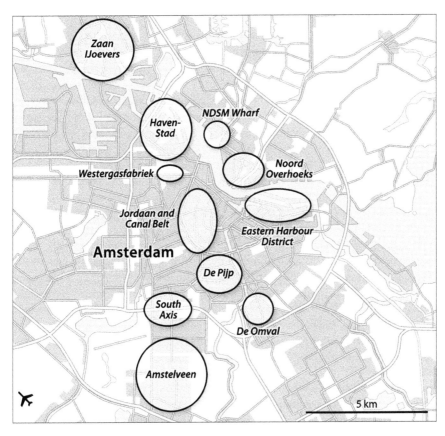

Figure 3.1 Creative hotspots and districts popular with creative or international creative knowledge workers, according to Amsterdam-specific literature and interviews

tend to have a stronger urban residential orientation than do students in economics, technical studies and sports (Musterd 2002). Similarly, a study conducted by Decisio (2008) among knowledge workers in the province of North-Holland found differences between the residential preferences of alpha, gamma and beta workers. Alpha workers tend to be found in urban cosmopolitan districts but do not have a large budget for housing. They therefore often prefer to have a combined living and working space. Beta workers generally have a larger budget for housing and more often prefer suburban areas with more space and comfort, while, on average, meeting places and culture are considered less important. Gamma workers often have a relatively high budget for housing and express quite mixed residential preferences. Young and ambitious gamma workers, especially those in dual-income households, tend to prefer highly urban living environments, whereas settled workers more often prefer high-quality suburban environments.

This is in line with the international studies that were presented in Chapter 2 (Van Oort, Weterings and Verlinde 2003; Lawton, Murphy and Redmond 2013). For international workers specifically, the presence of international schools is also important (Decisio 2008).

The Planning Department of the Municipality of Amsterdam has undertaken three consecutive studies (2006, 2008, 2011) in which the attractiveness of the city of Amsterdam for creative knowledge workers was measured. The first study concluded that creative knowledge workers are especially attracted to Amsterdam by a dynamic urban life with a high diversity of lifestyles and cultural and culinary amenities, as well as a high-quality urban public space. Compared to other categories of workers, knowledge workers are more demand oriented and have a stronger identification with their place of residence. Generally, knowledge workers consider the location of a dwelling more important than its size (DRO 2006). The second study (2008) had a stronger focus on relocation propensity and concluded that highly educated workers, and especially the younger groups, clearly prefer the highly urban residential milieus. Most decisions to leave Amsterdam are based on negative considerations, such as high housing prices and lack of living space. Although there is clearly an increasing group of family gentrifiers (see also Boterman 2012; 2013), many knowledge workers with small children are attracted to municipalities in the wider region because of more space inside and outside the house, the green structure and quiet. New developments on the urban edges, especially IJburg, Overamstel, Houthavens and Zeeburgereiland, have been constructed in order to increase the possibilities for this group to continue a residential career in the city (DRO 2008). The third study (2011) confirmed that, of all those knowledge workers in Amsterdam with a propensity to relocate, 66 per cent prefer to stay within the city, in particular because of the varied amenity structure. Knowledge workers relatively often mention satisfaction with the neighbourhood or the current distance to the workplace as a reason for not wanting to move (DRO 2011). Although the studies by DRO may indicate the stronger urban orientation of creative knowledge workers compared to other groups of workers, an important nuance is that only workers who were already living in the city of Amsterdam, and therefore were the most likely to have strong urban preferences, were included in the survey. This may give a biased view of the residential preferences of creative knowledge workers, since the voices of those living in the surrounding suburban municipalities were not heard. For that reason, the stated preferences analyses in the remainder of this book focus on people who work in the Amsterdam region but do not necessarily live there.

Bontje, Pethe and Rühmann (2008) found that for creative knowledge workers in Amsterdam there is a strong overlap between their residential preferences and activity patterns. Based on interviews, they concluded that creative knowledge workers generally expressed satisfaction with local amenities, services and infrastructure and many of them have a strong preference for inner-city areas. They value an authentic built environment and atmosphere, which they also enjoy in their leisure-time activities. Workers living in the inner city use urban amenities significantly more often than persons living in the suburban areas of the region.

Creative centres in the outer fringes of the region will likely attract different types of creative knowledge workers. Their study also found that, with respect to reasons for settling in Amsterdam, soft factors such as diversity played a more prominent role for recent graduates than for employees in creative knowledge sectors. A majority of creative knowledge workers came to Amsterdam for a new job, which confirms the continued importance of employment (Storper and Scott 2009) and is in line with earlier empirical studies in other European city regions (Brown and Męczyńsky 2009; Martin-Brelot *et al*. 2010; Andersen *et al*. 2010).

During the expert interviews, it was often mentioned that workers in creative industries have different preferences than technical workers in ICT. Broadly stated, whereas many technical workers, particularly those working in large companies, come to Amsterdam predominantly for work and do not care so much for living in a lively urban district, workers in creative industries generally attach more value to the soft side of the city. Creative workers tend to prefer living in the inner city and near to meeting places and specific (high culture) amenities. One respondent stated that for many creative workers, soft factors are equally as important as hard factors. ICT workers, in contrast, have more diverse residential preferences and generally attach more value to the hard factors such as employment and career prospects. Creative workers are, more often than other professionals, critical with regard to both their workspaces and – in particular – their residential locations. They often have a strong preference for the most central spots in Amsterdam, particularly the canal belt and the Jordaan district, and attach high value to the proximity of meeting places and nightlife amenities. Also areas with attractive historic buildings, including industrial heritage sites (e.g. Westergasfabriek, NDSM-werf and Overamstel in Amsterdam), are considered attractive. However, in particular the start-ups and the artists within the creative industries often have an income that is too low for them to be able to fulfil their wishes. The plans for enlarging the central urban milieu in the Structural Vision 2040 (Municipality of Amsterdam 2011) are expected to offer more opportunities for workers in the creative industries and 'new ICT' workers, at least for those who can afford the housing prices and rents, but are not particularly appealing for 'old ICT' workers, and very likely not for workers in other non-creative professions.

Outside the inner city, especially the neighbourhoods immediately surrounding the inner city, are living areas that are popular because of their proximity to the inner city, in combination with their characteristic nineteenth-century or early twentieth-century housing stock and the presence of lively street markets (e.g. Albert Cuypmarkt in De Pijp district and Dappermarkt in East). Besides these areas, Amsterdam has been very active since the 1990s in the revitalization and transformation of former harbour and industrial sites. The former docklands in the Eastern Harbour District, and Java-eiland in particular, are currently among the most expensive residential districts in Amsterdam. Old warehouses have been transformed into apartment blocks and new, modern architecture has been added. Also the Westergasfabriek area has been transformed from a former gas plant into a leisure district where bars and cinemas are located and music concerts are held occasionally. A similar development has taken place in Overamstel since 2006, around a former chewing gum factory, and in Amsterdam-Noord, at NDSM-werf, a former shipyard that has been in use as a creative hotbed and a mixed residential and leisure district for a number of years. Also the parts of Amsterdam-Noord close to the ferry are increasingly becoming popular residential districts, whereas until a few years ago, Noord was considered an unattractive borough. Adjacent to the Shell Technology Centre, a mixed functional area called Overhoeks has been developed with modern apartments and the new EYE film museum. Attractive old industrial heritage is considered to have high potential for either meeting places or the creation of creative hotspots. Similar developments are also taking place outside the core city, as in Halfweg (SugarCity), and in Zaandam (Zaanoevers) former factory buildings have been transformed into creative hotspots. No specific concentration neighbourhoods for international knowledge workers were identified, with the exception of a large Japanese community in the relatively affluent suburban municipality of Amstelveen, on the south side of the region.

Concentrations of knowledge workers in the Eindhoven Metropolitan Region

Although in the Eindhoven region research on the residential preferences of creative knowledge workers is generally lacking, a small number of studies have gained insight into the residential preferences of highly skilled knowledge migrants. Due to the economic structure of the region, many of these workers are working in technical professions. Buiskool and Grijpstra (2006) conducted a survey among international workers on their valuation of different aspects of living in Eindhoven. They found a clear distinction between workers at the technical university, who are younger and have lower incomes, and knowledge workers at private companies, who generally have higher incomes and encounter fewer difficulties in fulfilling their housing demands. Large concentrations of international knowledge workers exist in the city of Eindhoven and the adjacent suburban municipality of Veldhoven, while destinations outside the Eindhoven Metropolitan Region also appear to be popular residential locations: 's-Hertogenbosch and, to a lesser degree, the large cities of the Randstad. Almost half of the international knowledge workers in Buiskool and Grijpstra's study (42 per cent) were living in apartments. Excluding the (often younger) university workers, a majority of the international knowledge workers (55 per cent) were living in single-family dwellings. Most international knowledge workers were living in rented dwellings (around 70 per cent), while 20 per cent were owner-occupiers. For almost 10 per cent of the international knowledge workers, accommodation was provided by the employer. The survey signalled a demand for an greater diversity and volume of housing stock, and for 1- and 2-bedroom apartments and furnished flats in particular (Buiskool and Grijpstra 2006).

A later survey by Vriens and Van der Dam (2011) largely confirmed these findings and showed that most international knowledge workers seek housing in or close to the city centre, with a preference for independent housing, rented dwellings, apartments and studios. Also, all-inclusive and furnished dwellings were in high demanded. Their study found that workers at education institutions are less willing to pay high amounts for housing, most likely because of their generally lower incomes and younger age (under 30). However, housing in their preferred price category (up to €550 a month) is quite scarce outside the social rented sector. Workers in private companies generally earn higher incomes and this group hardly faces any problems with finding appropriate accommodation, since housing in higher price ranges is widely available in the region. In addition, some of the larger companies arrange housing for their foreign employees, are familiar with their wishes and have good contacts with suppliers of private rented dwellings (Vriens and Van der Dam 2011).

In the in-depth interviews, different opinions about the importance of housing for attracting knowledge workers were presented. Some interviewees questioned the importance of the housing stock, while stressing the employment opportunities. However, others mentioned that an attractive housing stock can make the difference to competitiveness with other regions with similar economic profiles. In that respect, the quiet and green living environments of Eindhoven were considered attractive for the technical group in particular, in line with earlier studies (e.g. Kotkin 2000). Many interviewees were sceptical about the statement that (international) knowledge workers have different residential preferences to others. Rather, they linked differences in residential preferences among creative knowledge workers to demographic factors, in line with a number of international studies presented in Chapter 2 (e.g., Lawton, Murphy and Redmond 2013). Some interviewees stated that many international knowledge workers are young and arrive in the Eindhoven region without a partner. These younger workers in particular prefer to live in the central parts of the city. A lack of highly urban milieus in the region was therefore often mentioned as a challenge that Eindhoven needs to keep working on.

Figure 3.2 shows the main concentration areas of knowledge-intensive and creative employment and the most popular residential areas for their (international) workers.According to the interviewees, there are no clear concentration areas of knowledge workers, neither native Dutch nor international. However, some parts of the city and region tend to be a bit more popular with international knowledge workers than others. The city centre and its surrounding neighbourhoods, including a number of new residential towers (*Vesteda-tower, Hartje Eindhoven*), as well as the districts near the international school and alongside the 'A2-highway axis' – the south-western part of the urban area, including the High Tech Campus and ASML – are the most popular. Workers in creative industries were regarded the most spatially concentrated occupation category. They are overrepresented in a limited number of districts with high symbolic value, in line with some of the literature (Markusen 2006; Smit 2012). These areas largely overlap with former industrial estates formerly used by Philips, but which have recently been transformed into new urban districts with a combined function as residential area and creative hotspots. The industrial heritage sites *Strijp-S, Strijp-R, Sectie C* and the *NRE-site* are the main examples of such districts. Strijp-S is also home to many cultural events, including the *Dutch Design Week*, which contributes to

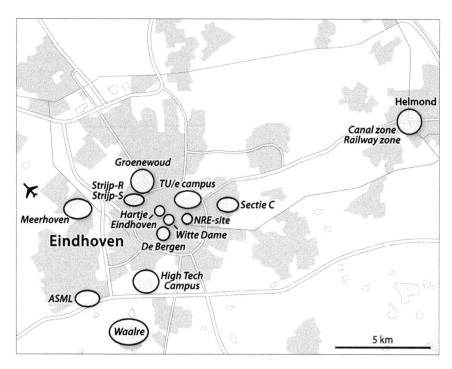

Figure 3.2 Eindhoven's creative and high-tech hotspots and residential locations popular
with creative and international knowledge workers, according to Eindhoven-
specific literature and interviews

its attractiveness for creative workers. Another example of a popular district is
De Bergen, which has transformed from an artistic district into an upmarket shopping street. In general, the southern part of the city is much more popular with
creative knowledge workers than the northern part. In addition, a concentration
of students in the Groenewoud district (Woensel-West), adjacent to Strijp-S, was
noticed by some.

International comparison: residential patterns of creative
knowledge workers in the Copenhagen and Helsinki regions

In an effort to put the Amsterdam and Eindhoven findings into a wider perspective, in this section the residential patterns of creative knowledge workers in the
two international case study cities (Copenhagen and Helsinki) are presented, again
based on region-specific literature and in-depth interviews with local experts.

Concentrations of knowledge workers in the Copenhagen capital region

Based on Andersen and Lorenzen's (2005) study on the Danish creative class,
creative knowledge workers in Denmark make up about 40 per cent of the Danish

labour force and have had stable localization patterns, also within regions. Creative people are over-represented in larger cities, and the largest concentrations are found in Copenhagen and Aarhus. Hansen and Winther (2010), in their study on the talents' proportion of municipal employment in Denmark, recognized a growing unequal distribution of talent in Denmark, with a vast concentration in the central and northern municipalities of the Copenhagen region, and also marked proportions in university cities elsewhere in the country, such as Odense, Aarhus and Aalborg. Within the Copenhagen region, polarization exists based on both industry and talent, with knowledge workers being over-represented in the central city and the northern and north-western 'corridors'.

Within the Copenhagen city-region, large concentrations areas of knowledge workers and knowledge intensive employment can be observed in the city of Copenhagen and Frederiksberg, and also in prosperous municipalities north and north-west of Copenhagen, such as Gentofte and Hellerup (Figure 3.3). The central city of Copenhagen is on the rise in terms of popularity among skilled workers (Andersen and Lorenzen 2005). Some of the interviewees confirmed the over-representation of creative knowledge workers in the Copenhagen region and some other larger cities in Denmark. In general, the residential patterns of knowledge workers seem to overlap with employment patterns and with districts with a large proportion of high-income households. Within the Copenhagen region, the corridor running from the city centre northwards was particularly mentioned as the major concentration of skilled workers.

Inside the city of Copenhagen itself, the most popular districts are those surrounding the city centre, where urban renewal has taken place: Vesterbro and Nørrebro. These areas have long been popular with students and business start-ups because of vacant spaces and relatively low rents, combined with a diverse population. Vesterbro, just west of the central station, used to be a seedy red-light district, but has been transformed into the trendiest neighbourhood of Copenhagen since the 1990s, due to a large-scale municipality-led urban renewal project. This renewal process involved a shift from public housing to collectively owned housing in private co-ops. Housing prices have exploded, apartment blocks and public space have been renovated and trendy fashion shops and 'hip' bars have popped up (Lund Hansen, Andersen and Clark 2001; Boterman 2012). The developments in this district in particular are also associated with the displacement of lower-income groups and other socio-economically vulnerable residents (Larsen and Lund Hansen 2008). Prices in Nørrebro increased because it is close to the university and city centre and because it is more internationally diverse than other parts of Copenhagen. Some of the new harbour developments (Holmen, Langelinie, Fisketorvet, Island Brygge) and the directly neighbouring city of Frederiksberg, where the Copenhagen Business School is located, were also mentioned as popular residential locations for highly educated workers.

The city has been transformed into a place for living, where both families with children and higher-income groups want to live. The municipality of Copenhagen is actively trying to attract high-income groups, including knowledge workers, through the revitalization of the city and the creation of urban residential milieus that are considered attractive by the more affluent residents. However, the newly

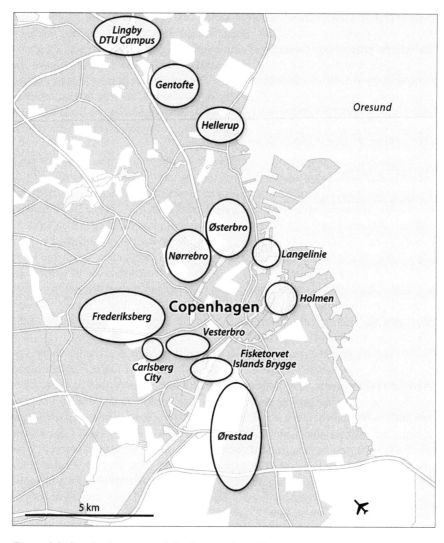

Figure 3.3 Creative hotspots and districts popular with creative and international
knowledge workers according to Copenhagen-specific literature and interviews

developed area of Ørestad, with some distinctive modern architecture, is not yet
very popular with Danish knowledge workers and housing prices are not as high as
in the central parts of the city. One of the local experts interviewed explained this
by the stronger preference among Danish knowledge workers for districts with
a vibrant street life and cultural amenities, which are largely lacking in Ørestad.
Rather, Ørestad is being transformed into a residential space for international
workers. It has a high availability of more expensive apartments that are more
easily accessible to people from abroad who have difficulty entering a housing

market dominated by social housing and co-ops. Planned huge investments have been reduced in size as a result of the crisis, thus opening up new opportunities for the area. In general, the international community is relatively small and under-researched in Copenhagen and therefore, as of yet, no other specific expatriate communities are known.

Two of the interviewees specifically outlined the different residential patterns of workers in the creative industries and workers in other knowledge-intensive sectors. One interviewee referred to a study in which the residential patterns of workers were mapped on the basis of Asheim and Gertler's (2005) different types of knowledge bases: 'synthetic', 'analytic' and 'symbolic'. Whereas the symbolic knowledge bases are generally associated with the creative industries, analytic knowledge bases include technical sectors such as the life-tech industries, which are have a big presence in Copenhagen and employ a large proportion of Copenhagen's knowledge workers. Urban policies aimed at attracting knowledge workers to Copenhagen are rather uniform and focus too much on the symbolic knowledge bases, whereas technical workers appear to have preferences with regard to amenities and living spaces that do not match this profile. The symbolic knowledge bases are mainly found in the inner city and the surrounding neighbourhoods of Vesterbro and Nørrebro. One of the interviewees explained the relatively high degree of residential concentration of creative workers, as compared to more analytical knowledge workers, by their generally higher need for face-to-face interactions, for which there are ample opportunities in inner-city districts.

Concentrations of knowledge workers in the Helsinki Metropolitan Area

A study on the location choices of knowledge workers in the Helsinki Metropolitan Area (Vaattovaara *et al.* 2010) found that most relocation decisions resulted from personal reasons, and people's personal trajectories in particular. Over 40 per cent of Finnish employees were born in the region, and the majority of Finnish workers and employees had been born, had family or had studied in the region. For the international knowledge workers, following a partner was an important driver of migration. Besides personal reasons, the quality of higher education and employment opportunities were identified in particular as major pull factors for knowledge workers who moved to the region (Vaattovaara *et al.* 2010).

Still, two-thirds of Finnish workers and 85 per cent of international migrants mentioned at least one soft condition as a reason for settling in the Helsinki region. In particular, safety, diversity of leisure and entertainment, the tolerant atmosphere and proximity to a natural environment were often mentioned. These factors were also often mentioned as reasons for remaining in the region. Soft factors in particular steer residential choices within the metropolitan region. In their survey, Vaattovaara *et al.* (2010) found that both Finnish and transnational knowledge workers attached most importance to the quality of their neighbourhood, the neighbourhood's atmosphere and the availability of private open spaces. Similar results were reported by Kepsu and Vaattovaara (2008), who found that much more than proximity to entertainment and the city centre, knowledge workers value a comfortable and welcoming neighbourhood and spend most of their free time at home – which often is located in a suburban neighbourhood – or in parks or other green areas. This may be due to the fact that a considerable proportion of knowledge workers in the Helsinki region are working in ICT or other technical sectors or in the public sector, rather than in highly creative professions. Based on previous studies (e.g., Kotkin 2000; Musterd 2002) and the interviews from the other case studies, this group can be expected to have a less clear preference for highly urban districts.

Figure 3.4 shows the main areas of concentration of knowledge-intensive workers, and also their main employment hubs. According to some interviewees, and in line with the findings from the other case studies, knowledge workers in the technical and creative sectors show different residential patterns. The residential patterns of knowledge workers in technical sectors such as ICT overlap to a large degree with their employment patterns. They are over-represented in the western part of the city and in the neighbouring city of Espoo, but under-represented in the eastern part of the city, which is far from their workplaces. People working in creative industries are more strongly concentrated in the inner city of Helsinki (e.g., the Design District) and the Kallio district adjacent to it. Another area that was mentioned during interviews was Arabianranta. Currently, the University of Art, Design and Architecture is located there, and it is also located close to one of the Helsinki University campuses. The design of the area's housing stock and public space sets it apart from other neighbourhoods of Helsinki. Different styles of modern architecture have been applied and many housing blocks have their own public art projects, which are paid for by the local community. According to some of the local experts, the intention was that this neighbourhood would become a creative hub. In practice, however, the area has attracted a number of artists, but in particular it has attracted households with families, many of whom are not employed in creative industries.

The area around the Cable Factory in Salmisaari has also developed into a creative hub (Bontje and Musterd 2009). In this district, many modern apartment blocks have been built. The harbour is being moved to the eastern part of the city and at its current site, Jätkäsaari, a new residential district is being constructed in order to accommodate the city's growing population.

Espoo has so far been particularly attractive to ICT and technical workers, and especially for families with children. According to one of the local experts, Espoo has most often been chosen as a residential location because of its proximity to work (many large companies including Nokia and Rovio are found there, as well as Aalto University) and the availability of larger dwellings, as compared to Helsinki. Creative workers have thus far not concentrated in Espoo, but the expansion of the metro system to Espoo is expected to lead to some changes, since this will improve connectivity to the inner city of Helsinki. Also, the planned relocation of the University of Arts, Design and Architecture from Arabianranta to Espoo is expected to have an impact on the creative character of Espoo.

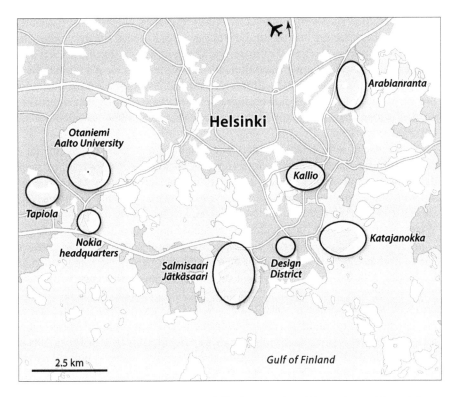

Figure 3.4 Creative and ICT hotspots and districts popular with creative and knowledge workers according to Helsinki-specific literature and interviews

Conclusions

In comparing the four city-regions, the main strengths of all four appear to be related to employment and education opportunities, while strengths on the soft side are highly diverse between the four cities. Amsterdam's main hard asset is its economic diversity, Eindhoven and Helsinki have strong specialized clusters and Copenhagen occupies a position somewhere in between. Amsterdam, Copenhagen and Helsinki benefit from large international airports and are 'talent magnets' because of their largest-city status and the accompanying concentration of large international companies and education institutes. Eindhoven's smaller scope – in terms of population, labour market, knowledge institutions and airport – may be a challenge for the city, but its high-tech cluster offers jobs that are unique in the Netherlands.

On the soft side, Amsterdam, Copenhagen and Helsinki are the main cultural centres of their respective countries, which is reflected in a rich supply of amenities. Eindhoven has a smaller supply of cultural amenities, due to its smaller size and its position as the fifth city of the country, but is distinguished by its large international events. With respect to authenticity, Amsterdam's main strength is its historic inner city, while the other cities focus especially on modern architecture and cultural events as ways to stand out from other cities. With respect to the social climate, the Dutch cities internationally have an image of tolerance and openness, whereas the Nordic cities have a reputation of being more closed societies. In all three countries, however, tolerance is under pressure, due to the rise of anti-immigration sentiment and populist right-wing parties, which may eventually harm the cities' attractiveness to international knowledge workers.

With respect to the relative importance of hard and soft conditions, the city-region-specific literature and the interviews with local experts point in the same direction as some earlier studies on the residential preferences of knowledge workers: the residential preferences of knowledge workers are highly diverse and steered by both their economic activities (Kotkin 2000; Musterd 2002; Van Oort, Weterings and Verlinde 2003) and their household situation or lifestyle (Andersen *et al.* 2010; Verdich 2010; Frenkel, Bendit and Kaplan 2013). Whereas creative workers relatively more often express the housing preferences that were presented by Florida (2002) – highly urban and diverse districts – knowledge workers in business services or technical sectors have housing preferences that do not differ much from those of the general population. The latter groups are attracted as much to urban as to suburban areas. Besides household situation and lifestyle factors, the relatively strong concentrations of, in particular, creative professionals in central urban districts may, according to some interviewees, be explained by the nature of their work, which (more than ICT or business services) requires face-to-face contacts on the 'scene'.

Many of the local experts interviewed confirmed that in their respective regions employment was the main reason why (international) knowledge workers chose to settle there, with housing being the main secondary factor. Still, in all cities it was mentioned that the soft conditions are more important for workers in creative professions than for those in other professions – sometimes even equally important as employment. In this sense it is interesting to note that in all four cities, albeit to varying degrees, the 'Florida-paradigm' still plays an important role and large-scale investments target highly urban residential milieus and amenities. Based on the region-specific literature and interviews, in line with the international literature, these developments serve the demands of sub-groups, rather than the entire population of knowledge workers. It is somewhat paradoxical that many cities, including Amsterdam and Copenhagen, are restructuring inner-city neighbourhoods with the construction of owner-occupied dwellings in the more expensive segment, often at the cost of social housing, and the cleaning up of public space. In the contexts of Denmark and Finland, having many high-income groups is beneficial from the city's viewpoint, since it brings in higher tax revenues. In the Netherlands this is much less of an issue because of the relatively low proportion of municipal taxes in the total tax take (10 per cent). Still, higher-income groups bring higher spending power to the municipality, which benefits the local retail and catering sectors. As a result, however, parts of the inner city become more attractive to people with higher incomes but less accessible for groups with lower incomes. Contrary to what is often presumed by policy makers, not all knowledge workers have high incomes. Rather, younger workers, especially those working in educational institutions (PhD-students) and professionals in cultural industries such as arts, have a lower or middle income. Still, according to a significant strand of literature and some of the interviews, these groups are the most likely to express a strong preference for living in highly urban districts. A danger related to recent developments in the regional housing markets is thus that knowledge workers in the lower-income segments are not able to find affordable dwellings in (relatively) central locations. As a result, these people will need to adapt their housing wishes in terms of location or size: either they will look for cheaper housing in surrounding municipalities, despite having an urban residential preference, or they will settle in smaller dwellings than preferred, in order to live in a central location. In both cases, there is a mismatch between stated and revealed residential preferences. More housing in mid-priced segments (e.g., private rent) is greatly needed in order to ensure the access of all knowledge workers to the city, but the development of such housing is unlikely to be accounted for by the market.

In addition, urban restructuring policies have led to previously diverse neighbourhoods in at least two of the four cities becoming more homogeneous and the loss of 'raw urban edges'. Following earlier literature (e.g. Peck 2012), this uniformity may, in the long run, make these neighbourhoods even less attractive to people in the creative industries.

In terms of international knowledge workers, the regional-specific literature and interviews do not suggest different residential preferences and patterns than for native workers. Rather, internationals seem to have different access to the housing market. Especially in cities with a large stock of social housing (e.g., Amsterdam and Copenhagen), they are restricted to the more expensive districts where there is more choice – if their income allows it – or to areas where short-stay agencies own housing. Hardly any districts with a clear concentration of international knowledge workers were identified (only Amstelveen in the Amsterdam region and Ørestad in Copenhagen were mentioned in particular). In addition to the provision of sufficient short-stay dwellings, this group is also likely to benefit from a larger supply in the middle-priced segment. After all, they need immediate access to dwellings and, due to short-term employment contracts, buying a house is not a viable option for many.

A final implication is related to international knowledge workers, and concerns the national, rather than the regional, policy level. Considering the relatively limited scale of the four city-regions and the countries in which they are situated, an international focus seems to be inevitable in order to be able to fulfil high economic ambitions. This concerns both the attraction of foreign direct investments, including international companies, and the welcoming of international knowledge workers, which can be influenced through government policies, including tax regulations and service delivery to expatriates, and through a general welcoming attitude toward international migrants.

Note

1 The 'triple helix' refers to cooperation between city governments, regional universities and the business sector.

References

Andersen, KV and Lorenzen, M 2005, *The geography of the Danish creative class; A mapping and analysis*, Copenhagen Business School, Frederiksberg.

Andersen, KV, Bugge, MM, Hansen, HK, Isaksen, A and Raunio, M 2010, 'One size fits all? Applying the creative class thesis onto a Nordic context', *European Planning Studies* 18(10), 1591–1609.

Asheim, B and Gertler, M 2005, 'The geography of innovation: Regional innovation systems' in *The Oxford handbook of innovation*, eds J Fagerberg, DC Mowery and RR Nelson, Oxford University Press, Oxford, 291–317.

Bontje, M and Musterd, S 2009, 'Creative industries, creative class and competitiveness: Expert opinions critically appraised', *Geoforum* 40, 843–852.

Bontje, M, Musterd, S and Pelzer, P 2011, *Inventive city-regions: Path dependence and creative knowledge strategies*, Ashgate, Farnham.

Bontje, M, Pethe, H and Rühmann, P 2008, *The Amsterdam region – A home for creative knowledge workers and graduates? Understanding the attractiveness of the metropolitan region for creative knowledge workers*, AMIDSt, University of Amsterdam, Amsterdam.

Boterman, WR 2012, 'Deconstructing coincidence: How middle-class households use various forms of capital to find a home', *Housing, Theory and Society* 29(3), 321–338.

Boterman, WR 2013, 'Dealing with diversity: Middle-class family households and the issue of "Black" and "White" schools in Amsterdam', *Urban Studies* 50(6), 1130–1147.

Boterman, WR and Van Gent, WPC 2014, 'Housing liberalisation and gentrification: The social effects of tenure conversions in Amsterdam', *Tijdschrift voor economische en sociale geografie* 105(2), 140–160.

Brown, J and Męczyńsky, M 2009, '"Complexcities": Locational choices of creative knowledge workers', *Built Environment* 35(2), 238–252.

Buiskool, B and Grijpstra, D 2006, *Attracting and embedding international knowledge workers in the Eindhoven region: A study on the composition, perceptions and expectations*, Research voor Beleid BV, Leiden.

City of Helsinki Urban Facts 2013, *Helsinki region trends; Current review of development in the region 2013*, City of Helsinki Urban Facts, Helsinki.

Decisio 2008, *Quick scan kenniseconomie in Noord-Holland – Input voor de provinciale structuurvisie [Quick scan knowledge economy in North Holland – Input for the provincial structural vision]*, Decisio, Amsterdam.

DRO 2006, . . . *Amsterdam, the place to be!*, Gemeente Amsterdam, Dienst Ruimtelijke Ordening, Amsterdam.

DRO 2008, *Thuis in de metropoolregio Amsterdam?!*, Gemeente Amsterdam, Dienst Ruimtelijke Ordening, Amsterdam.

DRO 2011, *A'dam en E.V.A. zoeken een woning!*, Gemeente Amsterdam, Dienst Ruimtelijke Ordening, Amsterdam.

Florida, R 2002, *The rise of the creative class and how it's transforming work, leisure, community and everyday life*, Basic Books, New York.

Frenkel, A, Bendit, E and Kaplan, S 2013, 'The linkage between the lifestyle of knowledge-workers and their intra-metropolitan residential choice: A clustering approach based on self-organizing maps', *Computers, Environment and Urban Systems* 39, 151–169.

Hansen, HK and Winther, L 2010, *The urban turn; Cities, talent and knowledge in Denmark*, Aarhus University Press, Aarhus.

Hospers, G 2003, 'Creative cities: Breeding places in the knowledge economy', *Knowledge, Technology, and Policy* 16(3), 143–162.

Kepsu, K and Vaattovaara, M 2008, *Creative knowledge in the Helsinki Metropolitan Area. Understanding the attractiveness of the metropolitan region for creative knowledge workers*, AMIDSt, University of Amsterdam, Amsterdam.

Kotkin, J 2000, *The new geography: How the digital revolution is reshaping the American Landscape*, New York: Random House.

Larsen, HG and Lund Hansen, A 2008, 'Gentrification – gentle or traumatic? Urban renewal policies and socioeconomic transformations in Copenhagen', *Urban Studies* 45(12), 2429–2448.

Lawton, P, Murphy, E and Redmond, D 2013, 'Residential preferences of the "creative class"?' *Cities* 31(2), 47–56.

Lund Hansen, A, Andersen, HT and Clark, E 2001, 'Creative Copenhagen: Globalization, urban governance and social change', *European Planning Studies* 9(7), 851–869.

Markusen, A 2006, 'Urban development and the politics of a creative class: evidence from a study of artists', *Environment and Planning A* 38, 1921–1940.

Martin-Brelot, H, Grossetti, M, Eckert, D, Gritsai, O and Kovácz, Z 2010, 'The spatial mobility of the "creative class": A European perspective', *International Journal of Urban and Regional Research* 34(4), 854–870.

Municipality of Amsterdam 2011, *Structuurvisie Amsterdam 2040; Economisch sterk en duurzaam [Structural vision Amsterdam 2040; Economically strong and sustainable]*, Municipality of Amsterdam, Amsterdam.

Musterd, S 2002, *De Nieuwe Amsterdamse Kernvoorraad; Woonmilieus in de Creatieve Culturele Kennisstad*, Bestuursdienst, Gemeente Amsterdam, Amsterdam.

O+S 2012, *Amsterdam In Cijfers 2012*, Gemeente Amsterdam, Bureau Onderzoek en Statistiek, Amsterdam.

Peck, J 2012, 'Recreative city: Amsterdam, vehicular ideas and the adaptive spaces of creativity policy', *International Journal of Urban and Regional Research* 36(3), 462–485.

Sleutjes, B 2013, *The hard and soft side of European knowledge regions, HELP UVA VU Report, no 1*, UvA, Amsterdam.

Smit, AJ 2012, *Spatial quality of cultural production districts*, Enschede: Ipskamp.

Storper, M and Scott, AJ 2009, Rethinking human capital, creativity and urban growth. *Journal of Economic Geography* 9, 147–167.

Vaattovaara, M, Bernelius, V, Kepsu, K and Eskelä, E 2010, *Creative knowledge and local policies in Helsinki. How to enhance the city's competitiveness*, AISSR, University of Amsterdam, Amsterdam.

Van Gent, WPC 2013, 'Neo-liberalization, housing institutions and variegated gentrification; How the 'third wave' broke in Amsterdam', *International Journal for Urban and Regional Research* 37(2), 503–522

Van Oort, F, Weterings, A and Verlinde, H 2003, 'Residential amenities of knowledge workers and the location of ICT-firms in the Netherlands', *Tijdschrift voor Economische en Sociale Geografie* 94(4), 516–523.

Verdich, M 2010, 'Creative migration? The attraction and retention of the 'creative class' in Launceston, Tasmania', *Australian Geographer* 41(1), 129–140.

Vriens, J and Van der Dam, S 2011, *Huisvesting van de International Knowledge Workers in Zuidoost-Brabant, Eindhoven; Een onderzoek naar woonwensen*, Gemeente Eindhoven, Eindhoven.

Website Region Hovedstaden, www.regionh.dk, Accessed 10 May 2013.

Part II

4 Housing and location preferences of higher educated workers in the Netherlands

An introduction

Marco Bontje, Sako Musterd and Jan Rouwendal

Higher Educated Location Preferences

The Higher Educated Location Preferences research project, which is the basis for this volume, came about in two phases. Part II of this volume focuses on the first phase, in which the stated and revealed preferences of higher-educated workers are analysed in general and in which a policy application tool is presented. Part III will focus on the stated and revealed preferences of higher-educated international migrants, including students.

The location preferences of higher-educated people are part of an on-going debate about urban and regional competitiveness and the attractiveness of cities. Higher-educated people are seen as a key factor in urban economic development. The debate involves questions like: how can cities and regions attract or retain the skilled workforce they need in order to remain or become internationally competitive? Does this require specific 'talented worker policies'? To what extent do higher-educated workers differ in their location preferences, as compared to other categories of workers? Are there differences within the category of higher-educated workers? Are such preferences reflected in their actual (residential) behaviour? A discussion of the literature (see Chapter 2) and of experiences (see Chapter 3) has suggested that there is some consensus about some of the answers to some of these questions. However, that discussion also showed that many questions remain open that require empirical study before they can be answered. In Part II we begin to fill in the gaps. Chapters 5–7 will revisit and elaborate on the debates addressed in Part I. The basis for this is several empirical analyses and modelling exercises focusing on the preferences of creative knowledge workers in general. People's preferences and their influence on actual behaviour can be analysed in various ways. A well-known and already mentioned distinction in the social and behavioural sciences that also applies to our research is between stated preferences and revealed preferences. *Stated preferences* refers to the preferences expressed by people, irrespective of whether they will eventually act upon those preferences. These preferences can be studied with different types of questions and/or choice experiments. In Chapter 5, where stated preferences are investigated, respondents were asked about their preferences in three different ways: by ranking photos of residential environments (without telling them where these photos were taken); by ranking names of residential environments in their city-region; and by responding to specific statements, such as 'I would rather have a big house in the suburbs than a small apartment in the city'. The comparison of the residential preferences of creative and technical workers shows how heterogeneous the overall category is. In widening the scope to the (new) middle class, the authors show that residential preferences are in fact multidimensional. A partial explanation of the heterogeneity of the responses is that photos contain only a part of the information that is used to make actual decisions about residential choice behaviour. For instance, no information about the price of the houses that were shown was supplied to the respondents. Responses were determined in part by respondents' assessments of affordability that were not made explicit in the research. Outcomes are very different for sub-sections or fractions of the new middle class, including creative knowledge workers. It will also be shown that there are important differences in terms of preferences between the metropolitan areas that are considered in this study.

Revealed preferences are the focus of Chapter 6. This is about actual spatial behaviour in and over various geographical spaces. The concept suggests that actual behaviour is a reflection of the preferences people have. Note, however, that these preferences are often conditioned by the respondents' assessment of the wider context in which decisions have to be taken, which is often left unspecified. For instance, respondents may express the wish to live in an apartment close to the city centre, while having only vague information about the prices of such apartments and the detached houses in the suburbs that were offered as choice alternatives. Imperfect information may result in substantial gaps between stated preferences and the actual choice behaviour that reveals preferences in the actual situation. In their study on residential behaviour Duncan and Newman (1976) noticed (already four decades ago) that fewer than half of those who said that they expected to move actually realised the move (p. 183). A 'realistic' stated preference may be closer to the revealed preference.

Imperfect information about real choice alternatives is just one reason why differences exist between stated and revealed preferences, and there are many others that are potentially relevant. When information problems are less likely to occur, because of careful design of the stated-preference study, such discrepancies are in principle important pieces of information, perhaps telling a story about the mismatch between the realised structure of housing and residential milieus and the structures and milieus that might be really needed. In any case, it is clear that we have to have a closer look at both the stated and the revealed preferences. In Chapter 7, attention turns to the integration of various pieces of knowledge and modelling outcomes, combined with projected population dynamics under certain scenarios. Various predictions of population change, for example, are evaluated in terms of the house-price effects they might have for certain areas. The information may be relevant for policy applications. In this introductory chapter we will now touch briefly upon the main themes addressed in each of the following chapters.

Stated preferences and revealed preferences

Concepts like 'place' (both in absolute and in relative meanings), 'space' and 'scale' take centre stage in research that focuses on stated preferences. Together they create multiple concrete and abstract contexts that in turn play a role when someone is to develop his or her ideas and tastes about preferences for settling in certain places and spaces. Multi-scalar considerations are relevant in this respect. People prefer certain territories over others (for example. one city over another, or a city over a suburb), but also within these territories, or beyond them, sub-spatial considerations will manifest themselves. Together with the profiles of those who express their preferences, this will shape certain social-spatial images that households strive for. The processes related to stating preferences do not necessarily result only in 'ideal-type', maybe even idealistic, outcomes. Depending on how surveys are designed, it is possible to approach respondents in such a way that they are likely to provide relatively 'realistic' preferences, while they are also capable of reflecting on trade-offs between various elements that play a role in the decision. For example, when both travel time to work and the 'atmosphere' of a residential area are seen as important factors in the decision to settle somewhere, individuals will likely, based on budget limitations, make a trade-off between these factors. In Chapter 5 several models of stated preferences are presented. Among the key findings is the fact that 'heterogeneity rules'. Suggestions in the literature that there would be one 'creative class' with a uniform preference for urban living are rejected, based on empirical analysis and a series of preference models.

In Chapter 6 revealed preferences form the starting point for the development of a series of logit-based sorting models. These are applied in the Netherlands and in the Greater Copenhagen area to uncover actual residential behaviour and to simultaneously investigate what residents are – apparently – willing to pay (extra) for a location close to certain urban and/or environmental amenities. Amenities relate to the general attractiveness of an area. This may not only have attracted people directly, but also may play a role in the decision-making processes of firms when they decide where to settle and what level of wages to offer. Firms may select places with amenities that people like, which will allow these firms, in compensation (trade-off), to reduce wages, but they may also select other places with fewer amenities, which will more or less force them to pay higher wages (see Roback 1982). In the trade-off process, besides wages and urban amenities in general, housing costs also play a role. Important points of departure in these modelling exercises are the optimisation of utility from the consumers' perspective, and striving towards market equilibrium from the housing-supply perspective. One key finding in Chapter 6 is that cities are important for finding a job, and also for finding ample consumption opportunities that people are willing to pay for. Another key finding is that urban amenities are not a substitute for an attractive labour market. These dimensions are in fact complementary.

The integration of knowledge: scenarios for housing and spatial planning policies

Chapter 7 reflects the ambition to 'translate' the analytical results into a hands-on tool for stakeholders in urban and regional development. The tool is designed for application in spatial development policy, housing policy, project and area development in the Netherlands and beyond. For this purpose, the results of the sorting models such as were presented in Chapter 6 were combined with long-term economic scenarios of the Dutch Central Planning Bureau and with the demographic prognoses of the Netherlands Environmental Assessment Agency (PBL) and Statistics Netherlands. These data were then combined with estimates on the projected future housing stock and future land use that are part of the GIS-based Land Use Scanner XL, developed by the PBL. A description is given of how the sorting models can be used to simulate the effects of different scenarios on house prices and the distribution of households over regions. In Chapter 7, several examples of applications are presented. Questions answered are: what happens with local dwelling prices if the demographics change; what happens if housing stock composition changes; what is the expected effect of an increasing urban orientation of households?

References

Duncan, GJ and Newman, SJ 1976, Expected and actual residential mobility. *Journal of the American Institute of Planners* 42, 174–186.

Roback, J 1982, Wages, rents and quality of life. *Journal of Political Economy* 90(6), 1257–1278.

5 'The' creative class does not exist

Contrasting the residential preferences of creative and technical workers in Amsterdam and Eindhoven

Willem R. Boterman and Marco Bontje

Introduction

The creative class is a much-contested concept, yet still very much in vogue among policy makers. Although a range of studies have built on, refined and improved this concept, there is still a tendency to under-estimate the heterogeneity of higher-skilled workers. Although various scholars, including Florida, also pay some attention to the heterogeneous nature of the creative class, much emphasis is placed on the lifestyles and preferences that these workers supposedly have in common. In this chapter we will focus on the residential preferences of higher-educated workers in general, and creative and technical workers in particular. Residential preferences play an important role in Florida's 'creative class' thesis. Florida (2002) claims that the 'creative class' have particular preferences in terms of their residential location and environment and their use of amenities that would set this 'class' apart from other segments of the working population. In his view the 'creative class' would have a strong preference for highly urban environments, including features like a diversity of functions, people and lifestyles, a high level of tolerance for this diversity, a vibrant nightlife, 'street-level culture', and 'third places' where the borders between work and leisure disappear. He suggests that urban economic strategies should focus on attracting the 'creative class', amongst others, by creating or improving the types of highly urban environments they demand. Initially basing his thesis mainly on data from US metropolitan areas, he has meanwhile expanded his 'creative class' research network to Canada, Europe, Australia and East Asia (e.g. Mellander *et al.* 2014).

While it is easy to understand why Florida's message became very popular among urban and regional policy makers, it is much more controversial in academic circles. Florida has gained some support from fellow academics. A significant part of this support is organised by him via his Creative Class Group and the Martin Prosperity Institute at the University of Toronto. Meanwhile, however, the criticism and counter-evidence is at least as substantial. The debate ranges from frontal attacks on the 'creative class' thesis and the way Florida promotes his message to more constructive reactions, and from identifying a range of theoretical, empirical and methodological problems to presenting counter-evidence. One of the key issues of debate concerns the relationship between 'class' and residential orientation. It has not been conclusively established that a 'creative class' exists, whether it is one 'class' or a heterogeneous gathering of sub-categories with varying residential orientations, and to what extent its members display different residential orientations than other higher-educated workers.

Internationally comparative research in Europe has demonstrated that the residential preferences of members of the 'creative class' are primarily determined by 'classic' factors such as position in the life course, education, availability of jobs, and social networks (i.e. partner; family) (Martin-Brelot *et al.* 2010; Musterd and Murie 2010; Lawton *et al.* 2013). Other European and North American scholars have also argued that, in contrast to Florida's ideas, jobs do not follow people, but people move to concentrations of relevant jobs (Hansen and Niedomysl 2009; Storper and Scott 2009). Furthermore, social networks play a crucial role in residential mobility within and between regions and countries (Grabher 2004; Martin-Brelot *et al.* 2010). The conclusion of most of these empirical studies is that *the* creative class does not exist and little evidence exists to support the idea that its members would display any particular common residential orientation.

In trying to unpack the broad definition of 'creative class', various scholars have argued for a more fine-grained categorisation of workers (Kotkin 2002; Pratt 2006; Hansen and Niedomysl 2009; Krätke 2010). Specific sub-groups (artists; designers; architects) may be more urban in their residential orientation, while more technical and professional workers have a more suburban orientation (Kotkin 2002; Musterd 2006). In fact, Florida himself also distinguishes between a 'super creative core' and 'creative professionals', but does not really connect this to possible differences in lifestyles or residential preferences. Next to, and partly overlapping with, these pleas for unpacking the 'creative class', two other related strands of debate should be mentioned here. First, what type of 'class', if any, are we actually dealing with? Are people with creative professions 'the new class', as Florida argues, or is it, rather, the rise of a new middle class, irrespective whether of they have a creative or non-creative profession? The debate on the supposed rise of a new middle class that would be much more urban oriented than the 'traditional' middle class (May 1996) goes back several decades and is closely linked to the debate about the gentrification of formerly derelict inner-urban areas (i.e. Ley 1996; Butler 1997; Bridge 2006). Second, as argued by Glaeser in particular (Glaeser 2005), but also by others (see Chapter 1), 'human capital' or 'skills' are probably better predictors of urban economic growth than Florida's 'creative capital'. Again, what makes creative workers so special compared to other skilled and higher-educated workers is put into doubt in this strand of the debate.

In this chapter we align with a more fine-grained categorisation of workers, highlighting the contrasting lifestyles and residential preferences of different sub-groups of higher-educated workers. We will compare workers in creative companies with workers in high-tech companies. Our analysis draws on self-collected data from a large survey (N = 2802) in the metropolitan areas of Amsterdam and Eindhoven, the Netherlands. The main research question is:

> To what extent, and in which ways do the residential preferences of technical and creative workers differ?

After reviewing the recent debates about the residential preferences of higher-educated workers, we will first discuss the findings of an earlier survey on this topic in some more detail: the results of the survey held in Amsterdam in 2007 as part of the Accommodating Creative Knowledge (ACRE) research project. We will then continue by introducing a new survey that forms the basis of our analysis, in which the residential preferences of creative and technical workers in the city-regions of Amsterdam and Eindhoven are compared. We will then also highlight a special feature of this new survey, as compared to earlier studies: the survey's focus on stated residential preferences rather than revealed residential preferences or residential satisfaction. This is followed by the main findings of our analysis. In the discussion and conclusions we will compare the earlier ACRE findings with our current findings and reflect on what our results may imply for the 'creative class' debate.

Literature

Residential preferences of the creative class

There seems to be a broad understanding among scholars that the original argument about the residential preferences of the creative class was too simplistic. Although the original definitions have been attacked from various angles and for different reasons, one that stands out is the broadness of the concept. By incorporating a very substantial part of the workforce into the creative class, much of its 'explanatory power' has been lost in the internal variation within this group. Even what Florida calls the 'super-creative core' is too diverse in terms of different residential preferences. This has in some instances led to the conclusion that creative class does not have a particular common residential orientation (Servillo *et al.* 2011; Lawton *et al.* 2013) and that other classical factors, such as household composition, income and social networks matter much more for residential decisions.

A number of scholars have therefore proposed more refined categories in order to grapple with this internal differentiation, bringing back the analytical value of categories of workers. Some have proposed to differentiate between creative workers and knowledge workers (Horwitz *et al.* 2003; Bontje and Musterd 2005); others have invented new categories such as 'the dealer class' to differentiate between real 'creative' workers and professionals working in finance, consultancy and real estate (Krätke 2010). Also, other studies have pointed to the importance of disassembling the creative class so as to test whether creative workers have a specific residential orientation. Van Oort and colleagues (2003), for instance, found that ICT workers do not differ strongly from other ('non-creative') workers in their (predominantly suburban) residential orientation. Kotkin (2002) even claims that skilled knowledge workers employed in high-tech industries in Silicon Valley prefer suburban areas. Their preferences are thus very different from, for instance, those of other members of the 'super creative core', such as artists and designers, who are found to be urban in their orientation (Markusen 2006; Musterd 2006). In a study investigating the location quotients of different employment groups, Arnoldus and Musterd (2002) found that of all architects and designers employed in Amsterdam more than 70% resided in the city, while of all accountants and consultants employed in Amsterdam, only fewer than 25% lived in an urban milieu.

The debate so far (see Chapter 2 of this book for a more detailed discussion) seems to point out that it makes sense at least to differentiate between people working in cultural and creative industries, on the one hand, and people working in knowledge-intensive industries, on the other. Moreover, the importance of personal and household characteristics is stressed; whether 'creative' or not, 'traditional' factors like age, household type, household income and gender matter when analysing residential preferences. In that respect, the 'creative class' and/or its sub-categories may not be that different from other segments of the working population.

Residential preferences of the (new) middle class

Although the middle classes have become almost synonymous with suburbia (Fishman 1987), urban living has gradually become more in vogue again among the middle classes. Gentrification in all its manifestations has rendered large parts of western cities a legitimate territory for middle-class habitation. Even though most middle-class families are still suburbanised, increasing numbers of (upper) middle-class families stay in the city when they have children (Boterman 2012a). Gentrification is sometimes discussed as a distinction strategy of a specific section of the middle class, commonly referred to as the new middle class (Ley 1996; Butler 1997), to set themselves apart from the more 'traditional' middle classes in the suburbs (May 1996; Bridge 2003).

As a number of scholars have argued, different middle-class fractions with other orientations of capital (cultural, economic, social) have various residential preferences and display diverging residential practices (Butler and Robson 2001; Bridge 2006; Boterman 2012a). Some class fractions are particularly urban, while others are more orientated towards the suburbs. Although the analysis relies on neo-Weberian or Bourdieusian class theory, it is common to measure the class fractions in terms of occupation or study (see, for instance, Ley 1996; 2003; Butler and Robson 2001, 2003; Atkinson and Bridge 2004; Bridge 2006; Boterman 2012b; Preteceille 2007).

This chapter follows these Bourdieusian conceptualisations of class, in which occupation plays a crucial role (Bourdieu 1984). We see the jobs people have and the sectors they work in as the product of the environments in which people acquired their dispositions (i.e. social milieu of the parental home; neighbourhood; school; higher education). What people do, their practices, is the product of the interaction of their historically accumulated experiences (habitus) and the social worlds in which they interact (field). Working in a specific sector such as creative or knowledge-intensive industries is both the outcome of previous experiences and a source for new experiences and a 'site' of habitus formation.

Living in the Amsterdam metropolitan area: attractive for creative knowledge workers? Results from the 2007 ACRE survey

Before we discuss the methodology and the results of the 2013 URD-HELP (Urban Regions in the Delta – project The Higher Educated Location Preferences) survey, we will first return to the results of an earlier survey on the residential preferences of creative knowledge workers, held in Amsterdam in 2007, because that may serve as an empirical framework for the new survey we will present. The URD-HELP survey that this chapter is mainly based on was, to some extent, a follow-up study of the EU 6th Framework project ACRE (2006–2010), in which 13 European city-regions were compared (the findings of the ACRE project are summarised in Musterd and Murie 2010 and Musterd and Kovacs 2013). The Amsterdam Metropolitan Area was one of these 13 city-regions. One of the main empirical data sources was a survey about the residential attractiveness of the 13 selected city-regions for people working in creative and knowledge-intensive sectors. In total, 2646 respondents took part in this survey, 235 of whom were in the Amsterdam Metropolitan Area. The Amsterdam sample of 235 consisted of 164 workers in selected creative and knowledge-intensive sectors and 71 recent graduates of the University of Amsterdam and the Rietveld Academy (higher education in the arts). Most of these recent graduates appeared to also be working in a creative or knowledge-intensive working environment. All 235 respondents were not only working but also living in the Amsterdam Metropolitan Area. However, the ACRE study does not allow for a 'one-on-one' comparison with the URD-HELP survey of 2013–2014, for various reasons. The ACRE survey had far fewer respondents in the Amsterdam Metropolitan Area and its focus was on 'revealed preferences' and residential satisfaction rather than on 'stated preferences'. Also, the ACRE 2007 sample of respondents was aimed at discovering the behaviour of specific economic sub-groups, which did not cover the entire creative knowledge sector. The survey was not aimed at obtaining a fully representative sample, either. In fact, the sample showed over-representation in some categories, such as people working in Amsterdam, higher-income groups, creative sectors, and males; and under-representation of people working in smaller cities or suburbs, lower-income groups, knowledge-intensive sectors, and females (see Bontje et al. 2008 for further details). Furthermore, the ACRE survey took place just before the credit crunch, while the URD-HELP survey was in the aftermath of that same crisis. Still, some of the results of the ACRE survey, in particular for the Amsterdam Metropolitan Area, are interesting and relevant to consider in connection with the URD-HELP survey results and with what would be expected based on Florida's creative class theory.

For the Amsterdam case, the ACRE survey confirmed findings from earlier studies by Arnoldus and Musterd (2002) and Musterd and Deurloo (2006): the creative class is not a homogeneous group in terms of residential location within metropolitan areas. Distinguishing between people working in creative industries and people working in knowledge-intensive industries, as these authors did, appeared to also make sense in the ACRE survey. Bontje and Kepsu (2013) compared Amsterdam with five other European cases in the same survey and found that, especially in Amsterdam, the differences in residential location between creative workers and knowledge workers in the sample were significant. In Amsterdam, 62% of the creative workers in the sample were living in the city core (within the A10 ring road), as compared to 49% of the knowledge workers. In the other five cases the differences between creative workers and knowledge workers were less pronounced, but also there, creative workers were more con-centrated in the city core than were knowledge workers. Amsterdam stood out in the ACRE survey in another respect: the importance that respondents granted to 'soft' factors like diversity, tolerance, urban atmosphere and urban ameni-ties. The general conclusion coming out of the ACRE survey was that personal networks and personal trajectories (born/grown up in region, studied in region, family/friends living in region) as well as 'hard' factors (factors related to the labour market – such as jobs available – and/or costs of living, travel and infra-structure) were much more important for decisions on residential location than were the 'soft factors' that Florida emphasises. This was also true for Amsterdam, but to a much lesser extent than for any of the other 12 European case studies. While in the other cases the 'soft' factors made up only between 1% and 12% of the most important reasons to live at the current location, in Amsterdam this proportion was almost 26%. Still, even in Amsterdam the personal networks/ trajectories factors (39%) and the 'hard' factors (35%) were mentioned more often than the 'soft' factors (Musterd and Murie 2010a). As in most other ACRE case study regions, the importance of personal networks and trajectories was strongly related to having already lived in the metropolitan area for a long time; in the Amsterdam case, often for more than 10 years. This result seemed to be at odds with Florida's description of the 'creative class' as being 'hyper-mobile' (Martin-Brelot *et al.* 2010).

The comparison between creative knowledge workers and recent graduates in the ACRE survey in Amsterdam also made clear that variables like age, gender, household composition, household income and lifestyle contribute to the hetero-geneity of residential situations, residential preferences and residential satisfaction within the 'creative class'. The recent graduates were generally younger, more often single or childless-couple households, and had lower household incomes than the creative knowledge workers. They were generally more urban oriented (strongly preferring living in or close to the inner city and making intensive use of urban amenities), and much less likely to move within the next few years than the creative knowledge workers. Moreover, also within the creative knowledge workers' sub-group, differences in age, household type and household income corresponded with differences in lifestyles, residential preferences and plans to move or stay put. Also gender differences appeared, especially with younger women having a stronger preference for living in or close to the inner city (Bontje *et al.* 2008). As will be shown below, many of these findings receive support from the current study, even though there were some methodological differences between the two studies.

Data, case study regions and methodology

The data used for this chapter are from the 2013 URD-HELP survey about the residential preferences of higher-educated workers in two metropolitan areas of Amsterdam and Eindhoven. The database contains 2802 individuals sampled from:

- two larger high-tech firms: Shell Technology Centre in Amsterdam and ASML in Veldhoven (Eindhoven metropolitan area);
- several creative industries firms (mainly advertising, but also graphic design and architecture) in the two cities;
- a reference group of other higher-educated workers, making use of the 'city panels' of the departments of research and statistics of Amsterdam, Almere and Eindhoven;
- a sample of foreign high-skilled workers obtained from the 'expat centres' of the Amsterdam and Eindhoven metropolitan areas. The comparison of foreign high-skilled workers (both from the expat centre sample and foreigners from the other sample sources) with native Dutch high-skilled workers will be the focus of Chapter 9 of this book.

The respondents from the high-tech firms and creative firms were selected because of their workplace in the Amsterdam or Eindhoven metropolitan areas; they did not necessarily also have to live in the same metropolitan area where they worked. The reference group, however, was both living and working in the Amsterdam or Eindhoven metropolitan areas. The survey consisted of an extensive online questionnaire investigating the respondents' residential preferences and personal backgrounds in great detail. Key targets of the survey were to assess the differences in residential preference of technical, creative and other high-skilled workers, as well as the differences between two metropolitan areas with very different economic profiles. Stated preferences questions were an important part of the survey: respondents were asked to choose in various ways from a range of residential environments (see Boterman and Sleutjes 2014 for more details about survey design and methodology).

The two case study regions, the metropolitan areas of Amsterdam and Eindhoven, have already been introduced in Chapter 3. Here we just stress that the Amsterdam metropolitan area has a very diverse but mainly service-oriented economy. Financial services and creative industries are among the key commercial service sectors of the region. Advertising, which is the creative sector we targeted in particular in this survey, is one of the most prominent segments of Amsterdam's creative industries. High-tech manufacturing and research and development are also represented in the regional economy, but play a much less prominent role than the commercial and public service sectors.

In contrast to the situation in Amsterdam, high-tech manufacturing is one of the key economic sectors in the Eindhoven metropolitan area. ASML, where many of the Eindhoven survey respondents are working, is one of the region's largest employers, together with Philips and several spin-off companies of Philips like NXP. The Technical University Eindhoven and local businesses collaborate closely in various institutional bodies such as 'Brainport Eindhoven' and in urban economic development projects like the High Tech Campus. The area has a high proportion of higher-educated workers and was named 'the world's smartest region' by the Intelligent Community Forum in 2011.

To address the main research questions, a range of models were built to assess the difference in residential orientation of class fractions within the professional and managerial middle classes. All respondents are higher-educated (at least a completed upper-vocational education). To assess the potential effect of the class fraction on preferences, the key independent variables are academic versus non-academic education; subject of university studies (technical, law, medicine, arts, etc.); educational background of parents; sector of work (i.e. technical; creative). Other (control) variables are demographic predictors such as nationality, gender, age, income, and household composition. In this chapter, we will mainly focus on the sector of work, on the one hand, comparing between technical workers, creative workers and other higher-educated workers; and the field of study, on the other hand, comparing between technical studies and other fields of study.

The models presented in this chapter assess the residential preferences in two dimensions: (1) characteristics of the dwelling (size and tenure); (2) characteristics of the residential environment to which we will refer to as *residential milieu* (e.g. urban – suburban – rural; amenities). The characteristics of the dwelling, such as size, number of rooms, tenure and net monthly expenses are asked quite straight-forwardly in the questionnaire. The characteristics of the environment are inquired about via various methods. The respondents were asked about their current residential environment; they were asked to evaluate various amenities at the level of the neighbourhood and at the city level; and they were asked to rank the various residential areas within the metropolitan areas of Eindhoven and Amsterdam (see Figures 5.1a and 5.1b). We were interested in particular in urban versus suburban residential preferences. The areas of Indische Buurt and Jordaan were selected as urban milieus in Amsterdam; Strijp S and Binnenstad were the urban milieus in Eindhoven.

Next to the ranking of area names, the respondents were also asked to rank images of ten different residential environments. For our comparison of urban and suburban residential preferences, out of ten images three were selected as urban environments and three as suburban (see Figure 5.2 for examples). Ranking of specific consumption practices is a methodology that is inspired by Bourdieu's study described in *Distinction* (1984). According to Bourdieu, the relative value people attach to certain goods or pieces of art is a good indicator of different social positions; in our analysis we assume that the same is true for certain types of homes and residential milieus. The rejection of certain symbolic goods or places may be an even better indicator of social position than the preference for other goods or places (see Bourdieu 1984, p 56 for a discussion of the role of rejection). Dichotomies such as urban versus suburban can be a useful tool for studying the positions people assume.

Analysis results

Altogether, ten models were built to analyse the differentiation in urban or suburban residential orientation of different segments of the higher-educated

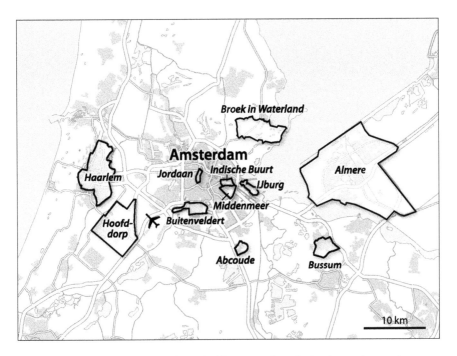

Figure 5.1a Residential areas to be ranked by respondents in the Amsterdam region

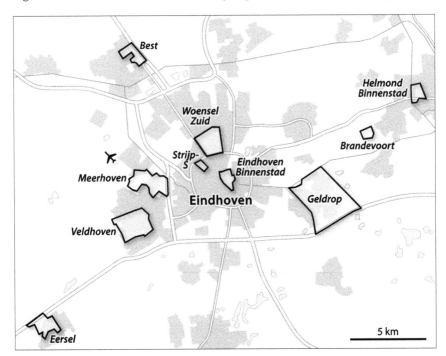

Figure 5.1b Residential areas to be ranked by respondents in the Eindhoven region

Figure 5.2 Examples of central urban and suburban residential environment photos (from a total of ten) to be ranked by respondents

workforce in the metropolitan areas of Amsterdam and Eindhoven. Each of these models had one dependent variable and 23 independent variables; moreover, models 1–6 had two versions, A and B, as will be explained below. Table 5.1 lists the dependent and independent variables used in these models and their descriptive statistics.

Table 5.1 Descriptives of dependent and independent variables used in the models

Dependent variables	N	Min	Max	Mean	StD
Ranking urban images	*1752*	2	9	5.022	1.73
Ranking suburban images	*1750*	2	9	3.948	1.79
Ranking urban locations	*1781*	1.5	9.5	4.203	2.60
Ranking suburban locations	*1781*	2	9	5.338	1.79
Rather large suburban house than small urban apartment	*1848*	0	1	0.5373	
Homeownership as priority	*1800*	0	1	0.2467	
Restaurants important	*1914*	0	1	0.5987	
Theatre important	*1914*	0	1	0.5303	
Museums important	*1914*	0	1	0.4587	
Speciality shops important	*1914*	0	1	0.4875	
Independent variables					
Gender = male	*1911*	0.00	1.00	.6010	
Age	*1914*	21.00	65.00	43.97	.39
Country of birth = foreign	*1914*	0.00	1.00	.1855	
Couple household (ref.)	*1914*	0.00	1.00	.3851	
Household with children	*1914*	0.00	1.00	.3981	
Single-person household	*1914*	0.00	1.00	.2168	
Number of higher-educated parents	*1890*	0.00	2.00	.7783	
Master's or PhD degree	*1914*	0.00	1.00	.4843	
Higher income	*1636*	0.00	1.00	.2133	
Lower income	*1636*	0.00	1.00	.1290	
Study Science/Technical (ref.)	*1722*	0.00	1.00	.4024	
Study Architecture	*1722*	0.00	1.00	.0354	
Study Law	*1722*	0.00	1.00	.0232	
Study Social	*1722*	0.00	1.00	.1678	
Study Medical	*1722*	0.00	1.00	.0679	
Study Economy/Business	*1722*	0.00	1.00	.1609	
Study Arts	*1722*	0.00	1.00	.0441	
Study Humanities	*1722*	0.00	1.00	.0662	
Study other	*1722*	0.00	1.00	.0319	
Occupation other (ref.)	*1705*	0.00	1.00	.4410	
Occupation technical	*1705*	0.00	1.00	.4352	
Occupation creative	*1705*	0.00	1.00	.1238	
Eindhoven region	*1914*	0.00	1.00	.6092	

Source: URD-HELP survey.

(Sub)urban orientation

The urban or suburban orientation of the survey respondents, expressed in their ranking of images of residential environments, is measured in two different models, each with an A and a B version. The A models estimate the effect of field of study; the B models estimate the effect of the sector of employment. The two types of variables could not be entered into one model because of too-high levels of collinearity and co-variance between the two.

Models 1a and 1b describe the mean ranking of three urban images. Ranking here implies that the lower the score, the higher the appreciation (rank 1 is highest, 10 lowest); models 2a and 2b describe the mean ranking of three suburban images. As becomes clear from Table 5.2, household composition has a clear effect: family households rank the urban images relatively low (compared to couples); singles, however, rank the urban images higher (compared to couples). For the suburban images, the opposite applies: families rank these images higher than do couples, while singles rank them lower than do couples.

While the respondents' household income has only a limited effect, the level of educational attainment of the respondents and that of their parents have a clear effect on urban or suburban residential orientation. Even though the sample contains higher-educated workers only, a significant difference could be identified between the academically educated (masters and PhD) and the more vocationally trained. The academically educated tend to rank urban images higher, and suburban lower. Also, respondents of higher-educated parents tend to prefer urban over suburban milieus.

The main distinction under scrutiny in this chapter is that between technically orientated workers and workers in 'creative industries'. In models 1a and 2a the effect of field of study is displayed. Compared to the reference category (technical studies and natural sciences), graduates from all other fields of study ranked urban images higher. in particular graduates in the social sciences, arts and humanities have a significantly higher appreciation of urban environments than do the technically educated. For the suburban images the picture is less clear. Only students of social sciences, humanities and architecture rank suburban images significantly lower than do technical graduates. Other graduates did not differ from the reference category. Finally, a clear effect could be discerned between the two urban regions of this research: respondents from the Eindhoven region generally ranked urban images lower and suburban images higher than did respondents from the Amsterdam region.

Models 1b and 2b estimate the effect of sector (technical and creative versus other lines of work). The results are in line with those for field of study. Compared to other higher-educated workers, technical workers are less likely to rank urban environments high, while workers in creative industries are more likely to rank them high.

Looking at the respondents' ranking of residential locations (names of city districts, towns and villages as shown in Figures 5.1a and 5.1b) instead of images, a similar pattern emerges (Table 5.3). Models 3a and 3b describe the mean ranking of three urban locations; models 4a and 4b describe the mean

Table 5.2 Linear regression models estimating the predictors of ranking of urban and suburban images

	Model 1a	Model 1b	Model 2a	Model 2b
Dependent variables	Ranking urban images[a]	Ranking urban images	Ranking suburban images	Ranking suburban images
Independent variables	Standardised B	Standardised B	Standardised B	Standardised B
Gender=female	−.006	−.056*	−.036	.006
Age	.026	.004	−.039	−.034
Country of birth = foreign	.033	.044*	.081***	.088***
Couple household (=ref.)				
Household with children	.095***	.090***	−.157***	−.149***
Single-person household	−.098***	−.125***	.122***	.118***
Master's or PhD degree	−.117***	−.137***	.082***	.097***
Higher-educated parents	−.059**	−.051*	.052**	.034
Higher income	−.005	−.015	−.047*	−.050*
Lower income	−.022	.016	.033	.015
Study Science/ Technical (ref.)				
Study Architecture	−.120***		.078***	
Study Law	−.077**		.041	
Study Social	−.196***		.133***	
Study Medical	−.059**		.040	
Study Economy/ Business	−.104***		.035	
Study Arts	−.157***		.043	
Study Humanities	−.141***		.070***	
Study other	.016		.021	
Occupation other (ref.)				
Occupation technical		.135***		−.081***
Occupation creative		−.203***		.078***
Eindhoven region	.166***	.149***	−.187***	−.179***
Model fit R²	*0.171*	*0.181*	*0.173*	*0.156*

Source: URD-HELP survey.

Notes: a Ranking here implies that the lower the score the higher the appreciation (rank 1 is highest, 10 lowest).

* p<0.1 ** p<0.05 *** p<0.01

ranking of three suburban locations. Models 3a and 4a show the effect of field of study; models 3b and 4b show the effect of occupation. Again, compared to couples without children, which is the reference category, households with children are more suburban oriented and singles more urban oriented. Both field of study and occupation have a clear effect, with those with technical studies and occupations having a more suburban orientation than those with other study backgrounds and/or creative occupations. The effect of educational attainment level found for the ranking of images also reappears for the ranking of locations, with the academically educated and those with higher-educated parents showing a stronger urban orientation. Household income again appears to have little effect on urban or suburban orientation.

Finally, comparing the results of ranking images and ranking locations, a seemingly paradoxical difference could be discerned between the two urban regions of this research. Respondents from the Eindhoven region generally ranked urban images lower than did respondents from the Amsterdam region. The urban locations, however, are more preferred in Eindhoven than in Amsterdam. Apparently the meaning attached to the locations in Eindhoven does not correlate to the images in the same way as it does in Amsterdam. Possibly the selected locations in the Eindhoven region are more contrasting to each other.

(Sub)urban preference in relation to dwelling size, dwelling type and tenure

Figure 5.3 demonstrates that a much larger proportion of technical workers than creative workers tend to prefer a large suburban home over a small urban apartment. The other statements do not indicate very big differences, although technical workers seem more often to prefer a homogeneous area than do the creative workers. To test whether the difference between technical and creative workers holds, we ran logistic regression models. Table 5.4 shows two models: model 5 (a and b) estimating the probability of preferring a large suburban home to a small urban apartment and model 6 (a and b) estimating the probability of mentioning homeownership in the top three most important aspects of residential choice (out of 21 options for either the dwelling or its environment).

For both the field of study and the line of work the effects are quite evident. Compared to technical graduates, all other studies predict a lower probability of preferring a large suburban home to an urban apartment. Compared to other workers, clearly technical workers prefer a suburban home, while creative workers tend to disagree with the statement more often. This may be related to the current tenure situation of the respondents. Of the main control variables, family composition is a strong predictor: households with young children agree with the statement, while singles disagree. Interestingly, the level of education of the respondents, and that of their parents, also has a negative effect on the preference for a suburban home. Income does not seem to play a role.

Table 5.3 Linear regression models estimating the predictors of ranking of urban and suburban locations

	Model 3a	Model 3b	Model 4a	Model 4b
Dependent variables	Ranking of urban locations	Ranking of urban locations	Ranking of suburban locations	Ranking of suburban locations
Independent variables	Standardised B	Standardised B	Standardised B	Standardised B
Gender = female	−.010	−.042	.034	.053**
Age	.108***	.090***	−.033	−.031
Country of birth = foreign	.004	−.009	.000	.005
Couple household (=ref.)				
Household with children	.143***	.116***	−.093***	−.076***
Single-person household	−.059**	−.101***	.087***	.117***
Master's or PhD degree	−.076***	−.098***	.095***	.107***
Higher-educated parents	−.069**	−.057**	.012	.003
Higher income	−.019	−.028	.013	.024
Lower income	−.020	.004	.043	.015
Study Science/ Technical (ref.)				
Study Architecture	−.130***		.070***	
Study Law	−.096***		.062**	
Study Social	−.200***		.187***	
Study Medical	−.109***		.078***	
Study Economy/ Business	−.128***		.097***	
Study Arts	−.143***		.116***	
Study Humanities	−.156***		.119***	
Study other	−.072***		.055**	
Occupation other (ref.)				
Occupation technical		.234***		−.204***
Occupation creative		−.125***		.087***
Eindhoven region	−.213***	−.244***	−.237***	−.210***
Model fit R^2	*0.141*	*0.155*	*0.184*	*0.198*

Source: URD-HELP survey.

Note: * p<0.1 ** p<0.05 *** p<0.01

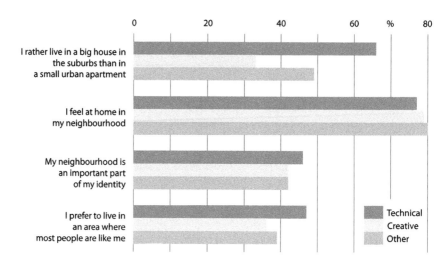

Figure 5.3 Proportion that (strongly) agree with statements about home and neighbourhood

Table 5.4 Logistic regression models of housing characteristics

	Model 5a	Model 5b	Model 6a	Model 6b
Dependent variables	Prefers large suburban home to small urban apartment	Prefers large suburban home to small urban apartment	Homeownership aspiration	Homeownership aspiration
Independent variables				
Gender=female	.782*	.710**	.653***	.664**
Age	1.001	.999	.992	.994
Country of birth = foreign	.743**	.803	1.257	1.188
Couple household				
Household with children	2.019***	1.953***	.965	.962
Single-person household	.637***	.584***	1.131	1.166
Master's or PhD degree	.618***	.565****	.750**	.728**
Higher-educated parents	.795***	.819***	1.019	1.034
Higher income	1.020	1.084	1.429**	1.479***
Lower income	1.024	1.034	.381***	.418***

Study Science/ Technical (ref.)				
Study Architecture	.371***		1.832*	
Study Law	.280***		1.468	
Study Social	.425***		1.083	
Study Medical	.583**		1.018	
Study Economy/ Business	.556***		1.183	
Study Arts	.369***		1.410	
Study Humanities	.378***		.985	
Study other	.403***		.901	
Occupation other (ref.)				
Occupation technical		1.842***		1.043
Occupation creative		.543***		1.127
Eindhoven region	1.848***	1.753***	1.036	1.171
Model fit *Nagelkerke R* ^{2}	*0.197*	*0.199*	*0.04*	*0.04*

Source: URD-HELP survey.

Note: * p<0.1 ** p<0.05 *** p<0.01

Regarding the preference for homeownership, the result is less clear. About a quarter of all respondents rank homeownership as one of their top priorities when selecting a dwelling and/or a residential environment. From Table 5.4 it appears that income and gender have the strongest effect on the preference for homeownership. Men are significantly more likely to include homeownership among their housing priorities. High-income households are much more likely and low-income households are much less likely than those on middle incomes to include owning a home as one of their priorities. Interestingly, academically trained respondents have a smaller chance of prioritising homeownership, as compared to the other higher-educated.

Of the key variables of this study, field of study does not seem to play a role in the aspiration to homeownership. Only students of architecture have a slightly stronger penchant to aspire to owning a home. There is also hardly any difference between the respondents from Eindhoven and Amsterdam.

Amenities

Opinions about regional amenities (Figure 5.4) are quite diverse: public safety, for instance, is considered (very) important by almost all respondents. Also, access to green areas and daily grocery shopping are amenities that most respondents consider important. In contrast with that, most cultural amenities are seen as much less important. Nonetheless, the offer of museums or classical concerts differs considerably between the different groups of workers. Cultural amenities are considered more important by creative workers than by technical workers. Compared to other higher-educated workers, creative workers do not seem to stand out. Most of the other amenities do not seem to be valued very differently.

Table 5.5 shows four models that describe the estimation of the importance of specific urban amenities. In these four models (7–10) only the effect of the sector of work is included (for field of study the effects are similar). The groups are not

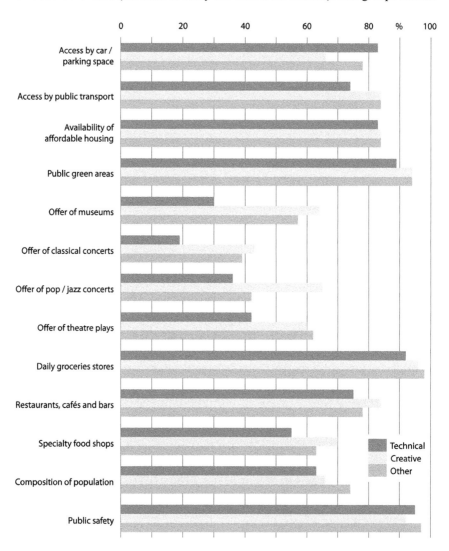

Figure 5.4 Proportion of respondents that find the amenities (very) important

Table 5.5 Logistic regression models of the importance of selected amenities

	Model 7	Model 8	Model 9	Model 10
Dependent variables	Restaurants, café (very) important	Theatre (very) important	Museum (very) important	Speciality shops (very) important
Independent variables				
Gender=female	1.591***	2.378***	2.174***	1.368**
Age	.971***	1.043***	1.050***	.992
Country of birth = foreign	1.517***	.861	1.966***	1.082
Couple household (ref.)				
Household with children	.630***	1.006	.846	.673***
Single-person household	.757*	.826	1.090	.785
Master's or PhD degree	1.241*	1.343**	1.493***	1.064
Higher-educated parents	.842**	1.086	1.072	1.020
Higher income	1.170	1.240	1.077	1.340**
Lower income	1.078	1.148	.824	1.089
Occupation other (ref.)				
Occupation technical	1.085	.670***	.504***	.773*
Occupation creative	1.872***	1.337	2.110***	1.424*
Eindhoven region	.547***	1.023	.561***	.581***
Model fit Nagelkerke R ^{2}	*0.107*	*0.150*	*0.256*	*0.07*

Source: URD-HELP survey.

Note: * p<0.1 ** p<0.05 *** p<0.01

significantly different for all amenities but, generally, creative workers are more likely to indicate that the urban amenities are important, while technical workers clearly have a lesser penchant to deem these amenities important. In particular, the offer of museums is valued very differently by the two groups. In addition to the core of our comparison, here also some interesting effects for control variables appear from the table. Gender has a strong effect on amenities, such as speciality shops, restaurants, and offer of museums and theatres. Women have a greater chance to appreciate these amenities than men. Also the household situation is a predictor for the evaluation of specific amenities: families with children, for instance, deem restaurants and speciality shops important less often than do singles or couple households. Finally, also income and level of education have some effect: speciality shops are more important for higher incomes, while academically trained workers attach more value to theatres and museums.

Conclusion and discussion

In this chapter the stated preferences of different groups of higher-educated workers have been investigated. The principal comparison made in this study was between employees of technical and creative firms in two Dutch urban areas: Amsterdam and Eindhoven. The results indicate that the residential preferences of higher-educated workers are differentiated between the worker groups. The differences in residential preferences occur along four dimensions: housing type, residential milieu, relative location and importance of specific amenities. These dimensions are not independent of each other and, moreover, they often point in the same direction. Together they make up a residential orientation that is the combined effect of the four dimensions.

For aspects of housing we found that higher-educated workers in high-tech companies have a preference for (semi-)detached housing, while higher-educated employees in creative companies (mostly advertisement companies) prefer apartments. Zooming in on trade-offs between aspects of housing, technical workers much more often than creative workers indicate that they rather have a large suburban house than a small apartment in the city.

Another key dimension is the appreciation of various amenities. In this respect too we demonstrated that differences exist between the worker groups: cultural amenities such as theatres, restaurants and museums are more important for creative workers than for technical workers. It should be noted, however, that despite these evident differences, most workers tend to agree that they are less important than other amenities such as public safety, public green areas and shops for daily groceries. Also, when amenities are compared to aspects of the dwelling and location they are generally considered less important.

Creative and technical workers also differ in their opinions about the importance of location. A location close to the city centre is a greater priority for creative workers than for technical workers. Living close to the workplace, in terms of accessibility, is more important to technical workers than for other workers.

Creative workers and technical workers also show considerable differences in terms of their preference for specific residential environments. Based on the ranking of pictures and areas, it seems that technical workers have a more suburban preference, as compared to other workers, while creative workers tend to favour urban milieus.

Our findings link to the academic debate about how to understand the relationship between residential location and economic activity (employment sector). This debate has until recently been inconclusive as to whether or not the creative class stands out from other higher-educated workers and whether or not it is urban in its residential orientation (Niedomysl and Hansen 2010; Lawton *et al.* 2013). The ACRE project, with which we explicitly entered into dialogue, found differences between knowledge workers and creative workers in Amsterdam and the other 12 case study regions of the project, challenging the supposed homogeneity of Florida's 'creative class', but found little evidence that these groups differed much from other higher-educated workers. The main conclusions of ACRE were that factors such as work, stage in the life course and social networks are more important for residential choices than 'soft factors', such as urban atmosphere, diversity and amenities. The HELP project confirms these findings of the ACRE project (Bontje *et al.* 2008; Musterd and Murie 2010). While the ACRE survey focused mostly on 'revealed preferences' and satisfaction with the residential and working environment, the HELP survey focused on 'stated preferences'. The fact that different survey designs and partially different methodologies led to largely similar results, at least in the European context, significantly strengthens the plea to unpack the 'creative class' into sub-categories of workers.

By making a more refined categorisation of workers in which technical and creative workers are opposed to each other, we did find support for some elements of the original idea of the urban orientation of the creative class, however. Perhaps more interestingly, we mainly found evidence of a distinct residential orientation of technical workers, who differ more clearly than creative workers from our reference group of other higher-educated workers. Reminiscent of studies by Musterd (2006) and Markusen (2006), specific groups of higher-educated workers do show distinct residential preferences. The association between high-tech and ICT workers and residential preferences that corresponds to a suburban residential milieu, as argued by Kotkin (2002) or Van Oort *et al.* (2003), is also demonstrated by our analysis.

Based on our sample in two contrasting urban areas, which basically show similar results, we argue that the lack of clarity in the international debate could be related to the variety and lack of precision in research designs. Different categorisations and definitions of creative class may have obscured the evident differences that exist between different groups of workers. The contribution of this study thus lies in the fact that a precise and narrow definition of occupation helps in understanding the residential preferences of higher-educated workers. At the same time this is a limitation of this study. By focusing on specific subsets of respondents we did not provide a statistically representative analysis of the preferences of all higher-educated workers. However, by selecting two groups of workers that we expected to differ most from each other, we did demonstrate that there is no one-size-fits-all approach to higher-educated workers. There is no such thing as *the* creative class.

This insight should be linked back to the literature on the (new) middle class and their role in the transformation of urban space. As various scholars have shown, the middle classes, particularly in larger metropolitan areas, are differentiated by their forms of capital (economic, cultural, social), as exemplified by their occupations (Bridge 2006; Butler and Robson 2003). Various middle-class 'fractions', with different occupations, are associated with specific tastes in consumption and residential preferences. Some class fractions, many belonging to the new middle classes, tend to prefer inner-city areas which offer a residential environment that suits their taste, distinction strategies and consumption lifestyle. Our study confirms the idea that people employed in creative industries belong to urban middle classes, while technical workers more often fit the image of the traditional middle classes (May 1996; Bridge 2003). Their residential preferences should hence be understood from a broader perspective on class and class reproduction.

References

Arnoldus, M and Musterd, S 2002, *Wonen in de regionale kennisstad.* Amsterdam: AME, Universiteit van Amsterdam.

Atkinson, R and Bridge, G (eds) 2004, *Gentrification in a global context: the new urban colonialism.* Abingdon, Oxon/New York: Routledge.

Bontje, M and Kepsu, K 2013, Creative knowledge strategies for polycentric city-regions. In: Musterd, S and Kovacs, Z (eds) *Place-making and policies for competitive cities*, 191–208. Chichester: Wiley-Blackwell.

Bontje, M and Musterd, S 2005, What kind of a place do the creative knowledge workers live in? In: Franke, S and Verhagen, E (eds) *Creativity and the city. How the creative economy is changing the city*, 166–175. Rotterdam: NAi Publishers.

Bontje, M, Pethe, H and Rühmann, P 2008, *The Amsterdam region – a home for creative knowledge workers and graduates? Understanding the attractiveness of the metropolitan region for creative knowledge workers.* ACRE report 5.1. Amsterdam: AMIDSt, University of Amsterdam.

Boterman, WR 2012a, Residential practices of middle classes in the field of parenthood, dissertation, Amsterdam: University of Amsterdam.

Boterman, WR 2012b, Residential mobility of urban middle classes in the field of parenthood. *Environment and Planning A* 44, 2397–2412.

Boterman, WR and Sleutjes, B 2014, *Stated residential preferences of higher educated workers in Amsterdam and Eindhoven.* HELP Report no. 2. Amsterdam: AISSR/Centre for Urban Studies.

Bourdieu, P 1984, *Distinction: a social critique of the judgment of taste.* Cambridge, MA: Harvard University Press.

Bridge, G 2003, Time-space trajectories of provincial gentrification. *Urban Studies* 40 (12), 2545–2556.

Bridge, G 2006, It's not just a question of taste: gentrification, the neighbourhood, and cultural capital. *Environment and Planning A* 38 (10), 1965–1978.

Butler, T 1997, *Gentrification and the middle classes.* Aldershot: Ashgate.

Butler, T and Robson, G 2001, Social capital, gentrification and neighbourhood change in London: a comparison of three South London neighbourhoods. *Urban Studies* 38 (12), 2145–2162.

Butler, T and Robson, G 2003, Plotting the middle classes: gentrification and circuits of education in London. *Housing Studies* 18 (1), 5–28.

Fishman, R 1987, *Bourgeois utopias: the rise and fall of suburbia.* New York: Basic Books.

Florida, R 2002, *The rise of the creative class, and how it's transforming work, leisure, community and everyday life.* New York: Basic Books.

Glaeser, E 2005, Review of Richard Florida's The rise of the creative class. *Regional Science and Urban Economics* 35 (5), 593–596.

Grabher, G 2004, Learning in projects, remembering in networks? Communality, sociality and connectivity in project ecologies. *European Urban and Regional Studies* 11 (2), 103–123.

Hansen, HK and Niedomysl, T 2009, Migration and the creative class: evidence from Sweden. *Journal of Economic Geography* 9 (2), 191–206.

Horwitz, FM, Heng, CT and Quazi, HA 2003, Finders, keepers? Attracting, motivating and retaining knowledge workers. *Human Resource Management Journal* 13 (4), 23–44.

Kotkin, J 2002, *The new geography. How the digital revolution is changing the American landscape.* New York: Random House.

Krätke, S 2010, 'Creative cities' and the rise of the dealer class: a critique of Richard Florida's approach to urban theory. *International Journal of Urban and Regional Research* 34 (4), 834–853.

Lawton, P, Murphy, E and Redmond, D 2013, Residential preferences of the 'creative class'? *Cities* 31 (1), 47–56.

Ley, D 1996, *The new middle class and the remaking of the central city.* Oxford: Oxford University Press.

Ley, D 2003, Artists, aestheticisation and the field of gentrification. *Urban Studies* 40 (12), 2527–2544.

Markusen, A 2006, Urban development and the politics of a creative class; evidence from a study of artists. *Environment and Planning A* 38 (10), 1921–1940.

Martin-Brelot, H, Grossetti, M, Eckert, D, Gritsai, O and Kovacs, Z 2010, The spatial mobility of the 'creative class': a European perspective. *International Journal of Urban and Regional Research* 34 (4), 854–870.

May, J 1996, Globalization and the politics of place: place and identity in an inner London neighbourhood. *Transactions of the Institute of British Geographers* New Series 21 (1), 194–215.

Mellander, C, Florida, R, Asheim, B and Gertler, M 2014, *The creative class goes global.* Abingdon, Oxon/New York: Routledge.

Musterd, S 2002, *De Nieuwe Amsterdamse Kernvoorraad; Woonmilieus in de Creatieve Culturele Kennisstad.* Amsterdam: Bestuursdienst.

Musterd, S 2006, Segregation, urban space and the resurgent city. *Urban Studies* 43 (8), 1325–1340.

Musterd, S and Deurloo, R 2006, Amsterdam and the preconditions for a creative knowledge city. *Tijdschrift voor Economische en Sociale Geografie* 97 (1), 80–94.

Musterd, S and Murie, A (eds) 2010, *Making competitive cities.* Chichester: Wiley-Blackwell.

Musterd, S and Murie, A 2010a, Synthesis: re-making the competitive city. In: Musterd, S and Murie, A (eds), *Making competitive cities*, 327–350. Oxford: Wiley Blackwell.

Musterd, S and Kovacs, Z (eds) 2013, *Place making and policies for competitive cities.* Oxford: Wiley-Blackwell.

Niedomysl, T and Hansen, HK 2010, What matters more for the decision to move: jobs versus amenities. *Environment and Planning A* 42, 1636–1649.

Pratt, AC 2006, Advertising and creativity, a governance approach: a case study of creative agencies in London. *Environment and Planning A* 38 (10), 1883–1899.

Preteceille, E 2007, Is gentrification a useful paradigm to analyse social changes in the Paris metropolis? *Environment and Planning A* 39 (1), 10–31.

Servillo, L, Atkinson, R and Russo, AP 2011, Territorial attractiveness in EU urban and spatial policy: a critical review and future research agenda. *European Urban and Regional Studies* 19 (4), 349–365.

Storper, M and Scott, AJ 2009, Rethinking human capital, creativity and urban growth. *Journal of Economic Geography* 9 (2), 147–167.

Van Oort, F, Weterings, A and Verlinde, H 2003, Residential amenities of knowledge workers and the location of ICT-firms in the Netherlands. *Tijdschrift voor economische en sociale geografie* 94 (4), 516–523.

6 Sorting models of household location and urban amenities

Mark Van Duijn, Jan Möhlmann, Ismir Mulalic and Jan Rouwendal

Introduction

Skilled workers and urban development

In earlier chapters of this volume it has been argued that highly educated workers are often regarded to be a crucial element of economic prosperity and growth in cities. In *The Economy of Cities* Jane Jacobs (1970) puts forward the thesis that human interaction is an important aspect of city life and crucial for our understanding of why people concentrate in expensive places with high densities. Economists such as Lucas (1988) picked up this idea, which was interpreted as human capital externalities. That is, interaction between higher-educated individuals generates benefits for society that exceed those accruing to the individuals. The high population density in cities stimulates interactions, and the external effects associated with them are an important source of agglomeration economies. Cities thus become more productive places and this process works continuously and generates growth. This process works better if higher-educated people interact. Empirical evidence confirming this hypothesis was provided by Rauch (1993).[1] Later studies include Glaeser and Maré (2001), who find that workers moving to the city realize important wage gains, especially when they are young. This suggests that cities foster skills. Glaeser and Maré (2001) show that these workers do not lose these gains when they later move to rural areas, which suggests that their sojourn in a city has permanently increased their productivity.

Consumer city

If it is true that the interaction of highly educated workers generates important external effects, it is clearly important for urban policy makers to know how they can attract such workers and, when they are present, make them stay. An important contribution to the economic literature on this issue was made by Roback (1982). The basic idea of Roback's paper is that of equilibrium: if identical workers live at different locations, they must be equally well off in all of them. The well-being of workers depends on wages, but also on the price of consumer goods, including housing, and on the presence of local amenities. There is a trade-off between these determinants: workers can, for instance, be compensated for high house prices by higher wages or better amenities.

Workers can be attracted to cities only if there are jobs and, although local labour markets may differ in many respects, it is generally the case that higher wages reduce the demand for workers.[2] However, if a city has good amenities it may continue to attract highly educated workers even when wages are not that high. This reasoning thus suggests an – at least potentially – important connection between urban amenities and economic prosperity.

Although urban economic theory has traditionally regarded the city primarily as the location of jobs, increasing attention is paid to the importance of consumer amenities for urban life. A pioneering contribution was Brueckner *et al.*'s (1999) answer to the question why central Paris is rich, while downtown Detroit is poor. Amenities make the difference, according to the theory developed by these authors. When the central city is attractive high-income households are willing to pay a lot for living there and contribute to a vital central city, whereas a lack of amenities makes the rich choose luxury houses in the suburbs, with the risk of a desolate inner city. Another seminal study is by Glaeser *et al.* (2001), who provide a large amount of empirical evidence that suggests that consumer amenities are important for cities. Later studies include that by Van Duijn and Rouwendal (2013), who show that cultural heritage – they use ancient inner cities as a proxy – is indeed an important attractor for cities. Their sorting model is of the same type as those used in this chapter.

In the next section the logit-based sorting model is introduced. This model has been the work-horse for investigating the importance of consumer amenities in a number of investigations that are discussed in the third section.

The logit-based sorting model

Sorting models

Although discrete choices have attracted the attention of economists at least since the 1970, sorting models are a relatively recent development in housing market analysis. Kuminoff *et al.* (2013) provide an excellent review that compares these models with hedonic price analysis. They distinguish various types of sorting models. The logit-based model that we use in this project is distinguished from others by the fact that it allows households to have preferences that permit any ranking of the choice alternatives based on their inherent characteristics (price is not included), whereas many other models require them to have basically the same ranking. Moreover, the model can easily deal with a large number of characteristics of households and choice alternatives and, in contrast to many other models, it can be estimated when the number of alternatives is very large.

One of the most important results of hedonic and sorting models is that they provide information about households' willingness to pay (WTP) for neighbourhood characteristics. This WTP is formally defined as the amount of money that takes the consumer back to his or her original level of utility after a change in one or more neighbourhood characteristics. It therefore expresses the trade-offs households are willing to make between experiencing these characteristics and money that can be spent on market goods. Since utility cannot be observed, it makes little sense to talk about the additional utility provided by neighbourhood characteristics, but WTP is easy to interpret and provides the essential information.

The logit model was used by psychologists before being made popular in economics by McFadden, who showed that it could be derived from the maximization of random preferences. McFadden (1973) is the seminal paper on the use of the logit model and other types of discrete choice models in applied economic analysis in which this result was proved and a detailed discussion of estimation of the model by maximum likelihood was provided. The logit model is still popular but its use has changed over time. Current practice pays more attention to unobserved aspects of the phenomenon that is studied and to potential endogeneity problems. This section provides an informal discussion of the logit-based sorting model, while a formal presentation is given in the appendix of this chapter.

The logit model

In McFadden's theory the utility of the actors – which we assume to be households, in this chapter – is the sum of a deterministic and a random part. The deterministic part is conventional and links household characteristics – which are important determinants of preferences – to characteristics of choice alternatives. In this chapter these alternatives are residential areas: neighbourhoods or municipalities. The deterministic part of the utility function indicates the quality of the match between the characteristics of the household and those of the neighbourhood. The random part of the utility is different. It is independent of the observed characteristics of the household and of the area. It is interpreted best as reflecting idiosyncratic tastes for these areas.

In some of the models to be discussed below, choice alternatives are not just residential locations, but a specific type of housing in such a location. For instance, households can choose between being a tenant or an owner-occupier in a particular location. Or owner-occupying households can choose between living in an apartment or a single-family house in a particular residential area. In such cases a choice alternative is a combination of a residential location and a type of housing. If the housing stock and all its characteristics are taken as given, one may take the extreme position that all existing dwellings should be treated as separate choice alternatives. Although this approach is feasible[3] it is often more convenient to assume that the level of the housing price at each location is given, whereas households can adjust the quality of their housing situation to their own preferences.[4] The work that is reviewed below follows the latter approach.

The random parts of the utilities are random only from the researcher's perspective. The households know their idiosyncratic preferences as well as the preferences that are reflected in the deterministic part of the utility function and take them both into account when making their choice among the residential areas. For the households, choices are therefore deterministic. However, for the researcher who knows only the distribution of the random part of the preferences, but not their specific values for any household, individual choice behaviour is random. That is, household choices can be predicted only as probabilities. An important advantage of the logit model is that these probabilities can be described as a simple function of the deterministic parts of the preferences. That makes the model relatively easy to handle.

The choice probabilities of the logit model imply that the alternative that offers the highest value of the deterministic part of the utility, and therefore the best match between the household and area characteristics, has the highest probability of being chosen. For all other alternatives the choice probabilities are positive, implying that there can always be idiosyncratic reasons why a household prefers to live in a particular area no matter how bad the area otherwise looks for this particular household. However, when the match between household and alternative as indicated by the deterministic part of the utility is bad, this choice probability will be very close to zero.

Heterogeneous behaviour and market demand

The logit model is primarily a model for individual behaviour and as such it is characterized by a property known as the independence of irrelevant alternatives. The best known consequence of this property is the so-called red bus/blue bus problem according to which the introduction of a new bus service which is exactly identical to an existing one except for the colour of the buses used (which is immaterial for the services offered) results in an increase in the probability that travellers choose the bus as their transport mode. This seems a priori unlikely, perhaps unless the existing buses were very crowded, since there is essentially nothing new to choose. The more general problem is that the independence of irrelevant alternatives restricts the way consumers react to changes in the characteristics of choice alternatives, such as their price. The model specification determines the reaction to these changes to a large extent, independent of the properties of the data at hand.

The recent literature has paid more attention to the use of the logit model for *market* demand (as opposed to individual demand) and from that point of view the independence of irrelevant alternatives is less of a problem. The reason is that differences in preferences among the individual actors may lead to variation in reactions to changes in the characteristics of the alternatives. Such differences are estimated and this implies that the reactions of market demand to changes in characteristics of alternatives are much more determined by the data than the reactions of the individual demands. For this reason, the independence of irrelevant alternatives is regarded as a less urgent problem when the model specification allows for a substantial amount of heterogeneity in the preferences.

It is common in the literature to model this heterogeneity through the use of a flexible functional form that specifies the utility attached to a choice alternative as the sum of an average utility and actor-specific deviation from that average. The latter are connected to the characteristics of the actor. For instance, in the context of neighbourhood choice, families with children are allowed to attach more value to the presence of parks than the average household; or higher educated people can attach more value to the presence of cultural heritage than the average household. All household characteristics can be crossed with all neighbourhood characteristics in this way. Through such a very general specification many types of possible heterogeneity are allowed and their importance can be estimated.

Unobserved characteristics and biased estimates

This specification of the utility function has yet another advantage. Estimation of the logit model then implies estimation of an alternative specific constant – representing the average utility – for all alternatives. This constant captures the impact of all observed characteristics of the alternative as well as that of possible unobserved (by the researcher) characteristics. This is an important issue, since it is in practice impossible to measure all relevant aspects of a house or neighbourhood. This is well illustrated by the fact that people often need to visit a house and the neighbourhood in which it is located before buying it, no matter how much information about the two has been collected before. Some characteristics are hard to measure, but are experienced almost immediately when visiting the location.

Incorporating the unobserved characteristics in the model is important for other reasons as well. If a house or neighbourhood is attractive (or unattractive) for reasons that are unknown to the researcher, then the housing price there is higher (or lower) than would be expected based on the observed information. If the presence of unobserved characteristics were not taken into account, this would be incorrectly interpreted as limited sensitivity of household to the price of housing. However, if the logit model is estimated with the alternative specific constants, these constants can, in a second stage of the analysis, be further analysed by methods that take into account the possibility that the housing price is correlated with the unobserved heterogeneity. In econometric terms, this is an endogeneity problem that is solved through the use of an instrumental variable.

Taking into account the possible presence of unobserved characteristics turns out to be not just a technical refinement, but often implies a substantial change in the values of the estimated parameters. It is common experience that the coefficient for the housing price increases substantially in absolute value when the instrumental variable procedure is used, which confirms the conjecture discussed above.

Finally, we mention that the estimated logit model can be used to derive an expression for the equilibrium housing price that is close to the hedonic equations that are often used. The sorting model can thus be viewed as being consistent with the hedonic approach, but it is much more comprehensive, since it also explains the location choices underlying the housing prices.

Applications

1 Introduction and overview

In this section we discuss a number of applications of the above-outlined modelling framework to questions concerning the relationship between educated workers and urban amenities. This subsection provides an overview of what follows. We start in subsection 2 with an investigation into the locational preferences of various household types in the Netherlands. The focus in this work is on housing in relation to jobs and other amenities. One important idea is that households with higher incomes, often related to more education, have better possibilities for realizing a satisfactory combination of housing, work and commutes than do otherwise comparable households with lower incomes. A second consideration is that this is especially important for households with two workers, since the higher income allows them to solve the co-location problem, which has been shown in the US to be an important driver for the choice of which metropolitan region to live in (Costa and Kahn 2002). The third and – for the purposes of the HELP project – most important aspect of this study was the investigation of the importance attached to other (non-work) urban amenities, relative to employment accessibility. The results confirm that households do not only appreciate the city because of its labour market advantages, but also attach substantial weight to consumption amenities.

In subsection 3 we delve a bit deeper into this issue by elaborating the role of conservation areas, which is the main indicator of urban attractiveness, in our sorting model. It is certainly true that the cultural heritage that is abundantly available in many historical Dutch cities is an important amenity in itself. However, the presence of this amenity also makes it more attractive for other amenities like shops, restaurants, cafés, theatres and music halls to locate in these cities. This is indeed the case and we can therefore conclude that our estimates of the strong preference for cities with historical districts reflect the value attached not only to the monuments and old buildings per se, but also to the endogenous amenities that are over-represented in its vicinity. Our findings thus confirm the importance of 'consumer city', especially for the higher-educated workers.

To provide an international perspective, subsection 4 discusses some results of the estimation of a sorting model for the Greater Copenhagen area, which can be considered as the Danish equivalent of the Dutch Randstad. The results confirm that in Denmark too, consumer amenities play an important role next to labour market considerations. Another issue, to which we return in other work for the Netherlands, is the unequal distribution of income groups over the Copenhagen metropolitan area. The higher incomes are over-represented in the north-eastern part of the area, whereas the lower incomes tend to live more often in the west. We link this phenomenon to the preferences of households with regard to the composition of the population in residential areas. This composition is thus, on the one hand, an important outcome of the choice process, but also, on the other hand, one of its driving forces. This interdependency has been taken into account when estimating the model, and the importance of this 'social interaction' phenomenon is clearly demonstrated. It suggests the possible existence of multiple equilibria and path dependence. However, further investigation of these issues was outside the scope of the Copenhagen study.

Before elaborating the social interactions issue for the Netherlands we turn to two other issues concerning the interpretation of the sorting model. The first one, discussed in subsection 5, concerns the question whether job accessibility is the appropriate indicator for labour market attractiveness. With competitive labour markets the wage should be a sufficient statistic for the attractiveness of a particular residential location. Although we know that labour markets are not perfect, the wage remains (of course) an important aspect and research (see Groot *et al.* 2011) has confirmed that there are non-negligible geographical differences in wages within the Netherlands. Using these research results, we investigated the robustness of our earlier investigation. The results show that wage differences can also be used as a labour market indicator and that the results with respect to urban amenities remain qualitatively unchanged. Wages and job accessibility are strongly correlated, a phenomenon that can be attributed to agglomeration effects.

Our finding that urban amenities are important drivers of location choice behaviour raises another question: can good amenities substitute for a strong labour market? This seems to be unlikely, for *a priori* reasons, but our results do not exclude this interpretation. To investigate the issue in some detail we have extended the sorting model with a cross-term for job accessibility and conservation area. A positive coefficient for this cross-term tells us that the impact of urban amenities is larger if the labour market is strong, whereas a negative coefficient suggests that consumers attach less value to these amenities when the labour market is strong, for instance because there is not so much time to enjoy the consumer amenities. The results are clear: consumer amenities are appreciated more in areas with a strong labour market. Without jobs, amenities are unable to add much to the attractiveness of a city. In subsection 6 we discuss this result and its extension to a more general, non-parametric specification.

In subsection 7 we return to the importance of the demographic composition of neighbourhoods for their attractiveness as a residential location. It is well known that in US cities the higher-income households tend to live in the suburbs, whereas in European cities the pattern is different: the rich are also over-represented in the city centres, especially when there are many amenities. In the Amsterdam metropolitan area this European pattern is also clearly visible in the owner-occupied sector. Including the proportion of high-income households as a possible attractor in the sorting model confirms the hypothesis that social interactions are also important here. This leads to interesting questions with respect to possible equilibrium configurations.

The presence of cultural heritage and associated endogenous amenities attracts higher-educated households to the city centre. Since these households often have higher incomes, this further increases the attractiveness of the centre. The 'social interaction' (people like to live where the rich live) therefore has a multiplier effect on the attractiveness of the centre. Moreover, simulations suggest that, depending on the initial situation and the parameter values, the social interactions help to determine the equilibrium configuration (where the rich can concentrate either in the suburbs or in the centre). These findings shed light on the successful policy of core cities of metropolitan areas since the 1980s to increase their attractiveness by targeting housing construction on high-income households.

Subsection 8 relates an exercise that investigates the consequences of a standard assumption in the sorting models literature: the absence of mobility costs. In the conventional set-up that has also been used in the work discussed thus far households are assumed to be able to locate everywhere. History does not matter. In practice, it is likely that the high costs of mobility (in monetary as well as in social and psychological terms) tend to tie households to locations that have been chosen in the past. Making unrealistic assumptions is not necessarily a bad thing: model building is useful exactly because it simplifies reality by neglecting many aspects that are irrelevant for the phenomenon of interest. However, treating immobile households as if they are perfectly mobile may well bias our estimates of the location preferences and this is the reason why we investigated this aspect in a separate (pilot) study for the Eindhoven region in the Netherlands. Our results show – not surprisingly – that mobility costs are large. What is more important is that including mobility costs has an impact of the estimated parameters of the utility function, both of the average household and of specific groups. Hence, WTP estimates are also affected, which implies that policy recommendations based on sorting models may also be biased. Further investigation of the importance of mobility costs in the logit model is therefore a relevant topic for further investigation.

Subsection 9 concludes our sequence of studies with an exploratory investigation into the relevance of making a distinction between technical, creative and other workers. The potential importance of this distinction is suggested by geographical literature, e.g. the stated preference survey conducted within this project.[5] To see if the suggested differences in location behaviour can be verified in revealed preference research as well, Möhlmann *et al.* (2015b) have used a classification of occupations to detect 'technical' as well as 'creative' occupations. Since occupations are – at least to some extent – chosen by the workers, they base the orientation of workers on their educational direction, which has usually been set once the worker enters the labour market. Their results show that the WTP for municipality characteristics differs significantly between creative and technical households.

2 Employment and amenities in the Netherlands

Weijschede-van der Straaten *et al.* (2015) study the locational preferences of various types of households in the Netherlands. Municipalities are their basic geographical unit of analysis and their focus is on the role of household heterogeneity. A main finding of their analysis is that education is an important determinant of differences in WTP for urban amenities among households. Table 6.1 gives the main results.

The first line of the table refers to a reference household's estimated WTP for a number of amenities. Accessibility to employment is measured as the shortest distance within which 100,000 FTE of employment can be found. The table shows that the reference household is willing to pay about €4,150 more for a standard house[6] if this distance is decreased by 1km. The reference household's WTP for proximity to a highway interchange and an intercity station is close to zero. The

Table 6.1 Average marginal WTP for location characteristics and deviations by household type, in 2009 euros

	Proximity to 100,000 FTE (km)	Proximity to highway interchange (km)	Proximity to intercity station (km)	Proximity to body of water (km)	Nature (percent)	Protected historical inner city (km²)	Ln(# of houses within region)
Marginal WTP of reference household (lower educated couple, one employed, no children, age 45–55)	4150	0	50	3300	350	3900	3150
Difference with reference household, other characteristics hold constant							
Single man	50	–150	250	700	0	0	1750
Single woman	250	50	250	450	0	100	3400
Youngest child <= 4	100	0	–100	–850	0	–250	–200
Youngest child 5–12	50	–50	0	–350	0	–450	–1000
Youngest child 13–24	–200	250	–50	300	0	–450	–950
Single, no employment	–200	–100	0	50	0	650	–1100
Couple, no employment	–250	50	100	850	0	–250	100

Couple, both employed	150	−150	0	500	0	−400	−250
Single, higher educated	500	450	200	400	50	550	2550
Couple, mixed education	250	50	150	200	50	400	850
Couple, higher educated	700	250	400	−250	50	850	3000
Age < 25	−450	350	0	800	50	600	2100
Age 25 − 35	−300	300	0	950	−50	150	1900
Age 35 − 45	−100	0	0	400	0	250	850
Age 55 − 65	−100	50	50	−150	−50	−300	−1000
Age >= 65	−250	−150	50	−650	0	−500	−1750

Source: Weijschede-Van der Straaten et al. (2015).

Note: Based on a weighted average price of a standard house of €208,700; WTP rounded to nearest €50.

reference household is willing to pay about €3,300 to reduce the distance to the nearest body of water (not including sea) by 1km, which implies that water is also considered an important amenity. This also applies to the amount of nature in the municipality, which increases the attractiveness of the municipality by about €350 per additional percentage point of nature. The penultimate column of Table 6.1 refers to the attractiveness of the city as a place to live. The area of the historic district is used as an indicator for this amenity. The Dutch Agency for Cultural heritage (RCE) has listed many of these districts for their outstanding value as cultural heritage and we have used the size of this listed area as our indicator for urban attractiveness. The reference household is willing to pay about €3,900 more for a standard house when it is located in a municipality that has an additional square kilometre of historic district. This number reflects not only the cultural heritage itself, but also the vivid city life that is usually associated with it, as visitors are attracted to these districts, which makes them also a preferred location for shops, restaurants, theatres and other urban amenities. The last column of the table gives the willingness to pay for municipalities with more owner-occupied houses, which is related to the higher number of individual house choices available in these regions, which increases the chance of a good match.

It should be noted that these results, as all other 'WTP' results reported in this chapter are based on the revealed preferences for owner-occupiers only. Rent control invalidates the revealed preference methodology for this segment of the housing market.

The table illustrates that cities are important not only because they provide access to dense labour markets, but also because city life is attractive in itself. Of course, this should not be interpreted as implying that cities can thrive without jobs; the point is, rather, that the inhabitants of cities are not only workers but also consumers and that they also take into account the consumption possibilities when choosing a residential location in the vicinity of their job.

The second part of Table 6.1 shows the deviations of the WTP of other types of households, relative to the reference household, when all other household characteristics remain constant. For example, the first line shows what happens to the WTP for each amenity when the household changes from being a lower-educated couple of age 45–55 without children (the reference household) to being a lower-educated single man of age 45–55 without children.

This part of Table 6.1 shows, for example, that couples in which both partners are employed have a higher WTP (+150) for proximity to employment than do couples in which one person is employed, which in turn have a higher (+250) WTP for proximity to employment than couples in which both partners are unemployed. Furthermore, young households and singles and couples with higher education, in particular, appreciate inner cities with a large amount of cultural heritage and the associated atmosphere. Households with children value these amenities less than do households without children. Note that 'power couples' still attach a higher value than the reference household to these urban location amenities even when they have children (since 850–450 > 0). This points to a potentially important aspect of location choice: it is not – perhaps we should say:

no longer – self-evident that the inner city is the wrong place to raise children. The times in which young households moved *en masse* to the suburbs may well belong to the past.[7]

3 Shops and cultural heritage

In the previous subsection we argued that our estimate of the WTP for historic urban districts should be interpreted as referring not only to cultural heritage per se, but also to the shops, restaurants, bars, theatres, music halls, etc. that are attracted to historic districts either because the ancient buildings provide an appropriate surrounding for the kind of services they offer or because large numbers of visitors are attracted to these areas (or both). In Van Loon, Van Duijn and Rouwendal (2014) we have focused on the relationship between historic districts and the number of shops. Table 6.2, which is taken from this paper, shows that there are more shops of all types in neighbourhoods that qualify as historic districts than in otherwise comparable neighbourhoods. The over-representation of antiques, art and culture is especially striking. The catering services include bars and restaurants. It is clear that theatres, music halls and museums are also over-represented in historic districts.

Note that the figures are adjusted for population size and population density. Thus the figures 'within and outside conservation areas' are comparable to each other. They are the average number of stores per neighbourhood. An average neighbourhood in this particular sample counts 2500 inhabitants and it has a population density of around 4000 inhabitants per square kilometre. We do not include neighbourhoods with a population below 100 and a population density

Table 6.2 Ratio of type of stores within and outside conservation areas for 2012

	Within conservation areas	Outside conservation areas	Ratio inside/ outside
Food stores	5.29	3.68	1.44
Fashion stores	9.19	2.63	3.50
Catering services	15.83	5.32	2.98
DIY	0.53	0.47	1.13
Antique and art stores	1.02	0.14	7.20
Sports and game stores	1.41	0.52	2.73
Flower and pet stores	1.18	1.03	1.15
Electronic stores	1.50	0.67	2.23
Furniture stores	2.67	1.35	1.98
Culture stores	2.16	0.54	4.00
Recreation facilities	0.94	0.54	1.75
Craft stores	5.99	3.03	1.97
Financial institutions	1.33	0.97	1.38
Private services stores	3.72	1.58	2.36
Vacant stores	4.80	2.18	2.20

Source: Van Loon, Van Duijn and Rouwendal (2014).

below 500. All this suggests that consumption patterns of urban citizens differ from those living elsewhere. The greater supply and variety of all kinds of services and commodities in urban areas has an impact on the way consumers spend their budget. Consumers who like the urban amenities are attracted to the city, but have to face the generally higher housing price prevailing there. See Rouwendal and Möhlmann (2015) for an analysis using consumer expenditure patterns.

4 Employment and amenities in the Copenhagen metropolitan area

A similar sorting model as discussed in subsection 1 above has been estimated for the Greater Copenhagen area (GCA).[8] The GCA is the political, administrative and educational centre of Denmark and accounts for more than 40 per cent of Denmark's GDP, one third of the Danish population, and 1 million jobs. Estimation is based on administrative register data for all Danish households with residence in the GCA for the year 2008, spread over 167 zones designed for the purpose of detailed traffic modelling. The study area is thus substantially smaller than that of the study discussed in subsection 3 above.

A 20 per cent sample of the population living in owner-occupied housing was used,[9] which gave us 41,099 observations. These consumers are distributed over 167 zones in which they can choose to live either in an apartment or other housing types (detached, terraced). In some zones we observe only other housing types (mainly on the outskirts of the study area) and in some zones only apartments (in the centre of the GCA), and the total choice set includes 302 elements.

We focus on 8 local amenities: (i) standardized house price, (ii) coastline (km), (iii) employment access, (iv) distance to the nearest motorway access (km), (v) distance to the nearest metro station (km), (vi) number of listed buildings per square kilometre, (vii) distance to the central business district, and (viii) proportion of higher-educated population. We include 10 socioeconomic variables: (i) age of the head of household, (ii) squared age of the head of household, (iii) a dummy indicating male head of household, (iv) three dummy variables indicating highest education obtained by the head of household, (v) a dummy indicating a single-person household, (vi) number of children in the household, (vii) household income, (viii) a dummy indicating that the head and his/her partner have the highest level of education (power couple).

In Table 6.3 we present the results of the second step of the estimation procedure. The first column shows the Ordinary Least Squares results, the second those of instrumental variables regression. The set of explanatory variables (location characteristics) differs somewhat from those used for the Netherlands, which is partly due to differences in available data. We used the number of conserved (protected, listed) buildings as an indicator of cultural heritage and (indirectly) also for other urban amenities like shops, restaurants, theatres, and the length of the coastline of a zone as an indicator for natural amenities.

We also included the proportion of higher-educated in the population as an indicator of an endogenous amenity. It is often argued in the literature that the attractiveness of living in a particular area is partly determined by the demographic composition of that neighbourhood. For instance, in sociology the phenomenon of *homophily*, that households prefer to interact with other households that are similar, is well known. In the urban economics literature the importance of this for location choice within the San Francisco Bay area was documented by Bayer *et al.* (2007). In this study we use a similar formulation.

As we noted earlier in this chapter, the demographic composition of location is as much the result of choice behaviour as it is one of its determinants. This means that we have to deal with the probable endogeneity of the proportion of higher-educated. For reasons that have also been detailed above, the price should also be treated as endogenous. Table 6.3 shows that dealing with endogeneity makes a huge difference for the estimation results.[10] We find a much larger (in absolute value) price coefficient and the coefficient for proportion of higher-educated becomes significant and also much larger once it is instrumented. This large value suggests that in the Copenhagen region the higher-educated tend to concentrate in particular areas. Maps show that this is indeed the case: the proportion of higher-educated is much larger in the north-eastern parts of the metropolitan region than elsewhere.

Table 6.3 Second-step estimation results: decomposition of the mean indirect utilities

	OLS	IV (2SLS)
Log (standardized house/apartment price)	−1.408***	−3.606***
	(0.552)	(0.577)
Coastline (km)	0.087**	0.115***
	(0.042)	(0.043)
Employment access	0.879***	0.840***
	(0.233)	(0.235)
Log distance to the nearest motorway intersection (km)	0.064	0.108
	(0.099)	(0.100)
Log distance to the nearest metro station (km)	0.113	0.111
	(0.116)	(0.117)
Number of conserved/protected buildings per sq.km	1.847***	1.852***
	(0.291)	(0.294)
Distance to central business district	0.019	0.015
	(0.021)	(0.021)
Share of higher educated	0.516	3.094***
	(0.887)	(0.919)
Dummy variable indicating non-apartment	1.896***	3.094***
	(0.326)	(0.339)
Constant	−1.879***	−1.195***
	(0.334)	(0.340)
R-squared	0.327	
No. of observations	302	302

Source: Mulalic and Rouwendal (2015).

Note: Standardized house/apartment price and share of higher educated are instrumented.

An important similarity between the results for the Netherlands discussed above and those for Copenhagen is the highly significant role of cultural heritage and the endogenous amenities associated with it. Although the size of listed historical districts may be a better indicator of this urban attractor than the number of monuments, the two are strongly correlated and we have also used the number of monuments per municipality as an alternative indicator in robustness analyses for the Netherlands. We always found strongly significant coefficients, as is the case for the Copenhagen metropolitan region.

5 Wages and job accessibility

The studies discussed above use job accessibility as an indicator of the quality of the local labour market. This is not necessarily the best indicator. Van Duijn and Rouwendal (2013) also use wage differentials between municipalities to deal with the attractiveness of the labour market in an alternative way. In their model they include many amenities (e.g. the area of historical inner cities, the area of nature, distance to the nearest intercity station) to make a clear distinction between employment and different types of amenities. The results of this residential sorting model show that wages and urban amenities are important determinants for the location choices of Dutch households. The results confirm households' high WTP for urban amenities and the presence of substantial heterogeneity of households. For instance, highly educated singles are willing to pay around 15 per cent more than the average household for living in a municipality where wages are 1 per cent higher.[11] In general, the higher-educated prefer to live in municipalities with higher relative wages, as compared to households with children and older households. Wages thus play a similar role to the job accessibility measures used in other studies. Wages also tend to be higher in places where job accessibility is good. In practice, the two local labour market indicators can therefore be taken as substitutes, although they clearly measure different aspects.[12]

6 Jobs and consumer amenities are complements

In the introduction to this chapter we briefly discussed the Roback (1982) model, which suggests that there is a trade-off between the wage, the housing price and urban amenities. Each of these variables has an impact on the utility of the consumer who is – according to standard economic theory – willing to accept (for instance) a lower wage if this is compensated by cheaper housing or better amenities.

An interesting related question is whether consumers are also willing to trade off job accessibility for urban amenities. Put differently, do consumers still attach a high value to cultural heritage and the related endogenous amenities if a city is located in an area with a lower density of jobs? The results discussed above for the Netherlands and Copenhagen are unable to provide a detailed answer because the models do not contain the interaction between job accessibility and cultural heritage. The question has therefore been investigated separately in an extension of Van Duijn and Rouwendal (2013), using job accessibility as an indicator for the local labour market. We introduced the interaction between the indicator for cultural heritage and the proxy for employment opportunities (the distance to the nearest 100,000 jobs) into the model as a new variable. Figure 6.1 shows the relationship between the average marginal WTP for an extra square kilometre of protected historic area and the distance to the nearest concentration of jobs. The graph shows that protected historic areas are especially valued in combination with good accessibility of jobs. The results thus show that investing in urban amenities is especially beneficial in areas where the labour market is dense. This can be interpreted as confirming the primacy of jobs in households' preferences. It also suggests that strategies to fight population decreases with better amenities are risky. Urban amenities are especially important in combination with and as a complement to a strong labour market.

7 Cultural heritage and social interactions

Earlier in this chapter the importance of the demographic composition of neighbourhoods was discussed and illustrated with estimation results for Copenhagen. In economics this phenomenon is often referred to as social interactions because the behaviour of some individuals influences that of others in their peer group directly, rather than only indirectly via the market mechanism and prices. In the

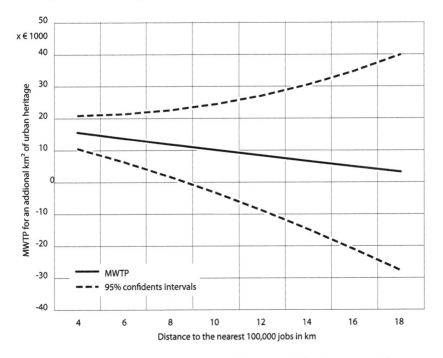

Figure 6.1 Interaction between marginal WTP for protected historic areas and distance to the nearest 100,000 jobs

case considered here the location choice of households is influenced by that of other households. Heterogeneity is essential for this phenomenon, since it is in particular the behaviour of one's peers or the members of one's reference group that matters.

The phenomenon has been investigated in some detail in Van Duijn and Rouwendal (2015), where the focus is on the impact of the proportion of higher-income households on the attractiveness of urban neighbourhoods. The study refers to the Amsterdam metropolitan area and uses administrative (register) data for all households in the year 2008. Household characteristics include(i) gross primary household income, (ii) household composition, (iii) socioeconomic category and (iv) age of the head of the household. In addition to the stand-ard exogenous neighbourhood characteristics (e.g. comparable house prices, employment, cultural amenities, transport facilities) we include the proportion of high-income households (those belonging to the highest quartile of the overall income distribution).

The results regarding the attractiveness of a historic inner city differ from those of the earlier studies, as we now have neighbourhoods (rather than the much larger municipalities) as our spatial units of analysis. Table 6.4 reports the marginal WTP for a limited number of local amenities. We find that historic inner cities are an important factor in the location decision of households in the Amsterdam area and that the willingness-to-pay figures of historic inner cities are reflected in the high house prices of the Amsterdam city centre. The average household pays around €40,000 more in terms of house prices for an extra square kilometre of historic city centre in the neighbourhood of residence. The higher the income of households, the more they are willing to pay to live in the historic city centre. Households that earn €10,000 more than the annual average are willing to pay

Table 6.4 Marginal WTP results from the SLS estimation

	(1) Mean		(2) Income (+10,000)		(3) Employed		(4) Retired	
Historic city centre (+km2)	40,274		2,175		1,300	(ns)	1,838	(ns)

Historic city centre
   in surrounding
   neighbourhoods (+km2)
	9,842		91		−84		−193	

High-income households (+%)	1,414		137		55		161	
Distance to nearest 100,000 jobs (-km)	644	(ns)	10	(ns)	−41		174	

Source: Van Duijn and Rouwendal (2015).

Notes: (ns) = not significant at the 5% level.
          Values in euros.
The significance levels of columns 2 to 4 are based on the first-step estimation procedure of the residential sorting model.

€2000 more for an additional square kilometre of historic city centre, as compared to the average household. We also find that social interactions are important. The average household prefers to live in a neighbourhood with a concentration of high-income households, and higher-income households prefer even more to live in such areas. According to our estimates, the average household is willing to pay almost €1500 for an additional percentage point of high-income households in the neighbourhood population. Households that earn €10,000 above the average are willing to pay another €137, i.e. almost 10 per cent more than the average household, for an additional percentage point of high-income households.

An interesting implication of these findings is that they suggest that urban amenities – indicated by cultural heritage – may have cumulative effects on household location. We discussed earlier that the WTP for cultural heritage and associated other urban amenities is higher among the higher-educated workers, who often have a relatively high income. This group therefore tends to become over-represented in areas that are relatively rich in cultural heritage, like the Amsterdam canal zone. The large proportion of high-income households contributes further to the attractiveness of the neighbourhood, especially for higher-income households. The social interaction effects thus tend to stimulate segregation between income groups in the metropolitan area. Interestingly, we see that the rich are over-represented in the ancient city centre – as in Paris – as well as in the suburbs close to the open space of the polders – which is similar to Detroit. A typical Dutch aspect is that this location pattern is especially present in the owner-occupied sector, as almost all rental housing is rent controlled[13] and accessible only to low-income households – although waiting lists for social rented housing in the Amsterdam city centre are extremely long.

8 Costs of residential mobility

One of the assumptions of the sorting model is perfect mobility of agents. Mobility costs do not play a role in the model and earlier location choices thus have no impact on current choices. Since mobility costs are in fact substantial it is important to investigate the possible bias introduced by this assumption. Households might be restrained from choosing their optimal location, due to mobility costs. Neglecting these costs may therefore lead to biased inferences about their location preferences.

We investigated this issue by analysing households' residential sorting behaviour within the local housing/labour market of Southeast North-Brabant (SNB), the region surrounding Eindhoven.[14] The SNB economy is highly specialized in knowledge-intensive production, such as high-tech manufacturing, making future regional growth heavily dependent on the ability of the region to retain and attract human capital-intensive firms and the associated skilled labour.

The locational characteristics considered are housing prices, natural amenities (natural and water coverage), urban amenities (the number of catering services) and various measures of accessibility. Household characteristics are highly educated households, marital status, presence of children and age of the head of the household. We capture the impact of mobility costs by introducing dummy variables in the utility functions of all residential locations except the one in which the household was living five years ago. If mobility costs are important, we expect a significant negative coefficient for this dummy, implying a reluctance of households to move. The cost of mobility is treated as a neighbourhood characteristic – albeit one that differs over households – and its coefficient is allowed to differ with household characteristics.

In Table 6.5 we report some descriptive statistics on movers. Slightly more than a quarter of the households observed in SNB in 2012 had moved between 2007 and 2012, implying that almost 75 per cent had stayed. The 10 per cent that moved within the boundaries of their original municipality are treated by us as non-movers, since our model does not distinguish between locations within a given municipality.

Table 6.6 reports the two sets of results of the first-step estimation of the sorting model (Gatto, 2013). The columns labelled (1) are the estimation results obtained when moving costs are not included in the estimation, and the columns labelled (2) are the estimation results obtained when moving costs are included. Since moving costs are individual-specific, they are included only in the first-step estimation of the sorting model. The impact of moving on utility is negative (as expected) and significantly different from zero. The loss in utility associated with moving is estimated to be higher for home-owners than for renters, which is plausible. Table 6.6 also shows that higher-educated, younger households and couples have lower utility losses when they move than does the average household. In contrast, older households and households with children under 18 have significantly higher mobility costs.

Comparison of the columns (1) and (2) suggests that moving costs is an important variable when we consider household location choice and that their incorporation can have a substantial impact on the coefficients estimated for other location characteristics, confirming our conjecture that willingness-to-pay estimates may be sensitive to the inclusion of this variable.

Moving costs are also included in an application of the sorting model by Möhlmann *et al.* (2015a). Their sorting model is also based on the Netherlands housing research survey (WoON 2012), but applied to 118 regions within the Netherlands. In the survey, households indicated whether they had moved within

Table 6.5 Descriptive statistics on movers (2007– 12) and sub-categories of movers

	Mean	Std. Dev.	Min.	Max.
Move within SNB to a different municipality	0.031	0.173	0	1
Move within original municipality	0.093	0.290	0	1
Move from outside SNB	0.028	0.164	0	1
Move but previous location unknown	0.114	0.318	0	1
Mover (total)	0.265	0.442	0	1

Source: Gatto (2013), based on WoON (2012).

Note: No. of observations = 1732.

the last two years. About 11 per cent of the relevant households indicated that they had moved at least once in that period. These households also indicated the municipality of their previous home. Based on this information, Möhlmann *et al.* (2015a) included a binary variable for moving as well as a distance variable in the logit specification. This allows the estimation of the fixed moving costs as well as the additional moving costs that households experience for moving over larger distances. The distances are calculated as Euclidean distances between the centres of the regions.

Preliminary results indicate that the fixed costs of moving to another region are about €57,000 for an average home-owner. Note that this is measured as a WTP for staying in the current region rather than moving to another region. This includes not only the monetary costs of moving (which are probably much lower) but also all other costs that people experience from changing their region. Also note that this is based only on moving to another one of the 118 regions in the model. Households that moved within the same region are not modelled as movers. The additional costs of moving to regions that are further away are preliminary estimated as about €500 per kilometre for home-owners.

The estimated moving costs are heterogeneous across different types of households. Couples, households with children and higher-educated households all experience higher fixed moving costs. The difference is about 6 per cent for couples versus singles, 10 per cent for households with children versus households without children and 7 per cent for higher- versus lower-educated households. Additionally, older households experience higher fixed costs of moving of about 1.3 per cent per year of age. The costs of moving over larger distances are higher for households with children (+29 per cent) and lower for couples (–33 per cent), higher-educated households (–39 per cent) and older households (–0.4 per cent per year). This implies that the last three groups are less inclined to move, but if they do move they tend to move over the largest distances. Households with children move less, and also over smaller distances.

9 Technical and creative higher-educated workers

A key feature of the sorting model is that it allows for heterogeneous preferences of households. The sorting models discussed so far have distinguished households based on household composition (couples versus singles and households with or without children), age and education level. The stated preferences research suggests that location preferences differ strongly between creative- and technical-orientated households (see Chapters 5 and 9). This can also be tested with a sorting model, provided that we have data on the educational orientation of workers. The previously discussed sorting models for the Netherlands are based on data from the housing surveys WoON 2009 and WoON 2012, which do not include data on the type of education. An alternative data source that does include these data is the labour survey (*Enquête Beroepsbevolking*) from Statistics Netherlands.

In Möhlmann *et al.* (2015b) the labour survey is used to estimate a sorting model which includes a measure for creativity of households relative to technical

Table 6.6 First stage results for homeowners: estimated parameters for interaction terms and moving costs

Municipality characteristics	Mean	Household characteristics			
		Highly educated households (1)	Age (+10 years)	Households with children (−18)	Couples
Standardized house price (€)		5.67419 *** (0.2581)	0.12215 *** (0.00749)	4.71692 *** (0.22943)	1.12390 *** (0.25863)
No. of shops		−0.00221 *** (0.00007)	−0.00006 *** (0.000002)	−0.00095 *** (0.00006)	−0.00083 *** (0.00007)
Nature (km2)		0.00150 (0.00095)	−0.00001 (0.00003)	−0.00136 (0.00094)	−0.03230 *** (0.00098)
Water (km2)		−0.23157 *** (0.01262)	−0.00625 *** (0.00038)	−0.01054 (0.01153)	0.01036 (0.01291)
Distance to 100,000 jobs (km)		0.06046 *** (0.00615)	0.00065 *** (0.00018)	0.03751 *** (0.00536)	0.05015 *** (0.00614)
Distance to intercity station (km)		−0.14177 *** (0.00602)	−0.00164 *** (0.00015)	−0.04968 *** (0.00469)	−0.02767 *** (0.00545)
Distance to motorway intersection (km)		−0.12346 *** (0.00386)	−0.00216 *** (0.0001)	0.01156 *** (0.00307)	−0.02543 *** (0.00359)

(2)

Standardized house price (€)		8.630421 *** (0.57764)	0.047589 *** (0.01801)	5.570084 *** (0.55125)	-5.727235 *** (0.63647)
No. of shops		-0.006405 *** (0.00017)	-0.000245 *** (0.000005)	0.000956 *** (0.00017)	-0.01291 *** (0.00226)
Nature (km2)		-0.04449 *** (0.00214)	-0.00096 *** (0.00006)	-0.005801 *** (0.00201)	-0.0051 *** (0.00019)
Water (km2)		-0.523477 *** (0.02836)	-0.027771 *** (0.00095)	0.302447 *** (0.02689)	-0.138238 *** (0.03265)
Distance to 100,000 jobs (km)		0.021503 (0.0134)	0.001874 *** (0.00043)	0.122163 *** (0.01299)	-0.310019 *** (0.01519)
Distance to intercity station (km)		-0.079744 *** (0.01192)	-0.002326 *** (0.00037)	-0.069554 *** (0.01095)	0.214774 *** (0.01301)
Distance to motorway intersection (km)		-0.059294 *** (0.00759)	-0.008194 *** (0.00025)	0.058145 *** (0.0072)	0.062597 *** (0.00841)
Moving costs homeowner	-8.355453 *** (0.02466)	0.616249 *** (0.04016)	-0.092124 *** (0.0014)	-1.543007 *** (0.04191)	0.248126 *** (0.04173)
Moving costs renter	-7.124961 *** (0.02979)				

Source: Gatto (2013).

houscholds. This measure is based on the field of education of the households. Each field of education was ranked from very creative (index 0) to very technical (index 1). They used the ranking of the field of education rather than the ranking of the occupation, since the former is believed to be a better indication for the intrinsic orientation of the worker, while occupations also depend on labour market conditions. Since regions can have different compositions of job types, the occupation is endogenous to the residential region. This problem is less severe for the field of education, since the field of education usually stays the same once a person has graduated, while the occupation may change several times. The ranking of the fields of education was determined by combining data on the field of education and the occupation of workers from the labour survey with creative and technical skill requirements per occupation.

The results of the sorting model estimated by Möhlmann *et al.* (2015b) show that location preferences are different between households with a technical or a creative field of education. Table 6.7 shows the WTP for several regional characteristics of the most creative and the most technical households, while keeping all other household characteristics equal to the reference household. For proximity to jobs (−12 per cent), proximity to an intercity train station (−36 per cent), the proportion of nature (−2 per cent) and the size of a protected historic city centre (−16 per cent), technical households have a lower estimated WTP than do creative households. For proximity to a highway interchange technical households are willing to pay more (+4 per cent). Since proximity to jobs and the size of a historic

Table 6.7 WTP of creative and technical households (in 2010 euros)

	Most creative field of occupation (given other household characteristics are equal to the reference household)	Most technical field of occupation (given other household characteristics are equal to the reference household)	Difference technical relative to creative
Proximity 100,000 jobs (km)	3250	2850	−12%
Proximity to intercity station (km)	650	400	−36%
Proximity to highway intersection (km)	950	1000	+4%
Nature (per cent)	850	800	−2%
Protected historic inner city (km²)	5750	4800	−16%

Source: Möhlmann et al. (2015b).

Note: Based on a weighted average price of a standard house of €211,000; willingness to pay rounded to nearest €50, percentage difference rounded to nearest percentage point.

city centre are strongly related to cities, the interpretation of these results can be that creative households have stronger preferences for living in urban environments than do technical households, which supports what was also found in the stated preferences research.

Conclusion

This chapter has summarized the results of several sorting models, as well as some additional research that has been carried out in the HELP project. The investigations have further established the usefulness of the logit-based sorting model for empirical research, and the connection with hedonic pricing analysis has been clarified. The estimated models have clarified our understanding of the role of urban amenities for the attractiveness of residential locations. Cities are important not only for work but also for consumption and our research has resulted in estimates of the WTP for these consumption amenities. The values reached for these figures depend on the geographical scale and the specification of the model. For instance, the implied WTP for an additional square kilometre of conservation area is lower if the model refers to municipalities than if it is estimated on neighbourhoods within the Amsterdam metropolitan area. We have shown that consumption amenities are not a substitute for an attractive labour market, but that the two variables must be seen as complements. Another important observation is that the attractiveness of neighbourhoods is not only a determinant of choice behaviour, but (at least partly) also a consequence of this behaviour. This underscores the importance of policies referring to, for instance, the construction of new housing. The research has also identified some loose ends. A potentially important one is the incorporation of moving costs, which calls for a generalization of the model to a dynamic setting. A second interesting issue that should be further investigated is the importance of heterogeneity within the group of highly skilled workers, notably the distinction between technical, creative and other high-skilled workers.

Appendix: The logit-based sorting model

This appendix provides a technical description of the logit-based sorting model.

1 The logit model with homogeneous consumers

Let $n = 1 \ldots N$ denote the choice alternatives. They are distinguished by characteristics X_n. The utility u_n attached by a consumer to each alternative is the sum of a deterministic part v_n and a random part ε_n:

$$u_n = v(X_n) + \varepsilon_n, n = 1 \ldots N. \tag{1}$$

The deterministic parts are identical for all consumers, but the random parts differ. They are regarded as random draws from a given probability distribution. Each consumer knows the draws that are relevant for him or her, but for the researcher these random draws are unobserved. The logit model thus takes into account that the researcher has imperfect knowledge of the consumer's preferences.

Although the researcher does not observe the outcomes of the draws for individual consumers, the distribution from which they are drawn is assumed to be known. If all the ε_n's are independent draws from the extreme value type I distribution,[15] the choice probabilities can be derived as:

$$\pi_n = \frac{e^{v_n}}{\sum_m e^{v_m}}, n = 1 \ldots N, \tag{2}$$

where π_n is the probability the consumer chooses and alternative n and v_n is used as shorthand notation for $v(X_n)$. This is the logit model.

It is conventional[16] to specify the deterministic part of the utility function as a linear function of the characteristics of the choice alternative:

$$v(X_n) = \sum_{k=1}^{K} \beta_k X_{nk} \tag{3}$$

In this equation the index k refers to individual characteristics of the choice alternatives and K is the total number of characteristics. The characteristics may simply be included as such, but transformations, e.g. the logarithm of the housing price, or interactions, can also be used.

Estimation of the model results in values for the coefficients β_k that reflect the importance the consumers attach to the various characteristics of the choice alternatives. The housing price is of course a relevant characteristic of each choice alternative and this provides the possibility of translating the intensities of preference into WTP. In the simple case in which the characteristics are included only untransformed and without interactions, this WTP is simply the ratio of the coefficient for that characteristic and the coefficient of the price. Estimating the

WTP for urban amenities is one of the main goals of the analyses reviewed in this chapter.

2 The logit model with heterogeneous consumers

An important property of the logit model is the independence of irrelevant alternatives. It says that the ratio of the choice probabilities of two alternatives depends only on the deterministic utilities of these two alternatives.[17] This property of the model has implications for the way the consumer is willing to substitute one choice alternative for another that are generally regarded as unrealistic. Researchers have therefore tried to find more flexible models that relax this property. An important development in this respect was the generalization of the logit model to situations in which the parameters β_k are random variables. This so-called mixed logit model can be interpreted as referring to a population of consumers that are heterogeneous not only with respect to the relevant values of the ε_n's, but also with respect to those of the β_k's. In a mixed logit model the latter are also regarded as draws from a distribution function. Although in a mixed logit model the independence of irrelevant alternatives is still present at the level of the individual consumer, it no longer holds for the population. Indeed, McFadden and Train (2000) show that under mild conditions *any* random utility maximization model can be approximated arbitrarily close by a mixed logit model, which suggests that the logit model is completely general if only one is allowing enough flexibility in the functions $v(X_n)$.

McFadden and Train's (2000) result suggests that the key to relaxing the restrictiveness of the multinomial logit model is to allow for heterogeneity among the actors. Even if one does not specify a completely flexible mixed logit model, taking into account that actors differ in preferences when estimating the model makes it more flexible and realistic. One obvious possibility, that will be used here, is to allow the coefficients of the utility function to differ with household characteristics. Taking specification (3) of the deterministic part of the utility function as our starting point, this generalization allows for consumer-specific values of the coefficients. That is, instead of β_k we should now use β_k^i, which is the realization of the coefficient for the k-th characteristic of the choice alternative for consumer i. It seems natural to allow for the possibility that these coefficients are related to consumer characteristics Z_i. Assuming linearity, we specify:

$$\beta_k^i = \alpha_k^0 + \sum_{l=1}^{L} \alpha_k^l \left(Z_{li} - \bar{Z}_l \right), \tag{4}$$

where Z_{li} denotes that the value of characteristic l for consumer i and $\bar{Z}_l$ is the average of Z_{li} in the population.[18] The formulation just discussed can be related to a mixed logit model in which the distribution of the parameter β_k^i in the population is determined by the distribution of the consumer characteristics. Randomly drawing a consumer from the population results in a realization of β_k^i.

The coefficient α_k^0 gives the value attached to characteristic k by the average consumer in the population, while the deviations from this average are determined by the coefficients α_k^l. When the latter coefficients are all equal to zero, we return to the logit model with homogeneous consumers that was discussed in subsection 1 above. A notable consequence of the generalization of that model implied by (4) is that the WTP for characteristics of choice alternatives becomes also dependent on household characteristics. For instance, if education is included as a relevant consumer characteristic, the estimated parameters reveal its impact on the WTP for location characteristics.

3 Estimating the model

Logit models can be estimated on individual data with the maximum likelihood method. McFadden (1973) showed that the likelihood function is globally concave. In practice the logit model is the only discrete choice model that can be conveniently used when the number of alternatives is large (hundreds or even thousands).

An important issue in estimating logit models that was brought to the fore by Berry *et al.* (1995) is that, in practice, researchers have incomplete information about the choice alternatives. They proposed to take this into account by adding an unknown alternative-specific variable ξ_n to the utility function. With this additional variable and allowing for individual-specific coefficients, the utility attributed to alternative n becomes:

$$v(X_n) = \sum_{k=1}^{K} \beta_k^i X_{nk} + \xi_n \tag{5}$$

Since the impact of unobserved characteristics of alternatives in (5) is not actor-specific, this formulation may still be regarded as restrictive. Nevertheless, its introduction was a major step forward in the application of logit models. The problem for estimation posed by (5) is that the new term ξ_n cannot be observed. To solve it, Berry *et al.* (1995) propose to rewrite (5), using (4), as the sum of an alternative-specific constant and a number of cross-terms:

$$v(X_n) = \delta_n + \sum_{k=1}^{K} \sum_{l=1}^{L} \alpha_k^l \left(Z_{li} - \bar{Z}_l \right) X_{nk} \tag{6}$$

with

$$\delta_n = \sum_{k=1}^{K} \alpha_k^0 X_{nk} + \xi_n. \tag{7}$$

Estimation then proceeds in two steps: first a logit model is estimated with the utility function specified as in (6) and then the estimated alternative-specific constants are analysed further by linear equation methods using (7). The unobserved heterogeneity terms ξ_n are the residuals of the estimating equation.

In the second step endogeneity concerns can also be addressed. An important one is that the housing price in a neighbourhood is likely to be correlated with its unobserved characteristics. Ignoring this problem implies the risk of underestimating the consumer's price sensitivity and it is indeed generally found that instrumenting prices results in substantially larger price coefficients. Other endogeneity issues arise when the demographic composition of a neighbourhood has an impact on its attractiveness.

Finding instruments for the endogenous variables is not an easy task. Berry *et al.* (1995) suggested the use of characteristics of competing alternatives as an instrument for the price in their model of the automobile market, but, in the context of neighbourhood location choice, the appeal of this argument is not so strong. Bayer and Timmins (2007) suggest computing an instrument using the logic of the model. The idea, for the case of prices, is to use the equilibrium prices that are predicted by the model in the counterfactual case in which the unobserved heterogeneity terms are all equal to zero. This procedure is used in the studies reviewed here for the housing price as well as for population proportions when they enter the utility function.

4 Relation with hedonic analysis

To discuss the relationship between sorting and hedonic price models, we assume that the price is the first location characteristic and write: $P_n = X_{1n}$. We can now invert the utility function (5) into something that looks like a hedonic price equation, apart from the fact that utility is one of the variables on the right-hand side. If individuals with the same characteristics would all reach the same utility level, no matter which location they chose, we could consider this as a 'fixed effect'. The logit model does not have this property, but there is a closely related property which guarantees that the distribution of the expected maximum utility of actors with a given set of characteristics is independent of the alternative that has been chosen.

Weijschede-van der Straaten *et al.* (2014) show that this property implies that we derive the following equation for the housing price at location n:

$$P_n = \sum_{k=2}^{K} \frac{\bar{\beta}_k}{-\bar{\beta}_1} X_{nk} + \frac{1}{-\bar{\beta}_1} \xi_n + C_n \tag{8}$$

where $\bar{\beta}_k$ is the average value of coefficient β_k^i, $k = 1 \ldots K$ in the population[19] and C_n is a term that reflects the heterogeneity of the actors and the supply of housing at n. The ratios $\frac{\bar{\beta}_k}{-\bar{\beta}_1}$ give the average WTP for characteristic k in the population, expressed in terms of the housing price. That is, they indicate how much the average actor is willing to pay for one unit of characteristic n. This agrees with the conventional interpretation of the coefficients in a hedonic price equation. Equation (8) thus establishes a link between sorting models and conventional hedonic price equations. Nevertheless, the two are not completely equivalent because the term C_n differs over the locations and may be correlated with the X_{nk} s, which suggests that hedonic analysis may lead to biased results. On the other hand, it should be observed that the problems with endogeneity of the housing price that are present in the logit model do not occur in the hedonic price equation.

Notes

1 See Moretti (2004) for a survey of the related literature.
2 The external effects generated by the interaction of highly educated workers may mitigate this effect, but should not be expected to provide full compensation.
3 See Bayer *et al.* (2007).
4 This ignores the costs associated with changing the quality of housing (Epple and Platt, 1998; Epple and Sieg, 1999).
5 See Chapters 5 and 9.
6 In our models we use the price of a standard house with a specific set of characteristics as an indicator of the housing price. The choice of the bundle of characteristics is arbitrary, but it guarantees that differences in the prices that we use do not reflect differences in quality.
7 See Boterman and Karsten (2014).
8 For details see Mulalic and Rouwendal (2015).
9 We ignore renters. This can be motivated by a nested logit approach in which the housing tenure choice is on the top of the utility tree and the choice of the combination of housing type (apartment or other) and the geographical area refers to the lower level.
10 An important message of this result is that the neglect of endogeneity issues may result in misleading conclusions. For instance, the smaller (in absolute value) size of the price coefficient tends to lead to *larger* estimates of the WTP for all amenities.
11 The average household is defined as a household where all characteristics are equal to the average values.
12 Further investigation of their relationship requires the development of a spatial labour market model with search. That is, a model in which the labour market does not clear and job seekers have limited information about vacancies, so that matching takes time.
13 This includes a large part of the stock of private rental housing.
14 This application is based on a masters thesis, "Locational Choice and Preferences with Costly Relocation", by M. Gatto, supervised by J. Rouwendal and M. Van Duijn in 2013.
15 This distribution, $F(\varepsilon_n) = \exp(-\exp(-\varepsilon_n))$, is sometimes also referred to as the Weibull- or Gnedenko-distribution.
16 Functions that are linear in the parameters are relatively easy to estimate and, if we allow for cross-products and powers of the characteristics, they can approximate any function arbitrarily closely.
17 It is easy to verify that $\pi_n / \pi_{n'} = e^{v_n} / e^{v_{n'}}$.
18 Note that the consumer characteristics Z_{li} may be transformations or cross-products of elementary consumers characteristics.
19 That is, $\bar{\beta}_k = \sum_i \beta_k^i / N$ where N denotes population size.

References

Bayer, P and Timmins, C 2007, Estimating Equilibrium Models of Sorting across Locations. *Economic Journal* 117, 353–374.

Bayer, P, Ferreira, F and McMillan, R 2007, A Unified Framework for Measuring Preferences for Schools and Neighbourhoods. *Journal of Political Economy* 115, 588–638.

Berry, S, Levinsohn, JA and Pakes, J 1995, Automobile Prices in Market Equilibrium. *Econometrica* 63, 841–890.

Boterman, W and Karsten, L 2014, On the Spatial Dimension of the Gender Division of Paid Work in Two-Parent Families: The Case of Amsterdam, the Netherlands. *Tijdschrift voor Economische en Sociale Geografie* 105 (1), 107–116.

Brueckner, J, Thisse, JJ and Zenou, Y 1999, Why is Central Paris Rich and Downtown Detroit Poor? An Amenity-based Theory. *European Economic Review* 43, 91–107.

Costa, DE and Kahn, ME 2002, Power Couples: Changes in the Location Choice of College Educated, 1940–1990. *Quarterly Journal of Economics* 115, 1287–1315.

Epple, D and Platt, GJ 1998, Equilibrium and Local Redistribution in an Urban Economy when Households Differ in Both Preferences and Income. *Journal of Urban Economics* 43, 23–51.

Epple, D and Sieg, H 1999, Estimating Equilibrium Models of Local Jurisdictions. *Journal of Political Economy* 107, 645–681.

Gatto, M 2013, Location Choice and Preferences with Costly Relocation: A Study on Household Residential Sorting for the Eindhoven Region. Master's thesis, VU University.

Glaeser, EL and Maré, DC 2001, Cities and Skills. *Journal of Labour Economics* 19, 316–342.

Glaeser, EL, Kolko, J and Saiz, A 2001, Consumer City. *Journal of Economic Geography* 1, 27–50.

Groot, S, de Groot, HLF and Smit, M 2011, Wage Differences in the Netherlands: Micro-Evidence on Agglometion Externalities, CPB Discussion paper 184.

Jacobs, J 1970 *The Economy of Cities*. New York: Random House.

Kuminoff, N, Smith VK and Timmins, C 2013, The New Economics of Equilibrium Sorting and Policy Evaluation Using Housing Markets. *Journal of Economic Literature* 51, 1007–1062.

Lucas, RE 1988, On the Mechanics of Economic Development. *Journal of Monetary Economics* 22, 3–42.

McFadden, D 1973, Conditional Logit Analysis of Qualitative Choice Behaviour. In: P. Zarembka (ed.) *Frontiers in Econometrics*, Academic Press, chapter 4, 105–142.

McFadden, D and Train, K 2000, Mixed MNL Models for Discrete Response. *Journal of Applied Econometrics* 15, 447–470.

Möhlmann, JL, Groot SPT and Rouwendal, J 2015b, Household Location Preferences and Field of Education. Working Paper in progress.

Möhlmann, J, Van Duijn, M and Rouwendal, J 2015a, Restricted Housing Supply, House Prices and Welfare: Evidence from the Netherlands. Working Paper in progress.

Moretti, E 2004 Human Capital Externalities in Cities. In: J. Vernon Henderson and Jacques-François Thisse (eds) *Handbook of Regional and Urban Economics* 4, 2243–2291, North-Holland: Elsevier.

Mulalic, I and Rouwendal, J (2015) Household's Location Choice and Transport Accessibility: Evidence from the Copenhagen Metropolitan Area. Working Paper in progress.

Rauch, JE 1993, Productivity Gains from the Concentration of Human Capital: Evidence from the Cities. *Journal of Urban Economics* 34, 380–400.

Roback, J 1982, Wages, Rents and the Quality of Life. *Journal of Political Economy* 90, 1257–1278.

Rouwendal, J and Möhlmann, J 2015, How Important Is Consumer City? A Comparison of Expenditure Patterns of Urban and Rural Consumers. Working paper in progress.

Van Loon, R, Van Duijn, M and Rouwendal, J 2014, Urban Resilience: Cultural Heritage and Store Dynamics. Working paper.

Van Duijn, M and Rouwendal, J 2013, Cultural Heritage and the Location Choice of Dutch Households in a Residential Sorting Model. *Journal of Economic Geography* 13, 473–500.

Van Duijn, M and Rouwendal, J 2015, Sorting Based on Urban Heritage and Income; Evidence from the Amsterdam Metropolitan Area. Tinbergen Institute discussion paper 15-030/VIII

Weijschede-van der Straaten, W, Rouwendal, J and Möhlmann, J 2014, The Impact of Education and Household Composition on Location Choice. Working Paper in progress

7 Integration and policy simulations

Jasper Dekkers, Jan Möhlmann
and Jan Rouwendal

Introduction

The main purpose of the sorting models that have been discussed in the previous chapter is to estimate the revealed preferences of households with respect to urban amenities.[1] These preferences reveal the value households attach to urban amenities and can be conveniently expressed in terms of their marginal willingness to pay (WTP) for them. Local governments that want to make their city more attractive to households should spend their limited budgets efficiently and therefore should concentrate on amenities that are appreciated. Since these amenities are usually not provided by the market, our estimations are useful for policy evaluation purposes. Preferences are generally regarded as a stable characteristic of households. It is therefore reasonable to expect that the measured preferences will also drive the allocation of households over residential choice alternatives in circumstances that differ from those under which the model has been estimated. This suggests that we can use the model to investigate the choices that will be made under such alternative, counterfactual conditions. The model can thus be used to simulate such allocations as well as the corresponding house prices, and inform policy makers about the consequences of possible changes in the provision of amenities.

Various aspects of such uses of the sorting model will be discussed in this chapter. In the next section we explain how to use the sorting model for counterfactual simulations. Since the changes involved in such exercises are, in general, not marginal, welfare analysis requires the use of compensating variations, and this topic is also discussed. The third section describes the model we use for these simulations and the required data inputs. The fourth section describes the results of the scenario simulations. In each scenario we change one of the inputs, like the composition of households, regional amenities, regional housing supply or household preferences, while holding the others constant. We present the differences from the resulting alternative equilibrium and the reference equilibrium, which is the given situation in 2012. The final section presents our conclusions.

Computing and evaluating counterfactuals with sorting models

Counterfactuals

In this section we discuss the computation of counterfactual allocation of house-holds over location choice alternatives with sorting models. A main characteristic of the sorting model is that it is a structural model. That is, the parameters that are estimated are thought of as stable determinants of choice behaviour. More specifically, when the environment changes – for instance, because of a policy change – these parameters do not change. It is this characteristic that makes sort-ing models useful for policy analysis.[2]

The sorting model is also an equilibrium model: at each location the supply of dwellings equals expected demand.[3] The multinomial logit model that has been discussed in the previous chapter has the attractive property that expected demand is equal to supply. This implies that the estimated model will 'automatically' rep-licate the situation for which it has been estimated, which in many cases provides a convenient reference for simulation exercises.

The equilibrium is achieved through the price mechanism. The house prices at the various locations adjust in such a way that expected demand remains equal to supply after one or more variables change in the model. This change may, for instance, be due to a policy intervention that attempts to make a particular loca-tion more attractive. The change in demand that results from this policy thus gives rise to changes in house prices. Although the two changes compensate each other in the sense that a new equilibrium is reached after the original disturbance, the choice probabilities of individuals may change. Heterogeneous households react in different ways to the policy change – some may be more attracted to the loca-tion whose properties have been changed than others – and their sensitivity to price changes will also differ.

For instance, Van Duijn and Rouwendal (2013) consider the impact of cul-tural heritage on the attractiveness of cities. After they have estimated a model of the type discussed in Chapter 6, taking the Dutch municipalities as the choice alternatives, they ask the question of what impact cultural heritage has on urban house prices in the Netherlands. To find the answer they change the value of their indicator for cultural heritage – the size of protected historic districts – so that it has the same value for all municipalities, thereby eliminating the impact of this amenity on choice behaviour. The result is that demand does not equal supply any more. Unsurprisingly, demand drops in municipalities that have a lot of cultural heritage – like Amsterdam – and it switches to locations that are attractive in other respects. Prices are then adjusted until a new equilibrium is reached. In this counterfactual equilibrium relative house prices in municipalities that have a lot of cultural heritage drop substantially, whereas they increase in others.

Computation of a counterfactual equilibrium is relatively easy when the price is the only location characteristic that is determined endogenously. Since choice probabilities in the logit model are always decreasing in the price of the alterna-tive to which they refer and increasing in the price of all other alternatives, there is only one price equilibrium.[4] If there is more than one endogenous variable – for instance the proportion of high-income households in a location may be a determinant of its attractiveness – the computation is somewhat more involved and there may be multiple equilibria.[5]

In order to use a sorting model to compute a counterfactual scenario, four main types of input are required: (i) household preferences, (ii) household characteristics, (iii) characteristics of the alternatives, and (iv) the number of dwellings available in each alternative. The next section will describe the data for each of these four types of input. Inputs (ii)–(iv) are needed to estimate the model, and estimation then results in input (i). If nothing is changed, the house prices predicted by the model will be equal to the original equilibrium prices. For the alternative situation this is not the case. In the alternative situation one or more of the inputs change. In policy simulations preferences are usually kept constant. This allows for the model to be used to see how house prices and the allocation of households over the housing stock change after the demographic composition of households changes (e.g. as a consequence of ageing), or after the characteristics of the choice alternatives change (e.g. because of a different geographical distribution of employment). Since the sorting model, in the way we use it here, is a distribution model, the total number of households must be equal to the total number of dwellings.[6] Information about the values of the inputs (ii)–(iv) in the alternative situations is often available from forecasts about demographic and economic development and the design of the policy to be evaluated.

It is also possible to simulate the consequences of a change in preferences, and this is indeed what we do in one of the examples discussed later in this chapter. Information about the new preferences can be derived from various sources. For instance, a stated preference analysis[7] focusing on a particular group of households may indicate that they differ in some respects from other people although this did not show up in the model's estimates. It may be useful then to consider what would happen if such preferences would be common in the population because the particular group can be regarded as forerunners, for instance because they are young.

Welfare analysis

The purpose of policy measures is often to improve the well-being of households. This means that it is important to assess the welfare impact of these measures for the population as a whole as well as for subgroups. To do so, the information about the marginal WTP that can be easily computed on the basis of the estimated coefficients is not sufficient. The reason is that the changes resulting from a policy measure are often not marginal. Some households will change location and the changes in prices and neighbourhood characteristics can also be substantial, as is illustrated by the simulation in Van Duijn and Rouwendal (2013) discussed above.

The conventional welfare measure for non-marginal changes is the compensating variation, which gives the amount of money (income) that can be taken from the consumer after the policy has been implemented so as to make his utility exactly equal to what it was before.[8] The compensating variation thus summarizes the impact of the policy on the well-being of a consumer in terms of a single number that can be interpreted as the value the consumer attaches to this policy.

In the sorting models that are discussed in this volume, income is not always included explicitly. However, the house price is always included and we can express the impact of a policy on welfare as a compensating variation expressed in this price. That is, we compute the change in the house price that would have the same impact on consumer welfare as the policy that we want to evaluate.

The welfare economics of discrete choice models have been investigated at an early stage by McFadden (1981), who also reviews the pioneering work by Small and Rosen (1981). A particularly useful result is that the change in the so-called logsum – the natural logarithm of the denominator of the expression for the logit choice probabilities – can, under certain conditions, be interpreted as the change in consumer surplus. However, one condition is that the utility function is linear in income,[9] while we would like to express the welfare measure into a change in the house price or its logarithm. If utility is nonlinear in the variable in which the compensating variation is expressed, this welfare measure cannot be determined as easily as was pointed out by McFadden (1999). The problem was investigated in detail by Dagsvik and Karlström (2005) and De Palma and Kilani (2003). They show that in general there does not exist a closed form expression for the compensating variation.[10]

In this chapter we use a somewhat different welfare economic concept: the relative change in all house prices that compensates for the change in the expected maximum utility of a group of households. This measure can be computed on the basis of the logsum. For instance, if the expected maximum utility of a group of consumers increases due to the implementation of a particular policy or a change in exogenous variables, our welfare measure gives the percentage increase in the house prices at all locations that would bring the expected maximum utility back to its initial level. Our welfare indicator is thus positive if the measure considered increases welfare and vice versa. Technical details can be found in the Appendix. It should be noted that our model considers housing only as consumption good. That is, house prices indicate the cost of living. Wealth effects do not play a role in our models.

The model and the inputs

In this section we discuss the model used in the policy simulations discussed later in the chapter and the inputs we use to define the alternatives to the reference situation.

The model and the reference situation

The household preferences used in this chapter are based on the estimation results of the sorting model that is estimated for the Netherlands by Möhlmann et al. (2014). This variant was estimated on a survey on housing from 2012 (BZK and

CBS, 2012). A novelty of this variant of the model is that we distinguish between three types of housing: apartments, terraced housing and detached dwellings.[11] This is implemented in the model by letting each combination of region and dwelling type form an alternative. This means that the number of alternatives is equal to four times the number of regions.[12] The number of regions is equal to 118 groups of municipalities.[13] This yields 472 alternatives, of which 3 x 118 owner-occupied alternatives and 118 rental alternatives. Including dwelling types is particularly relevant for policy, since in the Netherlands there are relatively strict land-use policies that influence both where dwellings are built and what type of dwellings are built.

The regional characteristics that are considered in the model are the distance to the nearest 100,000 jobs, the distance to the nearest intercity train station, the distance to the nearest highway intersection, the proportion of the region that is covered by nature and the size of the historic city centre. The values of these characteristics are determined by the group of municipalities to which they refer and independent of the housing type of the alternative. The house prices do vary between housing types within the same region.[14]

The household characteristics considered in the model are household composition, level of education and age. Household composition is indicated by a dummy for couples and a dummy for having children. In the case of a one-person household the variable for the educational level is one if the person is higher educated and zero otherwise. In the case of a two-person household this variable can also take on the value of 0.5 if one member is lower educated and one member is higher educated. When there are two adults in the household, the age variable is defined as their average age.

Table 7.1 shows the estimated WTP of each household type for each of the regional characteristics. It also shows the WTP of each household type for terraced housing and detached dwellings, relative to apartments. Note that these values apply to a standard dwelling with average characteristics. That is, the floor area, the number of rooms, etc. are all equal, although the housing type may be different. So the interpretation of the positive WTP for detached dwellings relative to apartments is that people would be willing to pay to live in a detached dwelling rather than an apartment, keeping all other household and neighbourhood characteristics constant. Higher-educated people attach more value to proximity to work and transport possibilities, to historic amenities and to terraced and detached housing.

Inputs for the counterfactual simulations

As a test scenario for the variants of the model framework we describe, we have chosen to use the Global Economy scenario (GE) for the year 2030 and to apply the model to the whole of the Netherlands. GE is one out of four scenarios that are often used in the Netherlands to simulate developments and answer 'what if' type of questions. The other three scenarios are Strong Europe (SE), Transatlantic Market (TM) and Regional Communities (RC). These scenarios are documented

Table 7.1 Average marginal WTP for location characteristics, and deviations by household characteristic

Characteristic	Average household	Couple vs single	Children vs no children	Age + 10	High education vs low education
Distance to 100,000 jobs (km)	−4186	−31	−252	−57	−544
Distance to intercity train station (km)	804	34	55	−5	−253
Distance to highway intersection (km)	−56	−150	−121	−12	−139
Nature (percent)	671	1	−3	19	1
Protected historic city centre (km²)	3812	−56	294	− 5	335
Terraced housing	−498	8977	15130	1112	895
Detached dwellings	38937	14090	17039	3916	6236

Source: Möhlmann et al. (2014).

in the 'Welfare, prosperity and quality of the living environment' (WLO) scenario study (CPB et al., 2006) (Figure 7.1).

A series of models is used to yield the input data for the GE scenario in 2030 that is necessary for the sorting model to run the scenario analyses. First, the projected future housing stock is obtained from the Land Use Scanner-XL model, a new version of the Land Use Scanner model developed by the Netherlands Environmental Assessment Agency (PBL) in co-operation with an Urban Regions in the Delta-projects.[15] The Land Use Scanner integrates future demand for space from various sector-specific models in a scenario setting and determines the results in an interactive demand–supply bidding process. The Land Use Scanner-model is GIS-based and has frequently been applied in different types of policy studies (see Koomen et al., 2011 for an overview). Hilferink and Rietveld (1999) provide a more

Figure 7.1 Four scenarios, placed on two axes with opposing forces: regionalization versus globalization on one axis, and economic development versus environmental protection on the other

extensive description of the model. To determine the housing stock in 2030 on a 100 x 100 meter grid cell level, the new version of the model takes into account the nationally projected number of dwellings to be built under a certain scenario; the regional capacities for realizing new dwellings outside existing urban areas; the potential for urban densification per region; and various other spatial planning restrictions (e.g., restriction on building in Nature 2000 areas).[16] For our purpose, we have received aggregated outcomes from PBL in the form of a future housing stock per municipality. This allows us to determine the impact of changes in the housing stock on the allocation of various household types over the municipalities.

Second, the Land Use Scanner-XL simultaneously delivers regional characteristics on future land use as an input for our sorting model, allowing for the calculation of the impact of changes in, for instance, the amount of nature in a municipality.

Third, projected data on household demographics are obtained from Hilderink et al. (2005), whose study on demographic developments in the Netherlands includes figures about household types, compositions, size and age for the four scenarios mentioned earlier. They use the PRIMOS-model for all calculations (see Den Otter and Heida 2003; Heida 2003 for more details about the model).[17]

Our sorting model is an equilibrium model that assumes equality of supply and demand. As we explained above, simulations are based on this equilibrium condition.[18] The output from the Land Use Scanner-XL does not connect in this way with the PRIMOS-output. We solve this problem by holding the number of households and dwellings constant, but varying only the proportions of different types of households and the proportions of the housing supply between regions.

Policy applications

This section describes five potential (policy) scenarios. Each scenario is compared with the base scenario. In the first four scenarios we vary only one component and in the fifth scenario we simultaneously change three components. The base scenario is based on the same data that were used to estimate the household preferences. The main data source is WoON 2012, which contains household characteristics and the distribution of housing supply in 2012. This survey contains individual households, but we aggregate them to 204 (17 x 2 x 2 x 3) household groups, based on 17 age groups (using 5-year intervals), households with or without children, singles and couples, and three groups based on educational level. Simulation of the base scenario results in predicted house prices that are very close to the actual house prices that were observed.[19]

We use the estimated preferences and the observed housing stock and characteristics per choice alternative as our reference. In this base scenario the predictions of the model for the number of households per alternative and the predicted equilibrium prices are the same as observed by WoON 2012. However, the predicted number of each type of household per alternative in the base scenario can deviate from the values observed by WoON 2012.[20] In order to make the outcomes of the model comparable we use the predicted household composition in the base scenario as a reference. The estimations of the scenarios will be reported as deviations from the estimation of this base scenario.

The scenarios that we simulated are (i) a change in the demographics of the household population, (ii) a change in the housing supply per region, (iii) a change in one of the regional characteristics (the proportion of nature), (iv) a change in household preferences for urban amenities and (v) a combination of the first three scenarios.

Household demographics

For this scenario we use the projected demographics for households in the Netherlands in 2030 in the GE scenario from PRIMOS. The main difference from the base model is a higher proportion of singles, which is 56 per cent in the PRIMOS model versus 42 per cent in the base model. Table 7.2 shows the proportions of the ten household types that we distinguish, in the base model and the PRIMOS model. We also separate each type into 17 age groups, but these are not shown here. The average age does not change much.

We use the PRIMOS household proportions and hold everything else constant and solve the model for a new equilibrium. We restrict the total value of the housing supply to remain the same, since the model can predict only relative house prices (between regions and between dwelling types). Compared to the base model, the average house price for apartments goes up by 1.1 per cent, while the average prices for terraced housing and detached dwellings go down by 0.1 per cent and 0.3 per cent, respectively (Table 7.3). This effect is probably mainly driven by the increase of singles households relative to couples. As shown in Table 7.1, singles attach a smaller premium to terraced housing and detached dwellings than do couples.

Due to differences in regional characteristics, some regions are more affected by the change in household demographics than others. Table 7.3 shows some of

Table 7.2 Proportions of the eight household types: base (2012) and GE scenario (2030)

	Base	PRIMOS
Single, no children, low educated	25%	33%
Couple, no children, low educated	17%	12%
Couple, low educated, with children	15%	12%
Single, low educated, with children	5%	5%
Couple, low/high educated, no children	7%	6%
Couple, low/high educated, with children	7%	6%
Single, high educated, no children	10%	17%
Couple, high educated, no children	5%	4%
Couple, high educated, with children	6%	4%
Single, high educated, with children	2%	1%

Source: Own calculations based on WoOn (2012) and PRIMOS projections obtained from Hilderink et al. (2005).

the variation in regional house price changes for each housing type. The predicted change in prices is positive for apartments and negative for detached dwellings in all regions. For terraced housing the predicted change is negative for most regions, but for some regions the predicted price change is positive. Since the largest deviation from the base model is the proportion of single households, this is likely caused by having characteristics that are relatively attractive to singles.

The effects of the PRIMOS scenario on the composition of households in the regions are summarized in Figure 7.2.

Computation of the multiplication factor k for all equilibrium house prices in the new (2030) situation shows that the change in market circumstances tends to make all groups of consumers somewhat worse off. More specifically, our computations show that all house prices must on average decrease by 0.10 per cent in the new situation to enable the consumers to reach the same expected maximum utility as with the current demographic composition. This is clearly a small number, but more interesting than the average are the differences between the various groups of consumers. The spread around the mean is limited: the standard deviation is 0.30 per cent, but this is large in comparison to the mean. For single-person households house prices must decrease by 0.37 per cent to 'make them as happy' as before the demographic change, and for households older than 50 this figure amounts to 0.30 per cent. Households with children experience an increase in utility: for them house prices can increase by 0.11 per cent to make them as well off in 2030 as they were in 2012.

To interpret these findings it should be noted that our computations refer to a situation in which the demographic composition of the Dutch population changes, whereas the composition of the housing stock remains unchanged. For instance, the proportion of apartments does not change although the proportion of single persons increases susbstantially.[21] The welfare consequences of this scenario, which can be considered as somewhat extreme since the model assumes that housing market does not change to accommodate the change in household composition, are found to be rather limited.

Changing the housing supply per region

We use the housing supply per region from the GE 2030 scenario from the Land Use Scanner XL. In order to keep the total number of households equal to the total number of dwellings, we change only the proportions of each region in the total

Table 7.3 Variation in change of house prices (in per cent)

Housing type	Average	Standard deviation	Minimum	Maximum
Apartments	1.14	0.09	1.01	1.57
Terraced housing	−0.09	0.11	−0.34	0.38
Detached dwellings	−0.32	0.05	−0.46	−0.13

Source: Own calculations.

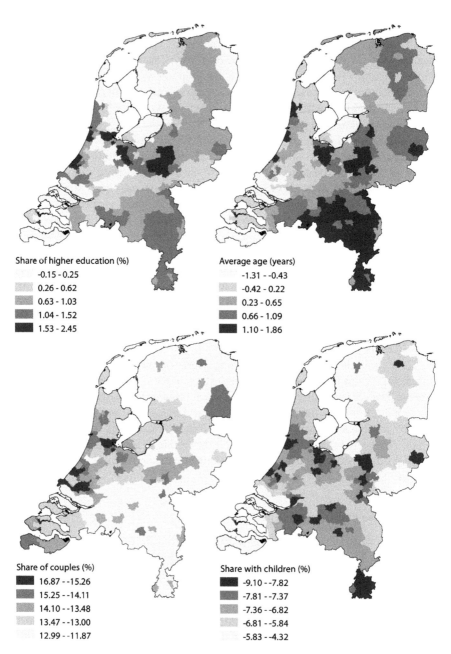

Figure 7.2 Changes in household composition per region, Global Economy 2030 versus base

Dutch housing stock while keeping the total size of that stock constant and equal to the number of households. The composition of the housing stock in terms of rental housing, apartments, terraced housing or detached dwellings for each region is assumed to remain the same as in the base scenario. In the 2030 scenario, the largest decrease in the proportion of the housing supply is 19 per cent (Zoetermeer) and the largest increase is 105 per cent (Beuningen, Druten, Overbetuwe).

Since our model deals only with relative house prices and not with the average price of housing (we restrict this to remain constant), the average prices of apartments, terraced housing and detached dwellings over the regions remains the same. However, spatial differences in house prices may change substantially, since the scenario adjusts the relative supply of housing while the demand for regional characteristics stays the same. Regions that experience an increase in their proportion of total housing stock will therefore experience a decrease in house prices and vice versa. The changes in house price between regions range between −3.1 per cent and +0.9 per cent.

The welfare impact of the change in the composition of the housing stock is also limited. On average there is again a decrease in welfare that could be compensated by house prices that are 0.10 per cent lower. For singles and households older than 50 there is on average a somewhat larger decrease in welfare: house prices have to decrease by 0.37 per cent and 0.03 per cent, respectively, to compensate them. Households with children gain: house prices could decrease by 0.11 per cent to compensate them. We thus find that – at least for the scenario considered here – the changes in the regional housing supply from the GE 2030 scenario have limited consequences for welfare.

Increasing the amount of nature

In this section we simulate the effects of a change of the proportion of nature in the regions. One of the reasons why we choose to change nature and not any of the other regional characteristics is that nature is more likely to change because of policy measures than some of the other characteristics. For example, the distance to highway intersections or to intercity stations is unlikely to change in many regions because traffic infrastructure networks are dense in the Netherlands. The second reason is that we have access to projections on the proportion of nature in 2030, which are obtained from the GE 2030 scenario of the Land Use Scanner-XL. The scenario for nature is likely related to the previous scenario on housing supply, since nature and housing are substitutes in the sense that land used for residential purposes can no longer be used for nature. Figure 7.3 shows the regional distribution of the proportion of nature in the base model (based on nature in 2003) and the projections from the GE scenario 2030.

Changing the regional characteristics will affect both the regional house prices as well as the distribution of different types of households over the regions. Regions in which nature declines relatively strongly will experience a decline in the house prices, since all household types have a positive WTP for nature (see Table 7.1). The distribution of household types will change, since some household types have a greater valuation of nature than others. However, Table 7.1 shows that the variation in WTP is small, which implies that the distribution of household types will not change much. The largest variation in the WTP for nature is caused by age. Since older people value nature slightly more than younger people,

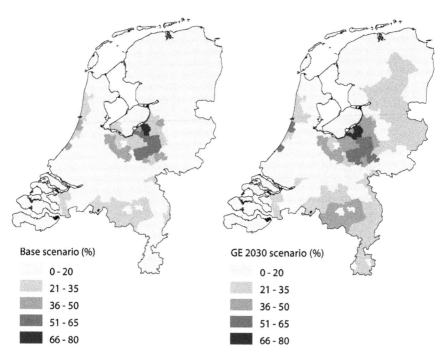

Figure 7.3 Share of nature in base and Global Economy 2030 scenario

regions that increase their proportion of nature are expected to experience a very small increase in the average age.

The results from the simulation exercise show a variation in relative regional house prices of between −5.60 per cent and +6.85 per cent. There is almost no variation in the predicted house price of different types of dwellings within the same region. The largest decrease (5.5 per cent) is predicted for the municipality Almere, where the proportion of nature goes down from 24 per cent in the base model to 11 per cent in the GE 2030 scenario. The largest increase (6.85 per cent) is predicted for the COROP region Zaanstreek, where nature is projected to increase from 5 per cent in the base model to 31 per cent in the GE 2030 scenario. Figure 7.4 shows the changes in average house prices per region.

When we consider the welfare consequences of the change in nature, we find larger figures than in the scenarios considered previously. If we look only at the changes in nature, and not at the changes in house prices that occur as a consequence, we find that welfare increases to the same extent as when house prices would decrease by 1.72 per cent.[22] Singles benefit a bit less (the increase in welfare is equivalent to a decrease in house prices of 1.50 per cent), households with children more (1.87 per cent) and households above 50 also benefit more than the average (1.87 per cent). These changes can be considered as the *ex-ante* effect of the policy.

The *ex-post* effect also takes into account the price changes that are needed to restore equilibrium in the housing market. Naturally, regions that have become more attractive face excess demand and a higher house price is needed to equilibrate demand and supply again. Since the average house price remains constant, regions that did not experience an increase in nature now benefit from a lower house price.[23]

Our computations reveal that the average welfare effect becomes greater after the change in the house prices has been taken into account. The reason that we find a higher welfare effect after the new prices are taken into account is that we consider only relative prices and assume that the average price level of housing stays constant. So, even though nature increases on average, the model assumes that average house prices do not increase. Relative house prices do change, which means that prices increase in regions where nature increases more than average and prices decrease in regions where nature increases less than average. After new equilibrium prices are taken into account the average compensation equals 2.3 per cent of the house prices. For singles the impact is smaller (1.87 per cent) and for households with children and the elderly it is larger (2.59 per cent and 2.55 per cent, respectively).

The effects of changes in household preferences

In this section we simulate what happens to the equilibrium if household preferences for urban amenities are increased. We did this by doubling the parameter

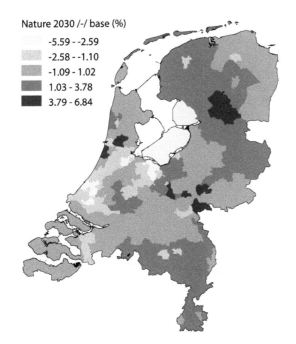

Figure 7.4 Change in average house price per region, nature 2030 versus base

for the size of the historic city centre for all households. Contrary to the previous two simulations, which were based on the GE 2030 scenario, this section is not based on any scenario. The point of this exercise is to give an idea of the order of magnitude of the effects of changing household preferences.

Doubling the preference for urban amenities will increase house prices in regions with large historic city centres. The largest average price increases are observed in The Hague (24.5 per cent) and Amsterdam (10.7 per cent), since these regions have the largest historic city centres. Many regions experience a price decrease, since they have either a small historic city centre or none at all. However, these price decreases are usually relatively small, since the average city centre is also small. The largest price decrease is 3.1 per cent. Similar to what was found in the previous section on nature, the price changes are very similar for different housing types within the same region. The changes of the average house prices per region are shown in Figure 7.5.

Adjusting household preferences can also influence the composition of household types. Since the preference for the size of the historic city centre was doubled for all households, the difference in preferences between household types also doubles. This means, for example, that higher-educated households will choose to live in urban regions more often than before, relative to lower-educated households. The results of the simulation show that the proportion of higher-educated households can increase by up to nine percentage points in The Hague. The largest

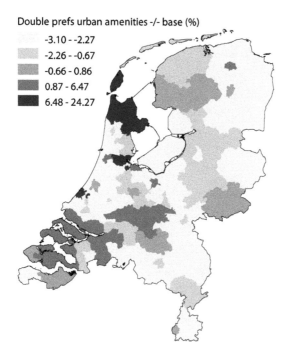

Double prefs urban amenities -/- base (%)

- ☐ -3.10 - -2.27
- ☐ -2.26 - -0.67
- ☐ -0.66 - 0.86
- ■ 0.87 - 6.47
- ■ 6.48 - 24.27

Figure 7.5 Change in average house price per region, double preferences for urban amenities versus base

decrease of the proportion of higher-educated households is almost one percentage point. The effects on the age of the population are relatively small: the largest decrease is 1.8 years (detached dwellings in The Hague) and the largest increase is 0.2 years. The reason why the average age decreases in The Hague is that age has a negative interaction with the WTP for urban amenities (see Table 7.1). Furthermore, the simulation results show for the proportion of households with children that the largest decrease is almost one percentage point and the largest increase is almost nine percentage points (The Hague). The proportion of couples hardly changes: the largest decrease is 0.2 percentage points and the largest increase is 0.7 percentage points.

For this scenario no welfare changes have been computed, since the changes in preferences are arbitrary.

Combining three scenarios

In the previous four sections we simulated what would happen when one type of input is changed while holding everything else constant. It is also possible to evaluate what would happen when two or more input types change at the same time. It is likely that multiple input types will change at the same time, for example because policies are made in reaction to changes in household demographics. Another example of two related types of input in our model is the proportions of nature and of the total housing stock. Since nature and housing are substitutes, an increase of the housing stock will often be associated with a decrease in the proportion of nature in the region.

In this section we adjust the household demographics, the housing supply and the proportion of nature simultaneously, according to input of the GE 2030 scenario from PRIMOS and the Land Use Scanner-XL. That is, we reconsider the changes studied in the first three subsections in a setting in which they all occur at the same time. It is possible that the combination of these three scenarios will reinforce effects in some cases or that effects will counteract each other in other cases. In this combined scenario, the average change in house prices over all regions is 0.24 per cent. However, the price changes differ strongly by housing type, see Table 7.4.

The table also shows that the standard deviation of price changes between regions is also much larger than in the previous scenarios. For the average change in house prices per region, the largest decrease is found in Almere (−6.6 per cent) and the largest increase is found for the region Rijnwaarden, Milingen aan de Rijn and Ubbergen (+7.8 per cent).

Table 7.4 Variation in change of house prices (in per cent)

Housing type	Average	Standard deviation	Minimum	Maximum
Apartments	1.13	2.47	−5.71	8.64
Terraced housing	−0.10	2.46	−6.84	7.49
Detached dwellings	−0.32	2.49	−7.18	7.36

Source: Own calculations.

We also observe changes in the composition of household types per region. These changes will be caused partly by changes in the overall household demographics of the PRIMOS model and partly by a different allocation of existing households over regions, due to the changes in the relative housing supply and the proportion of nature. For the proportion of higher-educated households we observe changes of between –0.4 percentage points and +0.6 percentage points. The average age of households changes by between –1.3 years and +1.9 years. Finally the proportion of households with children changes by between –3.2 percentage points and +1.6 percentage points and the proportion of couples changes by between –4.3 percentage points and +0.3 percentage points.

It may, of course, be expected that the welfare effects of the combined changes are close to those of the change in nature, since the other two scenarios were found to have a rather small impact on welfare. This is indeed the case. We now find an increase in welfare that is compensated by an increase in house prices of 1.73 per cent, which is somewhat smaller than the *ex-post* effect of the change in nature. For singles the impact is smaller (1.40 per cent), and for households with children and the elderly it is larger (1.96 per cent and 1.92 per cent, respectively).

Conclusion and discussion

This chapter has described how the sorting model can be used to simulate the effects of different scenarios on house prices and the distribution of households over regions. The model can be used to calculate a new equilibrium when household demographics, regional characteristics, regional housing supply or household preferences are changed. The model is very flexible in the sense that it can change any of these inputs simultaneously for any region, as long as the total housing supply is equal to the total number of households.

We simulated three aspects of the GE 2030 scenario, while holding all other inputs constant. The effects of the projected household demographics in this scenario on the prices of different types of dwellings are limited. Due to the changing composition of households, the price of apartments increases on average by 1.1 per cent, while the prices of terraced housing and detached dwellings decrease on average by 0.1 and 0.3 per cent, respectively. Note that this assumes that housing supply scales proportionally with the number of households. This means that we do not model a general upward or downward pressure on the housing market, but we estimate only relative price changes, while the overall average price of all dwellings stays the same. Larger relative price effects between regions can be expected from changing the relative housing supply proportions of the regions or from changing regional characteristics. When we use the predictions on regional housing supply from the GE 2030 scenario, relative house prices change by between –3.1 per cent and +0.9 per cent. Since we change the regional housing supply while keeping the demand for regional characteristics constant, an increase in the housing supply is always associated with a decrease of the regional house prices.

An example of a regional characteristic that is simulated in this chapter is the proportion of nature in the regions under the GE 2030 scenario. The model predicts house price changes that range from –5.60 per cent to +6.85 per cent between regions. The model predicts that prices of different types of dwellings within the same region move very similarly when regional characteristics are changed.

We also simulated the effects of changing household preferences. This simulation is not based on a particular scenario, but can be used to give an idea of the order of magnitude of these effects. We doubled the preferences for the size of the historic city centre of all household types. This is expected to lead to large relative price increases in regions with large historic city centres, like The Hague and Amsterdam. To compensate, many regions with a small or no historic city centre are expected to experience small price decreases. Finally, the results of this simulation predict relatively large changes in the regional distribution of some household types, which occurs because the difference in WTP between household types is also doubled.

Finally, the model also allows simulating what happens when several types of input are changed simultaneously. In this chapter we changed household demographics, the regional housing supply and the proportion of nature in each region simultaneously according to the GE scenario 2030. When changing multiple inputs of the model, it is possible that some effects will reinforce each other while others will counteract each other. However, in general we found more variation of the regional housing price differences than occurred when only one type of input was changed.

The chapter has demonstrated how we can use the models developed in the HELP project to investigate the consequences of possible changes in policy-relevant variables. The model can thus be used to answer a number of 'what if' questions. For instance, a local policy maker might be interested in what would happen if in the future more apartments, or more detached dwellings, were constructed in a particular region; and whether the outcome would be different if all other municipalities in the region were to realize the same shift in the composition of their housing stock. The model could be used to investigate the outcomes of these scenarios. The impact on the prices of the various housing types could be assessed, as well as the welfare consequences. The possibilities of the model are not restricted to this particular example, which is given here for concreteness only. The sections of this chapter provide alternative suggestions and they do not exhaust the model's possibilities.

Appendix: a welfare measure and its computation

The expectation of the maximum utility that is experienced by a group of consumers with the same deterministic parts of the utilities attached to the alternatives is given by the so-called logsum.[24] If we denote the deterministic part of the utility attached to alternative j in situation s as u_j^s, then the logsum in this situation is given as:

$$logsum^s = \ln\left(\Sigma_j e^{u_j^s}\right).$$

In our models the deterministic parts of the utilities are given by expressions of the type:

$$u_j^s = \alpha \ln p_j^s + \Sigma_m \beta_m X_{mj}^s .$$

In this equation p denotes the house price and m indexes other characteristics of the alternatives. We want to compare the logsums in two situations, 0 and 1, which can be interpreted as before and after the implementation of a particular policy. We introduce a variable k that is implicitly determined by the equation:

$$logsum^0 = \ln\left(\Sigma_j e^{\alpha \ln kp_j^1 + \Sigma_m \beta_m X_{mj}^1}\right).$$

The right-hand side of this equation gives the expected maximum utility that would be reached by a household if the characteristics of all choice alternatives were as in situation 1, except that the prices had been multiplied by a factor k.

To solve for k, we note that $\ln kp_j^s = \ln k + \ln p_j^s$ and elaborate the right-hand side of the equation as:

$$\ln\left(\Sigma_j e^{\alpha \ln kp_j^s + \Sigma_m \beta_m X_{mj}^s}\right) = \ln\left(e^{\alpha \ln k}\Sigma_j e^{\alpha \ln p_j^s + \Sigma_m \beta_m X_{mj}^s}\right)$$

$$= \alpha \ln k + \ln\left(\Sigma_j e^{\alpha \ln p_j^s + \Sigma_m \beta_m X_{mj}^s}\right)$$

$$= \alpha \ln k + logsum^1 .$$

Substitution of this result and solving for k then gives:

$$k = \exp\left\{\frac{logsum^0 - logsum^1}{\alpha}\right\}.$$

Notes

1 These preferences should be interpreted as referring to indirect utility functions and therefore incorporate the impact of the household's budget constraint.

2 Hedonic price models in general do not have this property. They describe a market equilibrium and the estimated coefficients should be expected to change when, for instance, the composition of the population or the housing supply changes.

3 Mathematically it requires: $\Sigma_i \pi_n^i = S_n, n = 1 \ldots N$ where π_n^i denotes the probability that actor i chooses location n and Sn is the supply of housing at location n.

4 A variant of the contraction mapping algorithm of Berry et al. (1995) may be used, for example.

5 Often a price equilibrium is computed while keeping the demographic characteristics at their initial values. Then the demographic composition of all locations at this price equilibrium is determined and plugged into the model. The price equilibrium is then computed again. This procedure is repeated until convergence occurs.

6 It is, in principle, possible to relax this property by introducing an outside alternative that corresponds to informal housing or postponing household formation and replacing the assumption of exogenous supply by a model of housing construction.

7 See Chapter 5 for a discussion of stated preference analyses.

8 See any microeconomics textbook for a discussion of this concept as well as the closely related equivalent variation and consumer surplus.

9 This limitation is closely related to the fact that Marshallian consumer surplus can be considered as an appropriate welfare measure only if demand does not depend on income.

10 For instance, De Palma and Kilani (2003) prove that the expected value of the compensating variation can be expressed in a one-dimensional integral of the choice probabilities.

11 Models that do not make this distinction assume implicitly that households can adjust the quality of their dwellings to their preferences. However, some quality characteristics are hard to change, and housing type (detached, terraced, apartment) is probably the main example of a fixed characteristic. The model we use here realistically takes into account that households cannot change it, while allowing for differences in other quality aspects within each type.

12 We distinguish the three dwelling types for owner-occupied housing. In addition, we include one alternative per region for rental housing.

13 We decided not to use the individual municipalities because the number of observations per municipality for specific housing types was sometimes small, especially in rural areas.

14 House prices for all choice alternatives were estimated by a hedonic price model.

15 This version is called Land Use Scanner-XL because it is integrated with the Tigris XL-model and thus simulates the relation between Employment and the Residential market in connection with a Transport model (LMS) in a more direct way than before.

16 For more details about the calculation of urban densities and the construction of dwellings outside existing urban areas, see Koomen et al. (2016). This co-production between the URD-AESUS and URD-HELP projects has formed the basis for the adaptations made to the Land Use Scanner-XL model.

17 We would have preferred to use the household scenario calculations from PBL's PEARL-model, since this model is also part of the Land Use Scanner-XL model chain, but unfortunately at the time of our analysis the divisions in household types between PEARL and the sorting-models did not (yet) match. The PRIMOS prognoses for the GE scenario are a few years older than the scenario projections for GE from the Land Use Scanner-XL, so small differences between the scenario versions occur, but these

do not hinder our purpose here to demonstrate the potential of using these tools for counterfactual simulations.

18 Formally, this means that all dwellings are occupied and all housing demand is served. However, it should be kept in mind that the model is estimated on the actual situation in 2009. A more appropriate interpretation is therefore that in the simulation the situation on the housing market is similar to that in 2009.

19 There is a small difference because we use aggregated household groups, rather than using individual households. If we include each household individually, the predicted house prices will be the same as observed. The reason that we use aggregated household groups is that for future scenarios we do not have individual households.

20 The estimations of the model do usually correctly predict over- or under-representation of certain household types in regions, but the observed variation of household composition is larger than predicted by the model, due to idiosyncratic preferences.

21 The assumption of a constant composition of the housing stock has been used to get a clear benchmark case. The model is able to deal with any other composition of the housing stock in 2030.

22 Recall that the wealth effect of house price changes is not included in our model.

23 The lower house price reduces housing costs and therefore increases welfare. To bring the households back to their original utility level, house prices would have to increase by the same amount. Our welfare measure thus takes on a positive value if house prices decrease.

24 See, for instance, Ben-Akiva and Lerman (1985).

References

Ben-Akiva, M and Lerman, S 1985, *Discrete Choice Analysis.* Cambridge, MA: The MIT Press.

Berry, S, Levinsohn, J and Pakes, A 1995, Automobile Prices in Market Equilibrium. *Econometrica* 63, 841–890.

BZK and CBS, WoOn2012: release 1.0 – WoonOnderzoek Nederland 2012, Ministerie van Binnenlandse Zaken en Koninkrijksrelaties en Centraal Bureau voor de Statistiek.

CPB, MNP and RPB 2006, 'Welvaart en Leefomgeving. Een scenariostudie voor Nederland in 2040', *Centraal Planbureau, Milieu- en Natuurplanbureau en Ruimtelijk Planbureau,* Den Haag.

Dagsvik, JK and Karlström, A 2005, Compensating Variation and Hicksian Choice Probabilities in Random Utility Models that Are Nonlinear in Income. *Review of Economic Studies,* 72, 57–76.

Den Otter, HJ and Heida, H 2003, Primos Prognose 2003. De toekomstige ontwikkeling van bevolking, huishoudens en woningbehoefte, *ABF Research,* Delft. Publication by the Spatial Planning Agency (RPB), November.

De Palma, A and Kilani, K 2003, (Un)conditional Distribution of Compensating Variation in Discrete Choice Models. Working paper.

Heida, H 2003 and Primos 2003, Prognosemodel voor bevolking, huishoudens en woningbehoefte. *ABF Research,* Delft.

Hilderink, H, den Otter, H and de Jong, A 2005, Scenario's voor huishoudensontwikkelingen in Nederland. MNP-RIVM/ABF Research/CBS/CPB/RPB/SCP report 550012005, Bilthoven/Delft/Voorburg/Den Haag.

Hilferink, M and Rietveld, P 1999, Land Use Scanner: An Integrated GIS Based Model for Long Term Projections of Land Use in Urban and Rural Areas. *Journal of Geographical Systems,* 1(2), 155–177.

Koomen, E, Dekkers, JEC and Broitman, D 2016, Analyzing and Simulating Urban Density; Exploring the Difference between Policy Ambitions and Actual Trends in the Netherlands (forthcoming) in *Spatial Analysis and Location Modeling in Urban and Regional Systems. Advances in Geographic Information Science Series*, ed. J-C Thill, Heidelberg: Springer.

Koomen, E, Hilferink, M and Borsboom-van Beurden, J 2011, Introducing the Land Use Scanner, Chapter 1. In: Koomen, E and Borsboom-van Beurden, J (eds) Land-use Modelling in Planning Practice. *GeoJournal Library* 101, 3–23. Dordrecht: Springer.

McFadden, D 1981, Econometric models of Probabilistic Choice. In: Manski, CF and McFadden, D (eds) *Structural Analysis of Discrete Data with Econometric Applications*, chapter 5, 198–271. Cambridge, MA: MIT Press.

McFadden, D 1999, Computing Willingness-to-Pay in Random Utility Models. In: Moore J, Riezman, R and Melvin, J (eds) *Trade, Theory and Econometrics: Essays in Honor of John Chipman*, 253–274. New York: Routledge

Möhlmann, J, Van Duijn, M and Rouwendal, J 2014, Restricted Housing Supply, House Prices and Welfare: Evidence from the Netherlands. Work in progress.

Small, KA and Rosen, HS 1981, Applied Welfare Economics with Discrete Choice Models. *Econometrica* 49(1), 105–130.

Van Duijn, M and Rouwendal, J 2013, Cultural Heritage and the Location Choice of Dutch Households in a Residential Sorting Model. *Journal of Economic Geography* 13(3) 473–500.

Part III

8 Housing and location preferences of higher educated international migrants in the Netherlands

An introduction

Jan Rouwendal, Sako Musterd and Marco Bontje

International migrants in the Higher Educated Location Preferences (HELP) project

A part of the HELP project, which is dealt with in Chapters 9–12, focused especially on international migrants. These include higher-educated workers and international students. Parts II and III have many similarities: both consider studies that have been performed from an urban geography and an urban economic perspective. Both also include analysis of stated and revealed preferences. The sorting model that has been extensively used in Part II now returns in Part III. In many respects we have studied the 'knowledge migrants' in the same way as we studied the whole population. However, there is difference in two respects. First, special attention will be paid to the preferences of international students. Second, we will not only go into stated and revealed preferences, as we did in Part II, but will also consider the settlement process. Where are highly skilled migrants settling when they first arrive and what are their next steps? We believe that these additions, together with the studies on stated and revealed preferences, provide a fairly comprehensive picture of the housing ambitions of highly skilled international migrants.

The significance of migrants for urban growth and urban development

For a long time it was more or less 'common sense' that in order to realize economic growth there had only to be greater amounts of labour and capital. However, Solow (1956) famously showed that these conventional production factors could not entirely explain modern economic growth. Since then, economists have paid much attention to developing and testing theories of endogenous growth; see Acemoglu (2009) for a review. Glaeser *et al.* (1992) argued that growth is, to a large extent, an urban phenomenon and they attempted to merge theories of agglomeration benefits with endogenous growth. Their results confirmed Jacobs' (1961) hypothesis that the presence and proximity of a variety of economic activities was particularly beneficial for growth. The main idea is that people pick up new ideas from interactions with others that carry out different activities. Later developments in the literature include Duranton and Puga's (2001) idea of 'nursery cities', which have a large amount of variation in economic activity and are particularly innovative. They are distinguished from other cities that are specialized in a limited number of activities. According to Duranton and Puga's theory, new activities – process innovations – start experimentally in a nursery city and, after they have proved to be successful, application on a larger scale occurs in other cities where the labour force is specialized and production is less expensive. This suggests, of course, that nursery cities in particular are the engines of economic growth in a country, or perhaps even on a larger scale.

Recognizing the possibility for new products and techniques requires skills and creativity. Education, knowledge and, in particular, networks of knowledge, are key to developing skills and knowledge in ways that are useful. It is therefore not surprising that the relationship between human capital and urban growth is usually found to be strong. This view is supported by Lambooy (1997), who, in a special issue of *GeoJournal* on the relationship between universities and cities, argued that 'in regions with universities the "normal" impact of salaries and teaching is important for the creation of regional income and the enhancement of the quality of the labour market. [But m]ore important for strengthening the economic base is whether the university and the related firms are able to build "knowledge networks" around clusters of knowledge-intensive production units of goods and services. A sufficient number of highly qualified knowledge workers and an efficient organization are very important for securing the opportunities of knowledge production' (p. 299). Duranton and Puga, who recently reviewed the literature on growth in cities, state that a one percentage point higher proportion of university graduates is associated with around 0.5 per cent population growth in the next decade (Duranton and Puga, 2013, p. 40).

The most likely channel through which higher-educated inhabitants have an impact on city growth is via productivity, but Diamond (2013) has recently argued that better-educated cities develop more attractive amenities, which in turn generate population growth.

The literature thus makes clear that the presence of a skilled labour force is important for the urban economy. A higher proportion of skilled workers is likely to be beneficial and can be achieved by the higher education of the native population or by an inflow of highly skilled migrants. In a globalized economy where, especially, international mobility of the higher-educated is becoming more important, attention to the attractiveness of cities for migrants is natural. Apart from being necessary so as to prevent a decline in the proportion of highly skilled workers by out-migration, a constant inflow of workers from various origins contributes to cultural diversity, which may contribute to further advantages in production as well as in consumption amenities (Ottaviano and Peri, 2006). The four chapters that follow study various aspects of the attractiveness of Dutch cities to highly skilled international migrants.

Comparing natives and migrants

It is conceivable, and to some extent probable, that the location preferences of migrant workers differ from those of natives. They are less familiar with the country and perhaps more oriented to proximity to their location of work. Contacts with other migrants from the same country may be important for them and may affect their preferences for residential locations. Their cultural background may differ from that of the native Dutch, and this too may have an impact on their preferences for housing and urban amenities.

The general picture that emerges from the research reported in the following chapters is, however, that migrant workers are similar to the Dutch in several respects (for example, Chapter 9). Yet they are not identical. They attach a somewhat higher value to typical urban amenities and services such as shops, which may be related to the absence of relatives and to the location of most of the jobs. They put more emphasis on the quality of public transport, which may be related to a lower propensity to own a car, especially among those who are staying in the Netherlands for a relatively short period, and live more often than do their native Dutch colleagues in a highly urbanized environment and in proximity to their workplace. As will be shown in Chapter 11, amenities such as job opportunities and accessibility, natural amenities and historic city centres, play a significant role in raising the attraction of municipalities. The proportion of migrants in a municipality also plays a role as an attraction factor. The Marginal Willingness To Pay (MWTP) for an additional proportion of migrants in a municipality is high for all skill and origin groups where proportions of migrants are low; but the MWTP decreases where proportions of migrants are high. The location preferences of skilled migrants show many similarities to those of skilled native workers. Further details are discussed in Chapter 11.

Affordable housing is also among the most important issues. This may be interpreted in different ways. One is that the social housing sector is not easily accessible to migrants, while it constitutes a very high proportion of total housing in larger Dutch cities. To have priority, one has to be on the waiting list for years, and this is generally not feasible for migrants. Further, the higher-skilled migrants in particular may simply earn too much to be part of the target group for social housing, to which 90 per cent of the available supply has to be allocated. Another interpretation therefore is that migrants look for rental housing that is not too expensive. It is well known that this segment of the housing market is of little importance in the Netherlands. On the one hand there is a large social rental sector that is accessible only to low-income households, and on the other hand there is an even larger owner-occupied sector that is less attractive to migrants who expect to stay in the Netherlands for a limited number of years. In the largest cities the private rental sector is not completely negligible, but it is expensive and appears to be mainly oriented towards the upper segment of the market. The special characteristics of the Dutch housing market appear to make Dutch cities less attractive to migrant workers.

Arriving and settling in the Netherlands

A potentially important way of attracting highly skilled people to Dutch cities is by offering possibilities to study in the Netherlands to young people from elsewhere (Chapter 10). Some of them will return to their home country but others may stay for prolonged periods, and even for the rest of their lives. A possible concern with the phenomenon of international student mobility is of course that it contributes to a 'brain drain'. On the other hand, the origin countries, especially among the developing countries, may benefit from students who return after having received a better education than their native country could offer them.

It appears that the proportion of foreign students who stay in the Netherlands after completing their studies has dropped somewhat in recent years, while their absolute numbers are increasing rapidly. The moderate drop may also be ascribed to increasing globalization, both of students who 'go abroad' and of students who come from a much wider array of origins than they did before. When they stay in the new country they usually remain in the vicinity of the higher education institutions that were the main reason for coming to the Netherlands. The initial concentration is related to the residential facilities that universities and institutions for higher vocational training offer to their students. When the students become active on the labour market, the settlement pattern diffuses slowly over time. After some years, the students become familiar with Dutch society and their preferences with regard to residential location become more similar to those of the native Dutch.

Migrants who arrive in the Netherlands after having completed their studies abroad – in their native country or elsewhere – show a similar residential location pattern to that of their Dutch colleagues from the beginning. Residential mobility is somewhat higher in the first years after arrival, especially among those who stay for a longer period, but there are no big changes in, for instance, the frequency of choosing an urban or suburban environment. Even the residential preferences that are associated with the type of job (and the industry in which a worker finds employment) are similar to those observed among the Dutch. It is evident, as will be shown in Chapter 12, that different orientations in terms of residential space are connected to economic sector (technical or creative), household attributes and duration of stay.

References

Acemoglu, D 2009, *Introduction to Modern Economic Growth*. Princeton: University Press.

Diamond, R 2013, The Determinants and Welfare Implications of US Workers Diverging Location Choices by Skill: 1980–2000. Working paper.

Duranton, G and Puga, D 2001, Nursery Cities: Urban Diversity, Process Innovation and the Life Cycle of Products. *American Economic Review* 91, 1454–1477.

Duranton, G and Puga, D 2013, The Growth of Cities. Forthcoming in: *Handbook of Economic Growth*.

Glaeser, EL, Kallal, H, Scheinkman, JA and Shleifer, A 1992, Growth in Cities. *Journal of Political Economy* 100, 1126–1152.

Jacobs, J 1961, *The Death and Life of Great American Cities*. New York: Random House.

Lambooy, JG 1997, Knowledge Production, Organisation and Agglomeration Economies. *GeoJournal* 41(4), 293–300.

Ottaviano, GIP and Peri, G 2006, The Economic Value of Cultural Diversity: Evidence from US Cities. *Journal of Economic Geography* 6, 9–44.

Solow, RM 1956, A Contribution to the Theory of Economic Growth. *Quarterly Journal of Economics* 70, 65–94.

9 Stated residential preferences of highly skilled international migrants

Bart Sleutjes and Willem R. Boterman

Introduction

Increasingly, the international migration of skilled workers has the attention of regional and national policy makers, as well as academics, because of the widely assumed positive contribution of human capital to economic development. Since a transfer of human capital generally implies the movement of people (Fratesi 2014), efforts to attract human capital are more complex than efforts to attract, for example, economic capital, and generally involve individual choices and preferences. Individuals' location choices often result from a combination of strategic factors – e.g., near to work or personal networks – and personal preferences. Higher education institutions play a very important role in influencing migration of the highly skilled: besides generating new human capital, universities attract talents from outside (Faggian and McCann 2006). Also, availability of jobs is an important attracting factor for higher-educated workers, and some regions are better at generating high-level jobs than others (Fratesi 2014). Further, especially for location choices within the region and for retaining knowledge workers, the housing stock and 'soft conditions' such as cultural and recreational amenities may also have some influence.

Migration of skilled workers from one place to the other has often been portrayed as 'brain drain', assuming permanent migration from less- to more-developed countries or regions (Bontje *et al.* 2009). However, through the internationalisation of national and regional economies since the 1980s, the idea of brain drain seems to have become less relevant (Beaverstock 1990; Bontje *et al.* 2009). Migration should be understood more in cyclical terms, with many skilled migrants eventually returning to their home regions (Vertovec 2007). Deregulation of the international financial markets and the relocation of production units outside of industrial producers' home markets resulted in the emergence of a large number of transnational production and service companies and the exchange of highly skilled professionals within these organisations. These 'expats' are often sent to a foreign branch for a short period, ranging from a few months to a few years. Expats generally have little choice with regard to their countries of destination, but are in a relatively privileged position, since they are often compensated through relocation services and earn higher salaries. Studies on expats in the financial services sector indicate that their mobility patterns are mainly between global cities, which are also increasingly located in emerging economies (Beaverstock 1994; 1996; 2002). Whereas migration previously occurred mainly from developing to advanced countries, the number of flows between advanced capitalist countries and from advanced economies to developing countries have been increasing. In addition, 'transnational migration' has resulted in the development of 'unbounded' international communities and social spaces (Bontje *et al.* 2009). Thus, the concept of 'brain circulation' seems more applicable to the current migration context in Western European countries, including the Netherlands (Pethe and Hafner 2013).

A dominant critique of the literature on brain circulation is the neglect of the migrant as an individual agent (Scott 2006). Technological progress has enabled small actors to become more internationally mobile, and highly skilled individuals may move between small and medium-sized companies as well, rather than between large multinationals (Bontje *et al.* 2009). Expats are over-represented in theoretical debates and empirical studies, although they are just a relatively small sub-category of all transnational highly skilled migrants. For many highly skilled workers, the move abroad was on their own initiative and steered by personal motives (Bontje *et al.* 2009). For this group of international migrants in particular, specific location factors may be relevant when making location choices; for example, the residential milieu, building style or the 'look and feel' of an area (Helbrecht 2004).

Since many cities in Europe are in competition with one another to attract international knowledge workers, and facilitating their needs is placed high on the political agenda of several local and regional governments, it is pertinent to obtain more insight into the residential preferences of this group and its sub-categories. This chapter will therefore present an investigation into stated choice for urban or suburban areas, specific dwelling types and amenities. The study compares the total group of international knowledge workers to higher-educated Dutch workers, and also takes the great heterogeneity within the international group into consideration. It focuses specifically on the Dutch city regions of Amsterdam and Eindhoven. The chapter focuses on the following research questions:

- To what extent are preferences for residential milieus and dwelling types different between Dutch and international knowledge workers, and between different groups of international workers?
- Which factors are the main considerations when looking for a new place to live, and what differences are there between Dutch and international workers and between different categories of international workers?

The second section of the chapter continues with a short review of literature on international migration of skilled workers in the two regions that are the focus of our study: the Amsterdam Metropolitan Area and the Eindhoven Metropolitan Region. After a short description of the data in the third section, the fourth section presents the outcomes of a quantitative empirical study on stated residential choice by highly skilled international migrants are presented. The focus of this study is on preferences for urban or suburban areas, specific dwelling types and the relevance of amenities. This section will first describe differences in stated preferences between Dutch and international knowledge workers in general, and then look at differences within the international migrant population, according to country of origin and sector of work.

Transnational migrants in the Amsterdam Metropolitan Region and the Eindhoven Metropolitan Region

Although only a limited number of studies have dealt specifically with the residential preferences of international knowledge workers, a number of recent studies have touched upon this topic. Several empirical studies have looked into the residential patterns of Amsterdam's workers in the creative and knowledge-intensive sectors, and, to a lesser extent, also those of international workers. This section outlines the main observations from these studies, and adds some insights from local expert interviews.

Residential preferences of international knowledge workers in the Amsterdam Metropolitan Area

In their study on different categories of labour migrants in the Amsterdam region, Pethe and Hafner (2013) addressed their demands and their location patterns. 'Corporate migrants' often work for transnational companies on a short-term basis, have much work experience within their company and belong to the highest-income groups. This group generally attaches more value to hard location factors, such as taxation and access to highways or airports (Pethe and Hafner 2013). The Dutch national government provides a number of conditions that are especially favourable for this group, including accelerated immigration procedures for the applicant and his or her family, generous arrangements for permanent settlement and tax incentives. Regarding the latter, the '30 per cent tax rule' offers a tax reduction to some highly skilled migrants, based on areas of expertise in high demand on the Dutch labour market (Hercog 2008). This group tends to settle in suburban locations close to the urban core, such as Amstelveen.

Next to labour migrants, there is a group of 'graduates', including students, recent graduates and 'lifestyle migrants', who often use social networks to find jobs and accommodation and generally have a moderate income. 'European free movers' often leave their country of origin after graduation or in the early stages of their career and are generally independent, single individuals with a mixed income structure. The free movers, and the highest-income segments in particular, express a clear preference for inner-city residential milieus, with housing in different price categories, and a need for assistance with essential administrative procedures (Pethe and Hafner 2013).

Finally, 'migrants from newly emerging countries' are a rapidly growing category of migrants in the Amsterdam region. Since the turn of the millennium,

Indian and Chinese companies, and professionals following in their footsteps, have expanded their markets into Europe, motivated by the shortage of IT professionals in many European countries, increasing trade between Chinese and European companies and the removal of barriers to migration from less-developed countries. Most of the Chinese and Indian workers are under 35 and, compared to other migrant groups, they are more often married and have dual-income households. They work in only a few sectors, including IT and trade. Their residential preferences range from inner-city housing (one third) to suburban medium-priced accommodation. When companies do not offer relocation services to their employees, information in English about access to housing is important for this migrant category (Pethe and Hafner 2013).

In previous empirical studies on the housing situation and preferences of international knowledge workers in Amsterdam, two main bottlenecks have come to the fore. First, housing costs are considered to be very high by a vast majority of highly skilled migrants, and by younger workers in particular (O+S 2006; Pareja-Eastaway, Bontje and d'Ovidio 2010; Decisio 2011). In this regard, it is important to note that while some (particularly expats) are assisted by their company through company-owned dwellings or housing agencies, others look independently for accommodation (Decisio 2010). Many internationals live in private rented dwellings, since, because of their short period of stay, they cannot apply for tax advantages related to home ownership (part of the mortgage rent can be refunded through the income taxes) (Decisio 2011). Second, the supply of dwellings does not always match the demand and this demand is different for various sub-categories of international knowledge workers. For example, a study by Regioplan (2005) among expats in the Randstad outlined differences in residential preferences between sub-groups of different nationalities. Whereas many Western expats prefer to live in mixed areas, Asians prefer to live among their fellow countrymen, and therefore in concentrated districts. In Amstelveen (south-west of Amsterdam), for example, a concentration of Japanese workers has emerged. The preferences for housing types and residential milieus also vary according to household situation and income. Expats with families tend to prefer suburban areas, such as Amstelveen or Het Gooi. For this group of internationals, space and quietness in and around the house, shopping facilities and the proximity to international schools are the most important factors. A survey among international knowledge workers in Amstelveen uncovered the fact that the safe and quiet living environment are the main attracting factors, but the availability of an appropriate dwelling, an international school and an international community were also valued positively (Gemeente Amstelveen 2008). For single internationals, especially those in Amsterdam, the (central) city is more attractive, and bars and restaurants are often used and they prefer to have them nearby (Decisio 2010; 2011). Dwelling size is problematic, especially for expats with higher incomes, who prefer large dwellings on spacious lots, but the availability of such types of housing in the Randstad is limited (certainly in the core city of Amsterdam and its immediately surrounding municipalities) and it is generally very expensive (Regioplan 2005).

There also seems to be a difference in residential preferences based on occupation. In general, creative workers are more frequently oriented toward central-urban milieus, with a combined living and working environment, whereas internationals in ICT or other beta professions mostly prefer suburban areas (Musterd 2006; Ernst & Young 2010; Decisio 2011).

Residential preferences of international knowledge workers in the Eindhoven Metropolitan Region

A small number of studies have gained insight into the residential preferences of highly skilled knowledge migrants in the Eindhoven region. However, no comparison with Dutch knowledge workers has been made. Buiskool and Grijpstra (2006) describe a survey among international workers on their valuation of different aspects of living in Eindhoven. A clear distinction can be made between workers at the technical university, who in general are younger and have lower incomes, and knowledge workers working for private companies. Most of the respondents included in Buiskool and Grijpstra's survey live in the city of Eindhoven, while outside Eindhoven the largest concentrations are found in Veldhoven (near ASML) or outside the region, particularly in 's-Hertogenbosch, but also as far away as the Randstad. Single-family dwellings are popular, especially among international workers working for private companies. University workers, who are generally younger, more often live in apartments. The majority live in rented dwellings and around ten per cent live in dwellings owned or rented by their employer (Buiskool and Grijpstra 2006).

In Eindhoven, the supply of housing and accessibility of the housing market are considered the main bottlenecks for international migrants. Concerning supply, the international knowledge workers expressed the need for increased volume, diversity and quality of accommodation in the Eindhoven region. In particular, there was a high demand for apartments with one or two bedrooms, and also for furnished flats. In terms of accessibility, the price of housing and long waiting lists at agencies were regarded as problematic, as was the lack of information in the English language (Buiskool and Grijpstra 2006).

Vriens and Van der Dam (2011) conducted a survey among international workers in Eindhoven which showed that most knowledge workers seek housing in or close to the city centre, with a preference for independent housing, rental dwellings, apartments and studios. Also, there was a high demand for all-inclusive housing: furnished dwellings with internet and telephone connection, and energy and service costs included in the rent. In the Netherlands, housing is usually offered vacant, which implies that international workers will need to buy furniture, sometimes for only a short period. Vriens and Van der Dam's study also found, in line with the previous study, that workers at education institutions in particular encounter problems with finding appropriate housing. Their lower incomes and younger age lead them to seek cheaper housing, and, in particular, affordable dwellings outside the social rented sector are only sparsely available. Workers in private companies, on the other hand, hardly face any problems with finding accommodation. In some cases the employer pays for housing costs, and their higher income enables them to search in more expensive segments of the housing market, in which there is a large offer in both the core city and the surrounding municipalities (Vriens and Van der Dam 2011).

Data

The empirical part of this chapter is based on a study on the stated residential preferences of highly educated workers, here with a focus on international workers. The empirical study overlaps with the one presented in Chapter 5 and draws on a large self-collected survey among 2,800 workers at two large technical companies (ASML Lithography in Eindhoven and Royal Dutch Shell in Amsterdam) and in advertisement companies in both urban regions. As stated above, this chapter has a special focus on the sub-group of international workers (n=354). We focus on the residential preferences of international migrants, measured preferences for urban or suburban residential milieus, specific dwelling types and local or regional amenities.

The chapter focuses on three aspects in particular. First, the preferences for urban or suburban residential milieus are presented, measured via the ranking of district names and photographs of distinct residential milieus. Second, we focus on the preferences for specific housing types: apartments as a typical urban housing type, and (semi)-detached housing as typical suburban housing. Third, the relative importance attached to various locational factors when making a location decision is taken into account, distinguishing between hard and soft factors. Respondents were asked to express their preferences regardless of their actual place of residence or their propensity to relocate. We assume that actual residential patterns, or 'revealed preferences', may result from a lack of choice. Therefore, we are interested in the preferences people would have if they had a choice between several options. This way, it becomes possible to see if the actual housing stock meets the demands of the target group. The internationals in the study sample are generally somewhat younger than Dutch workers (average ages 38 and 46, respectively). In total, 27 per cent of respondents have a household with children, but Dutch workers more often (35 per cent) than internationals (23 per cent). Since singles are more likely to prefer apartments and urban residential milieus, we controlled for single-person households as well. Of the total population, 21 per cent are single-person households, with only minor differences between Dutch and international workers.

Two measurements of income are included: one distinguishing low-income households (less than €35,000 per year) from all others, and one distinguishing high-income households (more than €100,000 per year) from the rest. In general, 14 per cent of all respondents belong to the lowest-income group, while 21.5 per cent belong to the highest-income group. Internationals appear to have somewhat lower household incomes than Dutch workers. This relates to the lower average age and lower proportion of family households among the international group. Finally, level of education is included by distinguishing those with university education (masters or PhD degrees) from the rest.

Within the sample of 354 international knowledge workers, we distinguish between workers in technical and creative sectors, and between workers from advanced economies and other, less-advanced economies. Table 9.1 shows that a majority of the workers belong to the technical occupation group. This means that they either have a job at a technical company or work in other types of companies but have completed a technical course of study. The number of creative workers within the international group (30) is rather low.

In terms of household situation, differences are small between occupational groups, although the reference category (not technical or creative workers) counts somewhat more households with children. Also, migrants from countries with advanced economies have children somewhat more often than those from other countries. With respect to age, technical internationals appear to be slightly younger than workers in other professions. Also, a much smaller proportion of technical workers are female (32 per cent), as compared to the creative professions (53 per cent) and the reference category (61 per cent). Creative internationals much more often belong to the lowest household income categories and much less often to the highest income categories. In contrast, technical workers more often have higher incomes. Technical workers are also more often university educated: 78 per cent, as compared to 50 per cent of creatives and 61 per cent of the reference group. Finally, a large majority (77 per cent) of the international technical workers were found in the Eindhoven region, while 87 per cent of the creative internationals worked in the Amsterdam region. This can be partly explained by the different economic profiles of the two cities. Creative industries account for 4 per cent of total employment in Eindhoven, but for more than 10 per cent of total employment in Amsterdam (Rutten and Koops 2014). Whereas Amsterdam is known for its diverse economic structure, dominated by financial and business services (26 per cent of regional employment), Eindhoven is known as a 'tech-pole', where high-tech industries account for 19 per cent of total regional employment (Sleutjes 2013).

Analysis: stated residential preferences of knowledge migrants

Preferences for urban or suburban residential milieus

As a measurement of preferences for urban or suburban areas, respondents were first asked to rank a list of names of residential districts from the district where they would want to live most (1) to the least popular district (10). These districts could be subdivided into inner-city, urban-edge or suburban districts. Based on the average ranking given to different districts in the Amsterdam Metropolitan Area (see Chapter 5 for a more detailed description of these districts) by different groups, the six most popular districts turned out to be exactly the same for Dutch and international workers. The three districts within the ring road in Amsterdam (Jordaan, Watergraafsmeer and Indische Buurt) and the City of Haarlem are the most popular choices (Table 9.2). However, although the Jordaan district in the centre of Amsterdam is the most popular district among both categories of

Table 9.1 Population characteristics of international knowledge workers

	Total response	Singles	Households with children	Average age	Female	Low household incomes < 35.000	High household incomes >100.000	Education: university or higher	Eindhoven
Technical occupation	157	24%	24%	34.1	32%	12%	22%	78%	77%
Creative occupation	30	17%	23%	41.6	53%	35%	4%	50%	13%
Other occupation	76	24%	29%	44.9	61%	26%	15%	61%	26%
From advanced economies	156	24%	29%	37.2	46%	13%	12%	67%	45%
From other countries	142	21%	22%	39.3	41%	25%	23%	74%	62%

Source: URD-HELP survey.

workers, it has a higher average ranking from international workers than from Dutch workers. Clearly, the suburban and rural residential milieus are the least popular districts for both groups of knowledge workers.

Internationals from advanced economies are somewhat more urban oriented than those from other countries. The Jordaan district, the most centrally located urban residential milieu is ranked higher by this group, and also the relatively centrally located Watergraafsmeer and Indische Buurt districts are somewhat more popular among them. At the same time, the urban-edge district of Buitenveldert is the second most popular district among internationals from other countries, while the suburbs of Almere/ Hoofddorp – the least popular areas among Dutch workers and migrants from advanced economies – are also relatively more popular with this group (Table 9.2).

In the Eindhoven region, the three least popular districts are the same for Dutch and international workers (Table 9.3). The inner city of Helmond – the second urban centre of the region – has by far the lowest ranking for both groups; Brandevoort, a newly built district with mostly single-family dwellings on the periphery of Helmond, and the village of Eersel are also unpopular with both Dutch and international knowledge workers. However, the differences between the two groups are greater with regard to the most popular residential locations. For Dutch workers, the inner city of Eindhoven has the highest average ranking, followed by the adjacent industrial heritage district Strijp-S. The suburb of Veldhoven, located close to the highway, the airport and some of the major employment clusters (ASML, High-Tech Campus) is the most popular location for international knowledge workers, and ranks third for Dutch knowledge workers. If a strategic location is more important for internationals than for Dutch workers, this may explain why the newly built district of Meerhoven, adjacent to Veldhoven on Eindhoven's urban edge, is slightly more popular with internationals than with Dutch workers. The second and third most popular locations for international knowledge workers are the two central urban districts: the inner city of Eindhoven and Strijp-S, which are on average ranked higher by internationals than by Dutch workers, despite the slightly lower position in their Top 10.

These results suggest that the residential preferences of both Dutch and international knowledge workers in the Eindhoven region are highly diverse. Whereas in the Amsterdam region the urban areas are especially popular, in Eindhoven both urban and suburban areas are highly sought after. A second overall conclusion is that the districts located close to the main high-tech clusters (ASML and the High-Tech Campus) where many internationals work are somewhat more popular with internationals than with Dutch workers. This suggests that, for internationals, proximity to work is at least as important as inner-city living.

In the Eindhoven region, differences in residential preferences between migrants from advanced economies and those from other countries are smaller than was the case in the Amsterdam region (Table 9.3). Still, the inner city of Eindhoven seems to be slightly more popular among migrants from advanced economies, whereas the suburban milieu of Veldhoven appeals somewhat more to migrants from other countries.

Table 9.2 Ranking of districts in the Amsterdam Metropolitan Area from most popular (1) to least popular (10): differences between Dutch and international workers

Rank	Dutch total	Avg. rank	Internationals total	Avg. rank	Internationals advanced economies	Avg. rank	Internationals other countries	Avg. rank
1	Jordaan (CU)	4.27	Jordaan (CU)	3.18	Jordaan (CU)	2.83	Jordaan (CU)	3.77
2	Watergraafsmeer (CU)	4.35	Watergraafsmeer (CU)	4.42	Watergraafsmeer (CU)	4.02	Buitenveldert (UP)	4.91
3	Haarlem (CU)	4.94	Haarlem (CU)	5.01	Indische Buurt (CU)	4.64	Haarlem (CU)	4.94
4	Indische Buurt (CU)	5.44	Indische Buurt (CU)	5.18	Haarlem (CU)	4.99	Watergraafsmeer (CU)	5.08
5	IJburg (UP)	5.55	IJburg (UP)	5.28	IJburg (UP)	5.34	IJburg (UP)	5.25
6	Buitenveldert (UP)	5.81	Buitenveldert (UP)	5.51	Buitenveldert (UP)	5.89	Almere/Hoofddorp (SU)	5.45
7	Broek in Waterland e.o. (RU)	5.83	Abcoude (RU)	6.26	Abcoude (RU)	6.05	Indische Buurt (CU)	6.04
8	Abcoude (RU)	5.89	Bussum (SU)	6.48	Broek in Waterland e.o. (RU)	6.64	Bussum (SU)	6.08
9	Bussum (SU)	6.03	Broek in Waterland e.o. (RU)	6.77	Bussum (SU)	6.72	Abcoude (RU)	6.57
10	Almere/Hoofddorp (SU)	7.01	Almere/Hoofddorp (SU)	6.92	Almere/Hoofddorp (SU)	7.88	Broek in Waterland e.o. (RU)	6.92

Source: URD-HELP survey.

Notes: CU: Central urban residential milieu
UP: Urban periphery
SU: Suburban residential milieu
RU: Village/rural residential milieu

Table 9.3 Ranking of districts in the Eindhoven region from most popular (1) to least popular (10): differences between Dutch and international workers

Rank	Dutch total	Avg. rank	Internationals total	Avg. rank	Internationals advanced economies	Avg. rank	Internationals other countries	Avg. rank
1	Binnenstad Eindhoven (CU)	4.15	Veldhoven (SU)	3.18	Binnenstad Eindhoven (CU)	3.63	Veldhoven (SU)	3.25
2	Strijp-S (CU)	4.25	Binnenstad Eindhoven (CU)	4.42	Strijp-S (CU)	4.02	Binnenstad Eindhoven (CU)	4.19
3	Veldhoven (SU)	4.56	Strijp-S (CU)	5.01	Veldhoven (SU)	4.1	Strijp-S (CU)	4.42
4	Woensel Zuid (CU)	5.55	Meerhoven (UP)	5.18	Meerhoven (UP)	5.03	Meerhoven (UP)	4.46
5	Geldrop (SU)	5.56	Woensel Zuid (CU)	5.28	Woensel Zuid (CU)	6.05	Woensel Zuid (CU)	4.74
6	Meerhoven (UP)	5.57	Best (SU)	5.51	Geldrop (SU)	6.23	Best (SU)	5.46
7	Best (SU)	5.64	Geldrop (SU)	6.26	Eersel (RU)	6.31	Geldrop (SU)	6.36
8	Eersel (RU)	6.57	Eersel (RU)	6.48	Best (SU)	6.74	Eersel (RU)	7.13
9	Brandevoort (UP)	7.08	Brandevoort (UP)	6.77	Brandevoort (UP)	7.08	Brandevoort (UP)	7.15
10	Binnenstad Helmond (CU)	9.0	Binnenstad Helmond (CU)	6.92	Binnenstad Helmond (CU)	8.4	Binnenstad Helmond (CU)	8.31

Source: URD-HELP survey.

Notes: CU: Central urban residential milieu
UP: Urban periphery
SU: Suburban residential milieu
RU: Village/rural residential milieu

A second measurement of urban or suburban residential preferences was done via a ranking of ten photographs (see Chapter 5), representing urban milieus and suburban milieus. The 'urban pictures' can in turn be subdivided into historic inner-city milieus and modern-medium and high-rise districts. Respondents had no knowledge of where these pictures were taken; they could in fact be anywhere in the Netherlands. The aim of this picture ranking was to investigate which types of residential milieus would be preferred by specific groups of knowledge workers, without a bias resulting from knowing the exact location.

Dutch and international workers both have highly diverse residential preferences (Table 9.4). One of the overarching conclusions from this picture ranking is that urban high-rise milieus are among the three least popular milieus for all categories, whereas suburban and central urban milieus are among the four most popular for all categories. However, there are also a number of differences between the two categories. Although for both groups the two most popular images represent suburban residential milieus, the picture ranked third contrasts highly between the two groups. Whereas the third most popular picture among Dutch workers is a farm house, internationals prefer an inner-city canal. This indicates that international workers are slightly more urban oriented than their Dutch colleagues. Dutch workers also appear to have a stronger preference for detached housing than do internationals.

Within the group of internationals, there are differences in residential preferences between those employed in the Amsterdam Metropolitan Area and those working in the Eindhoven Metropolitan Region. Table 9.4 shows that internationals in the Amsterdam region have a stronger preference for urban residential milieus than do workers in the Eindhoven region. Among the three most popular images with internationals in Amsterdam are two images of inner-city milieus, whereas the three most popular images among internationals in Eindhoven are all suburban. This regional difference may be due to a different population composition in Eindhoven. In Amsterdam, internationals had relatively more often moved to the region because of the social and cultural climate (10 per cent), whereas only 3 per cent of internationals in Eindhoven had moved for this reason. This may indicate that the type of worker that chooses to live in Eindhoven has other priorities than a vibrant inner-city life and is therefore in general less likely to have strong preference for a highly urban milieu than is the type of worker that chooses Amsterdam. However, the sample composition may also play a role, since relatively more technical workers were found in Eindhoven and more creative workers in Amsterdam, in line with the regions' working population.

Looking at the country of origin, internationals from advanced economies and other countries identify the same three most popular districts, but in a different order. Internationals from advanced economies have a stronger preference for a central urban milieu, while the two most popular residential milieus for migrants from other countries are suburban.

In general, residential preferences are rather mixed, but highly educated people tend to have a slight preference for suburban areas. Seventy per cent of the total

Table 9.4 The three most popular residential districts based on picture ranking; differences between Dutch and international workers and within international group

Rank	Dutch total	International total	International Amsterdam	International Eindhoven	International advanced economies	International other countries
a (SU)	2	1	2	1	2	1
b (SU)	8	7	9	6	8	6
c (HU)	10	10	10	8	10	9
d (CU)	4	3	1	4	1	3
e (CU)	5	5	3	7	4	7
f (CU)	7	8	6	10	6	10
g (SU)	6	6	7	5	7	5
h (SU)	3	4	5	3	5	4
i (SU)	1	2	4	2	3	2
j (HU)	9	9	8	9	9	8

Source: URD-HELP survey.

Notes: CU = Central urban residential milieu
HU = Highrise urban residential milieu
SU = Suburban residential milieu

sample of highly skilled workers, and 59 per cent of the international knowledge workers, has a first preference for a suburban residential milieu (Figure 9.1). Within the urban residential milieus, inner-city districts are clearly more popular than high-rise districts. Despite the fact that a majority have a first preference for a suburban milieu, international workers are more urban oriented than Dutch workers. The regression analysis in Table 9.5 shows that this difference is significant. International workers are more likely to have a first preference for one of the images of urban residential milieus than are Dutch workers, even after controlling for demographic factors, occupation and work region.

It is important to know to what extent location preferences are different for various categories of households, occupational groups, countries of origin and workplaces. The regression models in Tables 9.5 and 9.6 help to answer these questions. Single-person households, workers with a university education and workers in creative industries are more likely to prefer urban residential milieus, while households with children, technical workers and workers in the Eindhoven region have a stronger preference for suburban districts. Furthermore, there is a strong regional effect: workers in the Eindhoven region are less oriented toward highly urban residential milieus. Within the migrant population, creative knowledge migrants have a first preference for urban residential milieus significantly more often than do other occupation groups (Table 9.6, model a). Also, Western migrants more often have urban residential preferences than do migrants from other places of origin (model b).

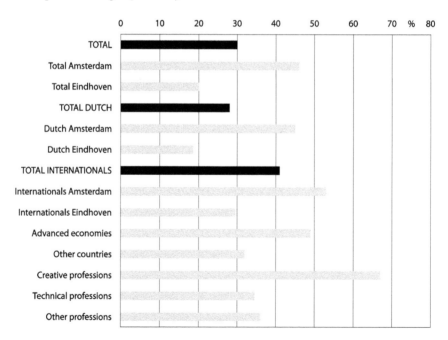

Figure 9.1 Preferences for urban, inner-city and suburban areas (differences between Dutch and international workers in the two cities)

Table 9.5 Urban areas first choice

Dependent variables	a) First preference urban area (All)	b) First preference urban area (Amsterdam only)	c) First preference urban area (Eindhoven only)
Independent variables	Exp(B)	Exp(B)	Exp(B)
Age	.990	.984	.997
Households with children	.539***	.673	.425***
Single-person households	1.501**	1.828*	1.321
High incomes	.977	.924	1.125
Low incomes	1.044	.838	1.208
University educated	1.684***	2.265***	1.229
Creative workers	2.850***	3.744***	2.166*
Technical workers	.521***	.390**	.665
Working in Eindhoven (ref. Amsterdam)	.320***	X	X
International worker (ref. raised in Netherlands)	1.488*	1.157	1.907**
Constant	1.128	1.240	1.907**
R-square	.201	.166	.085

Source: URD-HELP survey.

Note: *** $p<0.001$; ** $p<0.01$; * $p<0.05$

The popularity of suburban residential milieus is confirmed by a third type of measurement: the response to the statement 'I would rather live in a big house in the suburbs than in a small apartment in the city'. In general, 54 per cent of the respondents agree or strongly agree with this statement (Figure 9.2) and are believed to have stronger suburban preferences than those who do not. Again, differences between internationals and Dutch workers, on the one hand, and inter-regional differences between Amsterdam and Eindhoven, on the other hand, can be observed. Dutch workers in Eindhoven agree with the statement most often (62 per cent), whereas internationals in Amsterdam are the least likely to agree (31 per cent).

The model in Table 9.7 shows that the differences between Dutch and international workers, and between workers in the two city-regions, are also significant. Within the group of migrants, confirming our previous findings, Western migrants are less likely, and technical workers more likely, to agree with this statement (Table 9.8). In line with previous findings, households with children are more likely to agree with the statement. Having children clearly stimulates suburban residential preferences; only in Amsterdam, where the trend is that families with children increasingly prefer to stay in the city (Boterman 2013), this relationship is not significant. Furthermore, single-person house-holds generally prefer an apartment in the city over a larger house in the suburbs, and suburban preferences increase with age and are lower for workers who have completed a university education.

Table 9.6 Urban areas ranked as first choice: differences within the international knowledge migrant population

Dependent variable	a) First preference: urban milieu (with different occupation groups)	b) First preference: urban milieu (with different origin groups)
Independent variables	*Standardized B*	*Standardized B*
Gender = female	−.127	−.147
Age	−.025	−.015
Household with children	−1.154**	−.921*
Single-person household	.701	.536
High household income (> €100,000)	.549	.198
Low household income (< €35,000)	−.273	.080
Education: master's or PhD	.525	.504
Works in Eindhoven Metropolitan Region (ref. Amsterdam Metropolitan Area)	.550	−.949**
Occupation other sector (ref.)		X
Occupation creative sector	1.694**	X
Occupation technical sector	−.477	X
Country of origin: advanced economy (ref. other countries)	X	.696*
Constant	.634	.076
Model fit R²	.232	.179

Source: URD-HELP survey.

Note: *** $p<0.001$; ** $p<0.01$; * $p<0.05$

Housing preferences

In terms of housing preferences, international knowledge workers almost twice as often as Dutch skilled workers have a first preference for (upper level) apartments (Figure 9.3), while 38 per cent of the internationals have a first preference for (semi)-detached housing, nearly equal to the proportion of Dutch skilled workers (42 per cent).

Within the group of internationals, differences between Western and other migrants are relatively small, but differences are greater between occupational categories. Internationals active in the creative sector have a stronger preference for apartments (63 per cent first choice) than do internationals in technical (30 per cent) and other professions (33 per cent). At the same time, creative internationals much less frequently prefer (semi)-detached dwellings (13 per cent), which are particularly popular among internationals in technical occupations (50 per cent). An additional regression analysis shows that demographic factors also play a role in housing preferences, which is in line with expectations. The preference for apartments seems to decrease with age and is also lower for households with children. A preference for apartments is also less likely among internationals in the Eindhoven region, as compared to the Amsterdam Metropolitan Area.

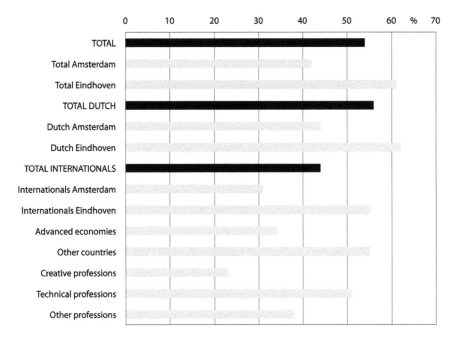

Figure 9.2 Response to statement 'I would rather live in a big house in the suburbs than in a small apartment in the city': differences between Dutch and international workers in Amsterdam and Eindhoven

Table 9.7 Rather a big house in the suburbs than a small apartment in the city: differences between Dutch and international workers in the two city regions

Dependent variables	a) Agree with statement (All)	b) Agree with statement (Amsterdam only)	c) Agree with statement (Eindhoven only)
Independent variables	Exp(B)	Exp(B)	Exp(B)
Age	1.016**	1.020*	1.014*
Households with children	1.777***	1.358	2.160***
Single-person household	.518***	.577*	.487***
High household income (> €100,000)	.964	.947	.992
Low household income (< €35,000)	1.128	.933	1.313
Education: master's or PhD	.599***	.443***	.743
Creative workers	.491**	.458*	.533
Technical workers	3.319***	2.968***	3.543***
Working in Eindhoven (ref. Amsterdam)	2.066***	X	X
International worker (ref. raised in the Netherlands)	.618**	.738	.533**
Constant	.386**	.410	.733
R-square	.201	.155	.162

Source: URD-HELP survey.

Note: *** *p<0.001; ** p<0.01; * p<0.05*

Table 9.8 Rather a big house in the suburbs than a small apartment in the city: differences within the international knowledge migrant population

Dependent variables	a) Rather a big house in the suburbs than a small apartment in the city (with different occupation groups)	b) Rather a big house in the suburbs than a small apartment in the city (with different origin groups)
Independent variables	Standardized B	Standardized B
Gender = female	.165	−.196
Age	.015	.004
Household with children	.846*	.970**
Single-person household	−1.017*	−.819*
High household income (> €100,000)	−.109	.174
Low household income (< €35,000)	.488	.193
Education: master's or PhD	−.730*	−.608
Works in Eindhoven Metropolitan Region (ref. Amsterdam Metropolitan Area	.499	.891**
Occupation other sector (ref.)		X
Occupation creative sector	−.770	X
Occupation technical sector	.968*	X
Country of origin: advanced economy (ref. other countries)	X	−.868**
Constant	−1.219	−.106
Model fit R^2	.213	.215

Source: URD-HELP survey.

Note: *** $p<0.001$; ** $p<0.01$; * $p<0.05$

Most decisive factors when making a location choice

In this section, the relative importance of hard and soft location aspects for making a location decision will be addressed. We will first take into consideration the importance attached to various regional aspects, on a scale from 1 to 4. After that, we present a ranking of location factors that are most decisive when choosing a new residential location. Here we distinguish between Dutch and international workers, on the one hand, and between different migrant categories, on the other hand.

In Figure 9.4, the importance of various regional characteristics and amenities for Dutch and international workers is measured on a scale from 1 to 4. A high ranking indicates that an aspect is on average considered important and a low average ranking stands for low importance. The most notable finding is that cultural amenities are clearly considered less important than public safety, daily

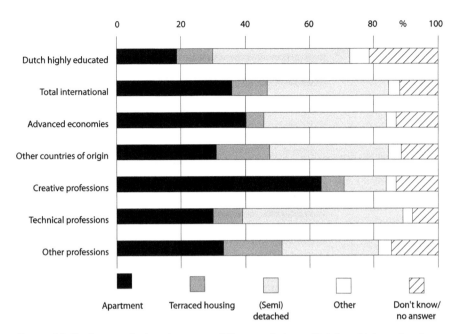

Figure 9.3 Preferences for housing types: differences between Dutch and international
knowledge workers and between different categories of internationals

shopping facilities and public green space, on the soft side, as well as accessibility
(by public transport) and the availability of affordable housing on the hard side.
Both for internationals and for Dutch workers, public safety is the highest-ranked
aspect at the regional level, followed by access to stores for daily grocery shopping. At the regional level, the role of soft conditions should therefore not be
over-rated. The cultural amenities are among the lowest-ranked aspects by both
Dutch and international workers, with only minimal differences between the two
groups. Although for most aspects differences in average ranking between Dutch
and international workers are small, we see that accessibility by public transport
and affordable housing are clearly regarded as more important by internationals
than by Dutch workers. In contrast, accessibility by car is clearly more important
for Dutch workers than for international workers.

An additional analysis has shown that, in general, both Dutch workers and
international workers are rather satisfied with almost all regional aspects, and
there are only minor differences between Dutch and international workers. The
only exception is 'availability of affordable housing'. Both groups, but especially international workers, are dissatisfied with this aspect. Dissatisfaction is the
greatest for internationals in the Amsterdam region and for those working in the
creative industries. The low rating, combined with the high importance attached
to this aspect, justifies structural policy attention to affordable housing.

A ranking of the most decisive location aspects confirms that soft location factors play, at most, a secondary role in choice of residential location. These factors

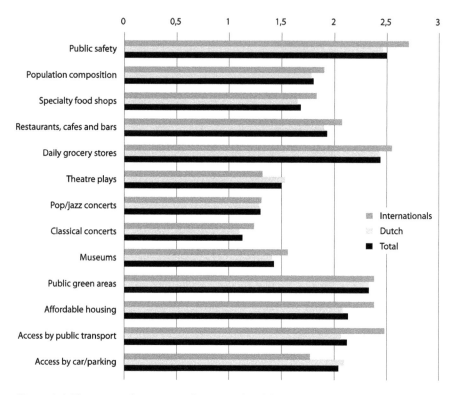

Figure 9.4 The average importance given to regional factors, on a scale of 1-4:
           differences between Dutch and international workers

can be subdivided into aspects of the house, the neighbourhood and the location
relative to amenities and networks. This has been done through a ranking from 1
(least often mentioned) to 21 (most often mentioned). Table 9.9 makes clear that
for both Dutch and international knowledge workers, a quiet residential environment is the most important factor. In general, the characteristics of the dwelling
itself, such as costs, space and ownership, appear to be more important than aspects
of the neighbourhood, which play only a minor role in the decision-making process. Only the make-up of the population (for Dutch workers) and the proximity
of daily shopping facilities (for internationals) are mentioned regularly among the
three most decisive factors, although both are not among the five most mentioned
aspects. In terms of location, proximity to work (especially for internationals)
and proximity to the city centre are mentioned often as decisive location aspects.
Opinions are varied between Dutch and international workers with respect to having a private garden: for Dutch knowledge workers, this is the main factor, together
with a quiet residential environment, but it ranks sixth among internationals.

    Within the group of international knowledge workers differences are greater.
Western migrants on average have a stronger preference for a central location
than do non-Western migrants: the distance to the city centre is more important

Table 9.9 Which aspects of the house, neighbourhood or strategic location are the most decisive when choosing a new place of residence? Ranking from 1 to 21, per category

	Dutch highly educated	*Total inter- national*	*Advanced economies*	*Other countries of origin*	*Creative professions*	*Technical professions*	*Other professions*
Dwelling characteristics							
Private garden	1	6	8	5	12	6	4
Building style and architecture	15	12	12	12	7	11	15
Being home-owner	5	3	1	4	2	3	5
No up or downstairs neighbours	9	15	18	11	9	15	12
Relatively low housing costs	4	2	4	2	2	4	2
Spacious dwelling	3	4	4	5	6	5	3
Open view	12	13	12	15	12	17	11
Characteristics of neighbourhoods and amenities							
Composition of neighbourhood population	8	10	11	8	9	12	6
Public green areas and parks	13	11	10	12	12	10	14
Quiet residential environment	1	1	3	1	4	1	1
Bakery, butcher, green grocer within walking distance	11	8	6	8	8	7	8
Good bookstore	18	16	14	16	12	13	15
Architecture and building period	21	21	21	21	20	21	21
Strategic location of dwelling							
Close to work	6	4	7	3	9	2	7
Close to highway	20	20	20	20	20	18	20
Close to public transport hub	14	9	9	7	4	9	8
Close to/in city centre	7	7	2	14	1	8	8
Close to relatives	16	18	16	17	12	18	17
Close to friends	17	17	15	17	12	13	19
Close to nature areas	10	14	16	8	12	15	12

Source: URD-HELP survey.

to them than a quiet residential environment. Also, home-ownership is more important to them than for the non-Western group. However, low housing costs, proximity to work and having a private garden are more important for non-Western migrants.

The various occupational categories also show different patterns. For example, creative workers tend to attach more importance to proximity to the city centre and public transport nodes, and less to a quiet residential environment, than do the other groups. For the technical occupation group, a location close to work is more important, while workers in other occupations attach more value to a private garden and a spacious dwelling.

Conclusions

This chapter has looked for answers to the following research questions:

- To what extent are preferences for residential milieus different between Dutch and international knowledge workers, and between different groups of international workers?
- Which factors are the main considerations when looking for a new place to live, and what differences are there between Dutch and international workers and between different categories of international workers?

The research findings in this chapter have shown that the role of soft location factors such as 'diversity' and 'tolerant atmosphere' in directly attracting and retaining knowledge workers has been greatly over-estimated by influential scientific literature (Glaeser, Kolko and Saiz 2001; Clark *et al.* 2002; Florida 2002) and by the policy agenda concerning international talent. However, if the concept 'amenities' is stretched to include aspects such as the intra-regional variation of quietness in the residential environment, safety, daily shopping facilities, accessibility and affordable housing, then amenities play a much more important role in location decisions. 'Soft' conditions in cultural domains, however, are regarded as important by only a minority, and this also holds for international knowledge workers.

Another interesting finding is that affordable housing is seen as an important regional factor, but as a problem as well, especially in the Amsterdam region, and to a larger degree by internationals than by Dutch workers. Internationals employed in creative industries are particularly dissatisfied with this factor. Recent trends, such as the sale of social housing to make the city more attractive to middle-income groups, might make the city even less accessible for this highly urban-oriented group of international workers.

Apart from a quiet residential environment, in particular the characteristics of the dwelling itself play a role in the decision-making process. With respect to the location of dwellings, proximity to work and – to a lesser degree – to the city centre are counted among the main considerations. In these domains, differences between Dutch and international workers are generally small. The main differences are related to having a private garden (more important for Dutch), home-ownership (especially for Dutch and Western migrants), low housing costs (especially non-Western migrants) the proximity to work (especially technical internationals) and proximity to the city centre (creative and Western migrants). International knowledge workers have significantly stronger urban residential preferences than do Dutch-raised workers. Not only do they more often have a first preference for urban milieus, but they also less often prefer a large house in the suburbs over a small apartment in the city. Internationals have a first preference for apartments twice as often as do Dutch workers. However, it should be noted that in absolute terms a majority of internationals have a first preference for a suburban residential environment as well, and the proportion of internationals that prefer a (semi)-detached dwelling is similar to the proportion that prefer an apartment. Thus, residential preferences are also highly diverse within the group of international knowledge workers. Just like the 'creative class' in general, the international knowledge workers are by no means a homogeneous group with uniform housing preferences.

In particular, the stronger orientation of technical knowledge workers toward suburban milieus and the stronger preference of creative internationals for urban milieus and apartments stand out. In addition, there are differences based on descent, since migrants from advanced economies have a stronger preference for urban residential milieus. Furthermore, household characteristics strongly influence residential preferences. In particular, households with children relatively often prefer suburban residential locations. In this respect, the findings of this study are in line with previous studies discussed in Chapter 2, which discussed the diversity within the creative class (e.g. Kotkin 2000; Markusen 2006; Andersen *et al.* 2010; Frenkel *et al.* 2013), and add to this knowledge a specific focus on international knowledge workers.

Finally, a large difference between the two regions comes to the fore with respect to preferences for residential milieus and dwelling types, even after controlling for personal characteristics, occupation and descent. In general, internationals in the Eindhoven region have a stronger preference for suburban residential milieus than do workers in the Amsterdam region. This reflects that both regions attract different types of workers.

We agree with Servillo, Atkinson and Russo (2012) and Borén and Young (2013) that no 'one-size-fits-all' policy should be implemented for attracting international knowledge workers. Also, for international knowledge migrants, it is important for policy makers to have a clear picture of the type of worker that is coming to their city or region, with respect to occupation, descent and household situation. Many urban policy makers stress the importance of urban residential milieus and cultural amenities. In the city of Amsterdam, enlarging the central urban residential milieu is one of the priorities of the planning department, and Eindhoven is also actively seeking to improve its image as a 'large urban centre' by adding high-density residential developments and stimulating cultural events. However, based on our study, these efforts are most likely to attract and retain only specific subsections of international knowledge workers, mostly those with one – or a combination – of the following characteristics: young, without children, from advanced countries and working in the creative industries. It should be noted that a majority of the international knowledge workers, and households with children and workers in technical professions in particular, prefer a single-family dwelling in a quiet suburban environment. It is thus important that any local or regional housing policy should strike a balance between urban and suburban residential milieus, with different types of housing, in order to satisfy the demands of the entire, heterogeneous group of international knowledge workers. Especially if a city has a technical economic profile (as in Eindhoven), investment in urban residential milieus should not be at the expense of the region's suburban qualities.

References

Andersen, KV, Bugge, MM, Hansen, HK, Isaksen, A and Raunio, M 2010, One size fits all? Applying the creative class thesis onto a Nordic context. *European Planning Studies* 18(10), 1591–1609.

Beaverstock, JV 1990, New international labour markets: The case of chartered accountants. *Area* 22, 151–158.

Beaverstock, JV 1994, Rethinking skilled international labor migration – World cities and banking organizations. *Geoforum* 25(3), 323–338.

Beaverstock, JV 1996, Revisiting high-waged labor-market demand in the global cities – British professional and managerial workers in New York City. *International Journal of Urban and Regional Research* 20, 422–445.

Beaverstock, JV 2002, Transnational elites in global cities: British expatriates in Singapore's financial district. *Geoforum* 33(4), 525–538.

Bontje, M, Pethe, H, Petrasch, F and Tuppinger, K 2009, *Amsterdam: an attractive creative knowledge region? The view of transnational migrants.* Amsterdam: AMIDSt, University of Amsterdam.

Borén, T and Young, C 2013, The migration dynamics of the 'creative class': Evidence from a study of artists in Stockholm, Sweden. *Annals of the Association of American Geographers* 103(1), 195–210.

Boterman, WR 2013, Dealing with diversity: Middle-class family households and the issue of 'Black' and 'White' schools in Amsterdam. *Urban Studies* 50(6), 1130–1147.

Buiskool, B and Grijpstra, D 2006, *Attracting and embedding international knowledge workers in the Eindhoven Region: A study on the composition, perceptions and expectations.* Research voor Beleid BV, Leiden.

Clark, TN, Lloyd, R, Wong, KK and Jain, P 2002, Amenities drive urban growth. *Journal of Urban Affairs* 24(5), 493–515.

Decisio 2010, *Internationals in Amsterdam: Kwantitatieve nulmeting in Amsterdam.* Amsterdam: Decisio.

Decisio 2011, *Internationals in de Metropoolregio Amsterdam, Literatuurstudie en analyse van de statistiek over de (huisvesting van) internationals in de MRA.* Amsterdam: Decisio.

Ernst & Young 2010, *Hoe woont de creatieve kenniswerker* [*What are the housing conditions of the creative knowledge worker?*].

Faggian, A and McCann, P 2006, Human capital flows and regional knowledge assets – A simultaneous equation approach. *Oxford Economic Papers* 52, 475–500.

Florida, R 2002, *The rise of the creative class and how it's transforming work, leisure, community and everyday life.* New York: Basic Books.

Fratesi, U 2014, Editorial: The mobility of high-skilled workers – Causes and consequences. *Regional Studies* 48(10), 1587–1591.

Frenkel, A, Bendit, E and Kaplan, S 2013, The linkage between the lifestyle of knowledge-workers and their intra-metropolitan residential choice: A clustering approach based on self-organizing maps. *Computers, Environment and Urban Systems* 39, 151–169.

Gemeente Amstelveen 2008, *De internationale dimensie van Amstelveen.* Gemeente Amstelveen: Staf Statistiek en Onderzoek.

Glaeser, EL, Kolko, J and Saiz, A 2001, Consumer city. *Journal of Economic Geography* 1, 27–50.

Helbrecht, I 2004, Bare geographies in knowledge societies – Creative cities as text and piece of art: Two eyes, one vision. *Built Environment* 30(3), 194–203.

Hercog, M 2008, The role of the state in attracting highly-skilled migrants; The case of the Netherlands. *Eipascope* 2008(3), 19–24.

Kotkin, J 2000, *The new geography: How the digital revolution is reshaping the American landscape.* New York: Random House.

Markusen, A 2006, Urban development and the politics of a creative class: Evidence from a study of artists. *Environment and Planning A* 38, 1921–1940.

Musterd, S 2006, Segregation, urban space and the resurgent city. *Urban Studies* 43(8), 1325–1340.

Pareja-Eastaway, M, Bontje, M and d'Ovidio, M 2010, Attracting young and high-skilled workers: Amsterdam, Milan and Barcelona. In: Musterd, S and Murie, A (eds) *Making competitive cities*, 192–207. Chichester: Wiley-Blackwell.

Pethe, H and Hafner, S 2013, Internationalisation and policies towards transnational migration. In: Musterd, S and Kovács, Z (eds) *Place-making and policies for competitive cities*, 239–261. Chichester: Wiley-Blackwell.

Regioplan 2005, *Spannend wonen? Woonwensen van expats in de Randstad Holland.*

Rutten, P and Koops, O 2014, *Monitor Creatieve Industrie 2014.* Stichting iMMovator Cross Media Network.

Scott, AJ 2006, Creative cities: conceptual issues and policy questions. *Journal of Urban Affairs* 28(1), 1–17.

Servillo, L, Atkinson, R. and Russo, AP 2012, Territorial attractiveness in EU urban and spatial policy: A critical review and future research agenda. *European Urban and Regional Studies* 19(4), 349–365.

Sleutjes, B 2013, *The hard and soft Side of European Knowledge Regions, HELP UVA VU Report, no 1.* Amsterdam: University of Amsterdam.

Vertovec, S 2007, *Circular migration: the way forward in global policy?* Oxford: International Migration Institute, University of Oxford.

Vriens, J and Van der Dam, S 2011, *Huisvesting van de International Knowledge Workers in Zuidoost-Brabant, Eindhoven; Een onderzoek naar woonwensen.* Eindhoven: Gemeente Eindhoven.

10 International students and the Netherlands

Or Levkovich, Jan Rouwendal and Carla Sá

Introduction

Recent years have witnessed the growth of international flows of students and, consequently, the international student migration phenomenon has gained importance as a research topic. Attracting international students and encouraging them to stay in the country of study is becoming an increasingly important target for regional policy, as human capital plays a central role in regional economic growth (Glaeser and Saiz 2003; Moretti 2012). In this chapter we investigate three main dimensions of international students' migration into the Netherlands. First, we examine the factors which influence the decision of foreign students to select the Netherlands for the purpose of their studies. We do so by estimating a gravity model over a cross-section of data of international student flows between OECD countries, and attempt to explain this flow using several destination-country characteristics. Second, we use data from NUFFIC, the Netherlands organization for international cooperation in higher education, to examine the choices of international students with respect to higher education institutions in the Netherlands and to compare them with the choices of local students. Finally, we use unique data from Statistics Netherlands to investigate the location preferences of international students in the Netherlands, their choice of residential municipalities during studies and after graduation, and their tendency to stay in the Netherlands after graduation.

Literature review

Three main theories have been pointed to as the ones explaining student choices in general and the mobility decisions of higher education students in particular (Sá *et al.* 2004; Van Bouwel and Veugelers 2010). Human capital theory states that students recognize the investment value of education; student migration decisions are taken when the expected returns and perceived benefits, such as future labour income and/or employability, exceed the costs. From the consumption theory perspective, price and income matter; students may then be guided by the attractiveness of the university location in terms of leisure offer and amenities. Student decisions can be analysed in the conventional signalling framework as well. Student mobility decision functions, in this context, as a sign of productivity.[1]

Most of the existing empirical evidence on international student mobility comes from studies on international migration as a whole, as well as from studies on interstate migration for the US (Bessey 2012). Most current literature on international student mobility refers to student flows from developing countries to industrialized countries (Van Bouwel and Veugelers 2010). A number of studies analyse student migration to a single country. The US is often the case (Lee and Tan 1984; Agarwal and Winkler 1985; Aslanbeigui and Montecinos 1998; Szelényi 2006; Dreher and Poutvaara 2011), as well as the UK[2] (Naidoo 2007; Soo and Elliott 2010), which comes as no surprise because these two countries are in the list of top international student destinations. Although less common, there is also some research on mobility to other countries, as, for example, Ireland (Bourke 2000) and Germany (Bessey 2012). There are also studies focusing on student mobility from a single country or from a group of countries. For instance, Hercog and van der Laar (2013) analysed the outgoing movements of Indian students, while Mazzarol and Soutar (2002) looked at the push and pull factors determining the decisions of Taiwanese, Indian, Chinese and Indonesian students to study overseas. More recently, Perkins and Neumayer (2014) have analysed international student flows based on a large sample of country pairs, in an attempt to approach a global sample. Empirical studies on international student mobility have mainly concentrated on its determinants and effects.

Determinants of international student mobility

The factors that influence the decision to study abroad, as well as the choice of a destination, are the two facets of student mobility under investigation (Mazzarol and Soutar 2002). The methodology applied varies across studies; for instance, count data models are used by Perkins and Neumayer (2013), whereas Van Bouwel and Veugelers (2010), González *et al.* (2011), Bessey (2012) and Felbermayr and Reczkowski (2012) estimate gravity models. The main determinants and motivations under analysis refer to the conditions in both the origin and the destination countries. Great benefits are attached to the experience of studying abroad, which individuals perceive as a boost to their careers either in their home countries or in the international job market (Hercog and van de Laar 2013). Obviously, such benefits vary with the quality of the institution attended.

Recent literature has devoted some attention to the role of institutional and programme quality (see, for instance, Van Bouwel and Veugelers 2010). Finding an overseas programme that is better than local programmes is essential to the decision to go abroad of students from Taiwan, India and Indonesia, although less relevant for Chinese students; but the quality of the education provided by the host country is very important for all students (Mazzarol and Soutar 2002). A positive effect of destination university quality is also found when a broader set of countries is considered: González *et al.* (2011) find a positive impact of quality on the decisions of Erasmus students, whereas Perkins and Neumayer (2013) achieve the same result using a larger sample covering countries from all regions. Soo and Elliott (2010) confirm the importance of quality rankings for student choice to study in the UK and, more interestingly, they conclude that Business Studies and Engineering students are influenced by different quality indicators (namely, subject-specific rankings). According to Mazzarol and Soutar (2002), it is not only the quality but also the reputation[3] of the institution where the student is to study that motivates student destination choices.

University quality is a subjective issue, such that there is not a consensual definition and measure for it. Measures based on the number and/or the quota of national higher education institutions in the top group of an international ranking such as the Academic Ranking of World Universities (also known as Shanghai ranking) are often used as proxies for quality (see, for instance, Van Bouwel and Veugelers 2010; González *et al.* 2011; Beine *et al.* 2013; Perkins and Neumayer 2013). Van Bouwel and Veugelers (2010) use, as robustness checks, alternative quality measures based on the number of citations received by each country's scientific publications (a proxy for research quality) and the number of institutions a country has in the *Times Higher Education Supplement* ranking (a proxy for the quantity of high teaching-quality institutions in the country).

Assessing the role of the migration costs is crucial for understanding the determinants of the international student mobility decision-making process. Distance is an apparent cost of migration, which has received ample attention in the migration literature. A common result, supported by several studies, is that distance deters student movements over space, as distant study destinations are associated with higher travel costs. Distance is usually operationalized by means of geodesic distance between country capitals or the most important agglomerations in the origin and destination countries (Van Bouwel and Veugelers 2010; González *et al.* 2011; Bessey 2012; Perkins and Neumayer 2013).

According to Bessey (2012), distance can also be seen as a rough measure of cultural similarity, because geographic proximity tends to imply similar language and values. The relationship between the host and the sending countries has been shown to determine student decisions. The migration costs are lower and, consequently, the student flows are stronger when moving between neighbouring countries and/or countries that have a common language (see, for instance, Van Bouwel and Veugelers 2010; González *et al.* 2011; Perkins and Neumayer 2013). Old colonial ties lower those costs as well (Lee and Tan 1984). This could happen because students have more and better information on countries to which their own country is linked, or because they perceive the institutions located in their former colonial master as more prestigious, or even because they are entitled for scholarships in those countries (Perkins and Neumayer 2013).

Knowledge and awareness of the host country are often gained via referrals by friends and relatives, which work as facilitating factors for student international mobility (Mazzarol and Soutar 2002). Pimpa (2003) further explores the influence of family and friends for Thai students and concludes that it influences the decision to study abroad, as well as the choice of country, city, university and study programme.

The size of the migrant network at the destination is known to reduce the migration costs. The stock of migrants from each country of origin living in the country of destination is often used as an indicator for this variable. Both the total migration stock and the stock of highly educated migrants have been used as such. Beine *et al.* (2013) found a strong network effect, which increases with the level of education of the network at destination.

Economic and social factors are among the most referred-to country push-pull factors, which have been taken into account in the majority of previous literature (Pimpa 2003; Shanka *et al.* 2006; Salisbury *et al.* 2009; Findlay *et al.* 2011). The socio-economic push-pull factors frequently include the gross domestic product (GDP) *per capita* ratio between the home and the host countries and the average schooling ratio between the two countries. The lower the GDP *per capita* in the country of origin relative to the host country (the US), the more attractive it is to migrate (Dreher and Poutvaara 2011). According to Perkins and Neumayer (2013), income in destination countries is among the most influential factors. Jena and Reilly (2013) showed that bilateral exchange rates are more relevant in determining student flows to the UK than the GDP *per capita* in the origin country.

The costs of education that students have to bear is an obvious determinant of students' decisions. Tuition fees are a non-negligible part of those costs, which has to be taken into account when analysing students' decisions. Despite several studies confirming the negative effect of tuition fees on the size of student flows (see, for instance, Van Bouwel and Veugelers 2010), the results are not consensual across studies. Beine *et al.* (2013) found a positive impact of the fees; it can be argued that this is due to the fact that fees act as a quality signal. Soo and Elliott (2010) found that fees hardly have any impact on application decisions; the impact of fees is significant only if the relationship is non-linear, and in that case it may depend on the university's quality. Fees are not the only education costs that students have to pay. Students are also sensitive to the living costs (including rent and food) at the destination, as they impact on the affordability of education (González *et al.* 2011; Beine *et al.* 2013).

Other factors, usually related to migration decisions, have also been taken into account in studies on the international mobility of students. For instance, differences in climate conditions are relevant for Erasmus students, which can be interpreted as the students' willingness to use those mobility programmes to facilitate their access to leisure activities (González *et al.* 2011). The level of democracy (from autocratic to democratic) determines different types of political regimes, with obvious consequences on students' mobility decisions. According to Perkins and Neumayer (2013), a lack of democracy in the country of origin encourages students to go abroad. Political stability in developing countries appears to play a role in the demand for student visas to the UK (Jena and Reilly 2013).

Effects of international student mobility

Studies on the effects of student mobility across borders have also analysed its consequences for future labour market performance in terms of returns and employability. In general, employees who have graduated abroad benefit from higher wages than home-country graduates would receive (see, for instance, Wiers-Jenssen and Try 2005; Rodrigues 2013).

But the consequences of international student migration go beyond labour market performance issues. Whether the student who went to study abroad returns to the country of origin after finishing his studies is of some concern, as it has important quantity and quality implications on the country's stock of human capital. According to the existing literature, studying abroad is an important predictor of subsequent migration, namely migration to work (Parey and Waldinger 2011; Dreher and Poutvaara 2011; Bertrand-Cloodt *et al.* 2012) or to take a PhD (Bertrand-Cloodt *et al.* 2012). Felbermayr and Reczkowski (2012) estimate an average of 70% student retention rate, which implies that the costs of educating foreign students are partly compensated by the availability of an important source of foreign skilled employees.

There is some evidence showing different behaviour for different types of students. First, there appear to be some differences according to the degree the student holds. Comay (1970), for instance, concluded that among Canadian BA graduates studying abroad the probability of returning home is about one third; whereas among PhDs who took their degree outside Canada that likelihood is between 20% and 25%. Nevertheless, a common result is that studying abroad may induce brain drain (see Oosterbeek and Webbink 2011, for a study based on Dutch data). Second, the most disadvantaged students are those who benefit most from experience abroad (see Parey and Waldinger 2011, for a study on Erasmus students).

Several factors may determine the decision whether or not to return to the country of origin, including individual and family factors, labour market features and country/region/city characteristics. The role of family and individual characteristics cannot be ignored. The student's gender, age, race and nationality are all characteristics that may make the student more ready to stay abroad. Students who find a partner in the host country are less likely to leave that country after finishing their studies (Bijwaard and Wang 2013).

Labour market reasons for staying abroad after a period of study have been the topic of a number of papers. Higher wages offered in the host country appear to increase the probability of non-return (see, for example, Gungor and Tansel 2008, for Turkish students). When a migrant student finds a job in the host country, she is less likely to go back to her home country (see, for instance, Bijwaard and Wang 2013, on a study on the inflow of foreign students to the Netherlands).

Country/region/city characteristics have been shown to have an impact on migrants' decisions on returning to home countries (Gottlieb and Joseph 2006; Brown and Scott 2012; Rodríguez-Pose and Ketterer 2012). When students from developing countries go to study in developed countries with, in general, more organized environments, return to the home country is less likely (Gungor and Tansel 2008). The social climate is crucial to foreign students' decision to stay after finishing their studies (Musumbaa *et al.* 2011). Students are more likely to return to rich and nearby countries, and to those countries that value their investment in education the highest (Felbermayr and Reczkowski 2012).

Empirical research has explored the role of other potential factors. For example, the time students spend abroad seems to play a role in their intentions to come back home. The longer they study abroad, the less likely it is that they will return to the country of origin (Gungor and Tansel 2008; Oosterbeek and Webbink 2011; Rodrigues 2012; 2013). Although students may change their minds afterwards, returning to the country of origin seems to be more likely for those who already had the intention to go back home (Soon 2010).

To sum up, the empirical literature has pointed to several determinants and consequences of international student migration, which will be addressed in the following sections.

Gravity model estimation

Empirical model

International students who decide to study abroad choose a host country based on several considerations. In this section we apply a gravity model to explain the factors which affect international student mobility between OECD member countries. The gravity model is inspired by Newton's theory: just as planets attract each other, and the effect becomes smaller when the distance between them is greater, so concentrations of population attract each other, in the sense that there will be flows of people and commodities between them, and here too the effect becomes smaller when the distance increases, although for human interaction it is not necessarily only the geodesic distance that matters. The gravity model is the workhorse for analysing trade and migration flows and it is likely that international student flows between countries also depend on distance, in a cultural as well as a physical sense, between origin and destination countries, and on various characteristics of the origin and destination countries (Karemera *et al.* 2000; Bessey 2012). The number of international students departing from each country of origin is known from national and international data reports. This allows a focus on the distribution of the student flow originating from any given country over the set of possible destinations. Applying a production-constrained gravity model assumes that outflows of students from countries of origin to various destinations are interdependent and that students who have decided to study abroad must choose between several competing destination countries. See Appendix C for a formal description of the model.

Choice of explanatory variables

In addition to the traditional variables which are used in the gravity model literature, such as population size, geographical distance and shared cultural or language characteristics, in this research we also focused on additional variables which are likely to attract international students. Such variables can be categorized into academic quality, economic indicators and quality of life (QOL) indicators. Academic quality in the destination country is likely to be an important factor in determining incoming student flows (Sá *et al.* 2004). Students invest effort in travelling to a foreign country to complete their academic studies, and would prefer to maximize the return on their effort, and their employment prospects, by studying in a top university. For the same reason, economic indicators in the destination country are likely to be of similar importance for student mobility, as they may imply better employment and wage prospects after graduation, or perhaps also better availability of study scholarships. QOL indicators relate to the attractiveness of the destination country in terms of sustainability, well-being and 'happiness'. Although this is difficult to measure at a country level, such indicators may well have a positive influence on student flows, as the QOL can be viewed as a country-level amenity.[4]

It is important to note that mobile students are a specific self-selected group that has initially decided to study in a tertiary education programme in a foreign country. Since the group of interest is mobile students, our model does not consider the initial choice of whether to study abroad. Accordingly, 'internal' flows, or the number of students enrolled in tertiary education programmes in the country of origin, are excluded from this analysis.

Data sources

Data concerning student flows is available through the OECD database. In this research we used international student flows in 2010, based on enrolment in all programmes for tertiary education. In the OECD database, student flows refer to the total number of students who are citizens of country *i* and are enrolled in a study programme in country *j*. Students are therefore identified as 'foreign students' if they are not citizens of the country in which they are enrolled to a study programme, a classification which may slightly differ between countries, as it depends on the immigration and naturalization policies of the reporting country. This group includes students who go abroad for a complete bachelor's and/or master's programme, but some exchange students may also be included.[5] Due to missing values for some reporting countries, not all countries were included as both origin and destination countries. The full list of countries included is specified in Appendix Table 10.A.

Economic indicators as well as population measures are also taken from the OECD country statistical profile database. Since country-level economic indicators are relatively correlated, we have included the GDP *per capita* (US dollars 2010) as the only economic indicator, which is used in the analysis to reflect the wealth and economic status of destination countries. Geographic indicators and languages data are available through the Centre d'Etudes Prospectives et d'Informations Internationales (CEPII), the French research centre in international economics. Distance is measured in kilometres between countries' largest populated cities or agglomerations. Distance is also expressed in terms of countries' shared official languages, common borders and EU membership.

In order to include countries' academic level, we use the number of universities in a country which are ranked in the worlds' top 200 universities based on

QS world university rankings for 2011.[6] For the QOL measure we use destination countries' score on the Happy Planet index (HPI) for 2012.[7] The HPI combines several indicators such as life expectancy and experienced well-being (based on data which was collected by surveys) that were used to determine the *Happy life-years* index developed by Veenhoven (1996), as well as each country's ecological footprint on nature. In order to better identify the effect of QOL, we separated the components of the HPI to include life expectancy and the level of well-being as separate variables in the analysis. However, due to a relatively high correlation between reported well-being and GDP per capita ($\rho = 0.7$), the reported well-being is excluded from the analysis in order to avoid a bias in the estimated coefficients. The full list of variables in the analysis is described in Table 10.1, and key statistics per destination country are reported in Appendix Table 10.B.

Results and analysis

The results of the gravity model estimation are described in Table 10.2. Column 1 presents the results of the basic gravity model equation, in which the flow of international students depends positively on the destination country's population size and GDP per capita, and negatively on its distance from the country of origin. The elasticity of student flows with respect to geographic distance is approximately –0.79, which implies that a 1% increase in distance is expected to result in 0.79% decrease in international student flows. As expected, the elasticities of flows to population and GDP are positive and statistically significant, and are estimated at approximately 0.7 and 2.42, respectively. Similarly, the attractiveness of destination countries is found to be positively dependent on their number of top universities. An additional university in the world's top 200 is expected to increase incoming student flows by approximately 4.4%.

Including several additional explanatory variables in the model (column 2) has a relatively small effect on the values of these coefficients. The most notable change was in the elasticity of student flows with respect to GDP per capita levels, which had dropped to 1.4, implying a 1.4% increase in student flow for every 1% increase in GDP per capita. The distance coefficient value dropped to –0.58 and is now interpreted as 0.58% decrease in student flow with every 1% increase in distance between population centres of origin and destination countries. Moreover, despite adding four additional variables to the analysis, the R^2 of the model increased from 0.63 to 0.69, which indicates that the added variables had a relatively small contribution to the explanatory power of the model.

The statistically significant coefficient value of 0.142 of the life expectancy suggests that a higher quality of life positively influences incoming international student flows, and an increase of one year in average life expectancy at birth is expected to increase the student flow by over 14%. The coefficient of about 0.58 for the EU variable implies that when both origin and destination countries are EU members, international student flows are expected to be 78% higher.[8] Similarly, a coefficient of 0.86 implies that a shared border between origin and destination countries is expected to increase student flows by about 136%, and a coefficient

Table 10.1 Variables used in the gravity model analysis

Variable	Mean	Standard deviation	Min.	Max.	Description	Source
Student Flow*	1425.93	7081.34	0.0	126498.3	International student flows between origin and destination countries	OECD (2011)
Distance*	5727.26	5257.86	59.6	19586.2	Distance in kilometres between origin and destination countries, as calculated between the most populated cities or urban agglomerations.	CEPII (2010)
Population*	37183.9	58965.4	318.0	309330.2	Population in destination country	OECD (2011)
GDP*	34186.1	13115	15603.7	86269.4	GDP per capita in destination country, US dollars 2010 prices and PPPs	OECD (2011)
Top Univ QS	5.71	10.22	0	54	Number of universities of destination country which are included in the world's top 200 universities ranking, based on QS ranking (2011)	QS World university Ranking (2011)
EU	0.416	0.493	0	1	Dummy variable which is equal to 1 if both origin and destination countries are EU members	CEPII (2010)
Border	0.062	0.241	0	1	Dummy variable which is equal to 1 if origin and destination countries share a border	CEPII (2010)
Language	0.076	0.265	0	1	Dummy variable which is equal to 1 if origin and destination countries share a common official language	CEPII (2010)
Life expectancy	79.40	2.95	68.8	83.4	Average life expectancy at birth, as collected in the 2011 UNDP Human Development Report and used in the HPI 2012 report	HPI (2012), UNDP (2011)

Sources: See final column.

Note: * Student flows, distance, population and GDP per capita variables are presented here in real values, but are estimated in the model in logarithm form.

Table 10.2 Estimation results

Variable	(1)	(2)
	ln (flow)	*ln (flow)*
ln (Distance)	−0.789***	−0.582***
	(0.0652)	(0.0841)
ln (Population)	0.705***	0.664***
	(0.0351)	(0.0334)
ln (GDP)	2.422***	1.418***
	(0.153)	(0.187)
Top Univ QS	0.0442***	0.0477***
	(0.00510)	(0.00457)
EU		0.582***
		(0.142)
Border		0.861***
		(0.202)
Language		1.515***
		(0.191)
Life expectancy		0.142***
		(0.0190)
Origin-specific constants	Yes	Yes
Constant	−20.84***	−23.61***
	(1.879)	(1.760)
Observations	1,326	1,326
R-squared	0.635	0.691

Notes: Robust standard errors in parentheses.

*** p<0.01, ** p<0.05, * p<0.1
<Estimation results>

of 1.51 implies that a common official language increases international student flows by roughly 350%. Although positive and statistically significant values for a shared official language are somewhat expected, as it eases immigrants' adaptation to a foreign country and its labour markets, this is still somewhat higher than what was previously found in gravity model literature which refers to immigration flows (Karemera *et al.* 2000; Letouzé *et al.* 2009; Adsera and Pytlikova 2012; Bessey 2012). However, it is possible that the coefficient of the shared language also captures the effect of a similar historical or cultural background of the destination and origin countries, which generally results in a relatively larger stock of immigrants from the same country of origin (Adsera and Pytlikova 2012). Accordingly, an existing community of migrants from the same country of origin is likely to offer a new immigrant some familiarity and support via network benefits. Another explanation for the high language coefficient, particularly for international students, may be that a shared official language plays a central role for students when choosing a study programme. Although many universities offer

programmes in English, and indeed many of the countries in the sample have English as an official language, proficiency in the destination country's language provides access to a much greater variety of study programmes.

Conclusion

In this section we have estimated a production-constrained gravity model in order to identify the determinants of international student mobility between OECD countries. Our analysis has focused on the attracting power of the destination countries, particularly with respect to academic level and economic and QOL measures. After controlling for population size and other geographical and language characteristics, we find that academic quality, economic status and QOL indicators have an effect on students' decision regarding where to study abroad. Although the measures of these indicators are difficult to compare, our results indicate that a high level of GDP per capita, a high number of top-ranked universities and a higher QOL (as reflected by life expectancies) all contribute to the attractiveness of destination countries from the perspective of international students.

International students and Dutch higher education institutions

Introduction

Having identified several factors that affect the destination choices of international students within OECD countries, we now examine the factors that determine the higher education institution (HEI) of such students within the Netherlands. The choice of HEI has some similarities with the choice of destination country, which was examined in the previous section, as both depend on HEI characteristics and the provision of amenities in the destination country. In this section we use unique data from NUFFIC, the Netherlands organization for international cooperation in higher education, to examine the choices of students from different nationalities between 39 Dutch HEIs, and to compare the importance of several HEIs' and municipalities' characteristics in the students' decision-making process.

Data

The data specifies the number of enrolled students in each Dutch HEI during the 2011–2012 study year, by nationality. During this period, students of 168 different nationalities were enrolled in Dutch HEIs and attended full-time programmes in 10 fields of study (Table 10.3).

In order to allow for identification of group preferences, we formed aggregated nationality groups, based on largest origin groups and following Gupta *et al.* (2002; Table 10.4). Data about HEI characteristics and available study programmes was taken from the StudieKeuze123 database.[9] Data on municipality characteristics was taken from Statistics Netherlands.

Table 10.3 Fields of study in Dutch HEIs – local and international students (2011–12)

Field of study	Dutch students		International students	
Economics and Business	175,550	28.7%	21,488	38.3%
Behavioural and Social Studies	107,661	17.6%	9,180	16.4%
Technical Studies	91,477	15.0%	6,982	12.4%
Languages and Culture	43,310	7.1%	6,393	11.4%
Health Studies	66,808	10.9%	3,988	7.1%
Agriculture and Environmental Studies	13,910	2.3%	2,223	4.0%
Natural Sciences	18,269	3.0%	1,807	3.2%
Law	26,281	4.3%	1,806	3.2%
Education	65,266	10.7%	1,199	2.1%
Interdisciplinary/Other	2,196	0.4%	1,065	1.9%
Total	610,728		56,131	

Source: NUFFIC (2011–12).

As Table 10.3 shows, students' preferences for fields of study differ between local and international students. These differences are likely to result from the fact that some fields are more internationally oriented than others, such as science,

Table 10.4 Nationality groups

Description	Abbr.	Number of students	Nationalities included
Netherlands	NL	586,137	
Germany	DE	24,783	
Eastern Europe	EE	7,324	Poland, Romania, Czech Republic, Russia, Serbia, Hungary, Former Soviet countries
China	CN	4,230	
Latin Europe	LE	3,245	France, Italy, Portugal, Spain
Belgium	BE	2,345	
Anglo cultures and Northern Europe	AN	3,450	USA, Australia, UK, Canada, Ireland, New-Zealand, South Africa, Denmark, Finland, Norway, Sweden, Switzerland, Austria
Former Dutch colonies	DC	1,609	Indonesia, Suriname
Traditional guest workers migration countries	GW	1,529	Turkey, Morocco
Rest of the world	RW	3,225	
Total		637,877	

Source: NUFFIC (2011–12).

economics and social studies, as compared to law and education, and therefore appeal more to international students. However, differences in preferences
for study fields also exist between nationality groups, as shown in Table 10.5.

Table 10.5 Ranking of fields of study among nationality groups (2011–12)

Group	Abbr.	Rank	Study field	% students from a nationality group	% students studying in top 3
Netherlands	NL	1	Economics and Business	28.70%	61.40%
		2	Behavioural and Social Studies	17.60%	
		3	Technical Studies	15.00%	
Anglo cultures and Northern Europe	AN	1	Languages and Culture	26.80%	60.30%
		2	Economics and Business	22.50%	
		3	Behavioural and Social Studies	11.00%	
Belgium	BE	1	Technical Studies	21.00%	56.50%
		2	Languages and Culture	18.90%	
		3	Economics and Business	16.70%	
China	CN	1	Economics and Business	63.60%	91.20%
		2	Technical Studies	19.90%	
		3	Agriculture and Environmental Studies	7.70%	
Former Dutch colonies	DC	1	Economics and Business	34.00%	68.70%
		2	Technical Studies	26.40%	
		3	Behavioural and Social Studies	8.30%	
Germany	DE	1	Economics and Business	41.10%	77.10%
		2	Behavioural and Social Studies	26.50%	
		3	Health Studies	9.50%	
Eastern Europe	EE	1	Economics and Business	44.60%	71.10%
		2	Languages and Culture	15.00%	
		3	Technical Studies	11.50%	
Latin Europe	LE	1	Languages and Culture	28.20%	65.50%
		2	Economics and Business	25.40%	
		3	Technical Studies	12.00%	
Traditional guest workers countries	GW	1	Economics and Business	36.80%	74.70%
		2	Behavioural and Social Studies	19.20%	
		3	Technical Studies	18.80%	
Rest of the world	RW	1	Economics and Business	31.60%	74.30%
		2	Technical Studies	30.40%	
		3	Languages and Culture	12.30%	

Source: NUFFIC (2011–12).

Economics and Business is the most common field of study for most nationality groups, including Dutch students. This field is one of the top three choices among all groups. Notably, over 63% of the international students from China chose to study Economics and Business during 2011–2012, the highest proportion among all groups. Technical studies (Engineering, ICT, computer science) also rank high among most groups and are most popular among students from former Dutch colonies (26.4%), Belgium (21%) and China (19.9%). In the other groups, the proportion of students who chose a technical field of study is somewhat comparable to the proportion among Dutch students, which is approximately 15%. Additionally, Language and Culture studies appear to be relatively popular among students from European and Anglo-cultures, and Behavioural and Social studies are relatively popular among students from Germany, Turkey and Morocco (traditional guest-worker migration countries).

Model

To estimate international students' choices of Dutch HEIs we use an Alternative specific logit model. The model predicts the probability that an individual from group i will select HEI j, following a list of variables that describe HEI characteristics and the provision of urban amenities in the municipality in which the HEI's main campus is located.[10]

In the absence of disaggregated micro-data, we identify international students only by their nationality. Since groups of students from the same country of origin can hardly be assumed to be homogeneous in their preferences for HEIs and fields of study, we focus the interpretation of the coefficients on urban amenities. Students from the same country of origin can be similar in their evaluation of these amenities, although they choose different types of education. For instance, preferences for the presence of an existing community of migrants, or proximity to the border (for German and Belgian students), and local employment opportunities may be common to students originating from a particular country.

The list of explanatory variables can be divided into two main categories – HEI characteristics and urban amenities. While HEI characteristics differ between every HEI, some HEIs are located within the same municipality and therefore share the same urban amenities (e.g., the city of Amsterdam has six different HEIs). Moreover, some HEIs have campuses in several municipalities. However, here we assume that each HEI has one municipality affiliation, related to the location of its main campus. In this analysis we examine Dutch and international students' choices of 39 HEIs (see description in Figure 10.1).

HEI characteristics included here are the number of full-time programmes, ratio of students to teaching staff and whether the institution is a university (WO), and the HEI's field of specialization. The first variable, the number of full-time programmes, relates to the size of the HEI, as well as the diversity of programmes which it offers. The number of English programmes is also assumed to be an important factor but is not included in the analysis, due to suspicion of reverse causality.[11]

Higher education in the Netherlands is offered in two main types of institutions – universities that offer scientific-oriented programmes and research education (WO, *Wetenschappelijk Onderwijs*), and higher vocational colleges, which offer higher professional training (HBO, *Hoger Beroepsonderwijs*). In order to control for preferences for WO or HBO institutions, we use a dummy variable that indicates whether a HEI is a WO or HBO.

Although tuition fees are very likely to be an important factor in the choice of HEI and study programme, they are not included as an explanatory variable in this analysis. This is because tuition fees vary between different study programmes, and students from EU and non-EU countries are required to pay different fees. Since this analysis is based on aggregated HEI, study field and nationality data, it is difficult to observe which rate of tuition fee was required from the international students in the sample.

Urban amenities variables include the number of official monuments in a municipality in logarithmic form, which represents the historical and cultural heritage of a certain municipality. Since cultural heritage is very often linked with leisure consumption, cafés and restaurants (Van Duijn and Rouwendal 2013), this variable is also used to estimate the preferences of international students for such amenities. In addition, we also include variables such as the percentage of nature coverage in a municipality, and a dummy variable which indicates whether an HEI is located within 20 kilometres of the Belgian border (for Belgian students) or German border (for German students).

The percentage of immigrants in a municipality was also added so as to reflect students' preferences for a local community of migrants. Since the data allows identification of the percentages of migrants from Western or non-Western nationality groups, we were also able to estimate the preferences of students from different nationality groups for communities of people of relatively similar origin. The definition of Western and non-Western immigrants is very broad, and was necessary due to data limitations and the need to aggregate several nationalities into one group. Although it may be used to examine how the presence of a community of migrants from a somewhat similar origin can affect the choices of students, in some cases this identification may be inaccurate. The percentage of migrants variable refers to 'Western immigrants' for groups from Anglo-cultures and Northern Europe, Eastern Europe, Latin and Southern Europe, Belgium and Germany, and 'non-Western Immigrants' for groups from China, Indonesia and Surinam (former Dutch colonies), Turkey and Morocco (traditional guest-worker origin countries) and the rest of the world.

Since many students are likely to be attracted to possible employment opportunities, we introduce a province-level location quotient (LQ) for employment in financial or ICT industries. These variables indicate whether these industries form the main economic activity in the region of the HEI. The concentration of such industries in a certain area indicates employment opportunities, but it can also have a positive effect on the quality of studies in a certain HEI, through the effect of knowledge spill-over from various local industries. The LQs of financial and ICT industries were chosen for this analysis, since they are most common fields of study among international students (see Table 10.3).

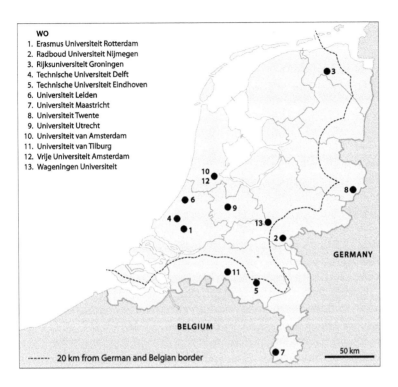

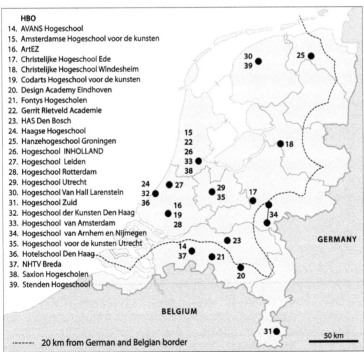

Figure 10.1 HEIs in the Netherlands

International students' location decisions in the Netherlands

The results of the estimation are presented in Table 10.6. The reported coefficients represent a preference of a certain origin group for a specific amenity. With regard to the preference of the base group (local Dutch nationality students), see a full explanation of the interpretation of the coefficients in Appendix C. As expected, HEIs which are located within 20 kilometres of the border with Belgium or Germany are positively and significantly affected by that location. Coefficients of 1.364 and 0.961 (Table 10.6a), respectively, imply that a student from Belgium is 3.9 times more likely to prefer an HEI if it is located within 20 kilometres of the Belgian border, and a German student is 2.6 times more likely to prefer institutions in similar proximity to Germany (Table 10.6b, top). Compared with the preferences of Dutch students, a student from Belgium is 10 times more likely to choose an alternative HEI within 20 kilometres of the Belgian border. A German student is 5 times more likely to choose an HEI within 20 kilometres of the German border, as compared to a Dutch student (Table 10.6b, bottom).

As expected, the coefficients of an existing community of migrants (Perc. Migrants) are positive and statistically significant for all origin groups, implying that international students attach positive value to a community of migrants, given all other amenities remain constant. Coefficient values between 0.0155 (China) and 0.086 (Belgium) imply that an additional proportion of migrants in a municipality would raise the probability of a certain HEI's being chosen by between 1.5% and 9%, given all other attributes remain constant. When compared with the preferences of local Dutch students the interpretation changes somewhat (Table 10.6b, bottom). Compared with local students, students from Belgium, China, Germany and Latin Europe are more likely to choose HEIs in municipalities with higher percentages of migrants, while students from an Anglo-culture, Northern Europe, Eastern Europe, former Dutch colonies, Morocco and Turkey are less likely to choose HEIs in municipalities with higher percentages of migrants.

Examining the preferences for industry specialization in the vicinity of an HEI, it appears that students from China, former Dutch colonies and Eastern Europe have positive preferences for ICT industries, while only students from China have a positive preference for a concentration of financial industries. When compared with local students, Chinese students are 10 and 12 times more likely to choose an HEI which is located in areas specialized in ICT or financial industries, respectively.

Conclusions

In this section we have explored the preferences of international students from different origins for Dutch HEIs. Using nationality group as the only distinctive personal characteristic, we find that all international students have positive preferences to study in a municipality with a higher percentage of foreigners. Additionally, we found statistically significant coefficients for LQs for ICT and financial industries, indicating that knowledge spill-over between HEIs and industries, as well as future employment opportunities, can be viewed as appealing

Table 10.6a Multinomial logit regression results – aggregated nationality groups (see Table 10.5 for the description of column codes)

	AN	BE	CN	DC	DE	EE	LE	GW	RW
N Fulltime programmes	-0.00577***	-0.00632***	-0.00935***	-0.00534***	-0.00235***	-0.0100***	-0.0109***	-0.00943***	-0.0161***
	(0.000602)	(0.000824)	(0.000541)	(0.000861)	(0.000253)	(0.000403)	(0.000612)	(0.000974)	(0.000641)
Ratio students-personnel	-0.178***	-0.228***	0.0444***	0.0412***	-0.0594***	0.00591	-0.219***	0.00537	-0.140***
	(0.00706)	(0.0109)	(0.00931)	(0.0145)	(0.00427)	(0.00696)	(0.00645)	(0.0119)	(0.00754)
University (WO)	-0.239***	-0.631***	1.246***	1.495***	-0.106***	1.570***	-0.586***	0.183	0.615***
	(0.0796)	(0.105)	(0.0850)	(0.138)	(0.0380)	(0.0699)	(0.0721)	(0.125)	(0.0790)
ln (Monuments)	0.475***	0.264***	-0.493***	-0.162***	-0.00957	0.184***	0.247***	0.101**	-0.337***
	(0.0321)	(0.0321)	(0.0245)	(0.0426)	(0.00989)	(0.0207)	(0.0289)	(0.0513)	(0.0251)
Nature coverage	0.0134***	-0.0433***	-0.00386	0.0131**	0.0179***	0.0230***	-0.0108***	0.00146	-0.0148***
	(0.00389)	(0.00707)	(0.00288)	(0.00549)	(0.00113)	(0.00254)	(0.00388)	(0.00556)	(0.00382)
LQ (ICT)	-0.122***	-0.452***	0.150***	0.200***	-0.607***	0.318***	-0.173***	-0.221***	0.357***
	(0.0474)	(0.0685)	(0.0394)	(0.0649)	(0.0202)	(0.0309)	(0.0473)	(0.0745)	(0.0483)
LQ (Finance)	-0.385***	-0.488***	0.265***	-0.106	-0.632**	-0.425***	0.108*	0.0134	0.493**
	(0.0699)	(0.0879)	(0.0534)	(0.0980)	(0.0263)	(0.0437)	(0.0642)	(0.115)	(0.0596)
Perc. Migrants	0.0707***	0.0860***	0.0155***	0.0363***	0.0438***	0.0709***	0.0347***	0.0528***	0.0244***
	(0.00918)	(0.00982)	(0.00192)	(0.00315)	(0.00314)	(0.00618)	(0.00850)	(0.00304)	(0.00233)
Border proximity	–	1.364***	–	–	0.961***	–	–	–	–
	–	(0.0650)	–	–	(0.0214)	–	–	–	–

Notes: Perc. Migrants indicates the percentage of Western immigrants (AN, BE, DE, EE, LE, and non-Western immigrants (CN, DC, GW, RW) Border proximity indicates that an HEI is within 20 km of the Belgian border (for B) or the German border (for D).

Standard errors in parentheses; *** p<0.01, ** p<0.05, * p<0.1.

<Estimation results>

Table 10.6b Odds ratios for international students' location decisions

Odds ratio		AN	BE	CN	DC	DE	EE	LE	GW
$\dfrac{Pr_{i,j}}{Pr_{i,h}}$	N full-time programmes	0.99	0.99	0.99	0.99	1.00	0.99	0.99	0.99
	Ratio students-personnel	0.84	0.80	1.05	1.04	0.94	1.01 (ns)	0.80	1.01 (ns)
	University (WO)	0.79	0.53	3.48	4.46	0.90	4.81	0.56	1.20 (ns)
	Ln (Monuments)	1.61	1.30	0.61	0.85	0.99 (ns)	1.20	1.28	1.11
	Nature coverage	1.01	0.96	1.00 (ns)	1.01	1.02	1.02	0.99	1.00 (ns)
	LQ (ICT)	0.89	0.64	1.16	1.22	0.54	1.37	0.84	0.80
	LQ (Finance)	0.68	0.61	1.30	0.90 (ns)	0.94	0.65	1.11 (ns)	1.01 (ns)
	Perc. Migrants	1.07	1.09	1.02	1.04	1.04	1.07	1.04	1.05
	Border proximity		3.91			2.61			
$\dfrac{Pr_{i,j}}{Pr_{Dutch,j}}$	N full-time programmes	0.26	2.55	9.22	0.56	1.93	0.11	3.62	0.32
	Ratio students-personnel	0.22	2.04	9.73	0.58	1.83	0.11 (ns)	2.94	0.32 (ns)
	University (WO)	0.20	1.36	32.36	2.50	1.74	0.54	2.03	0.39 (ns)
	Ln (Monuments)	0.42	3.34	5.69	0.48	1.92 (ns)	0.13	4.68	0.36
	Nature coverage	0.26	2.45	9.27 (ns)	0.57	1.97	0.11	3.62	0.32 (ns)
	LQ (ICT)	0.23	1.63	10.82	0.69	1.06	0.15	3.08	0.26
	LQ (Finance)	0.18	1.57	12.13	0.50 (ns)	1.82	0.07	4.07 (ns)	0.33 (ns)
	Perc. Migrants	0.28	2.79	9.45	0.58	2.02	0.12	3.79	0.34
	Border proximity		10.02			5.06			

Note: (ns) indicates that the figure is based on a significance level of less than 5%.

<Estimation results>

by international students from several origin groups. In the next section we will explore further the location preferences of international graduates.

Location preferences (choice of residential municipalities) of international students during studies and after graduation, and their tendency to stay after graduation

After graduation, international students face a choice of whether to stay and find employment opportunities as immigrants in their host country, or to return to their home country (or go to a third, different host country). The decision to stay in the country of study depends on several factors, which can be grouped into several categories. First, the personal characteristics of the international graduate, such as country of origin, age or family status, can have an effect on the decision whether or where to stay (Bijwaard and Wang 2013). Second, labour market characteristics – such as wages, employment possibilities or international orientation of the market – may encourage graduates to stay and take advantage of the local employment opportunities. Third, country- or city-level amenities can also influence the decision to stay. Amenities were found to be an important factor in determining migration decisions (Gottlieb and Joseph 2006; Brown and Scott 2012; Rodríguez-Pose and Ketterer 2012). Historical and cultural amenities, social amenities like an international environment, or physical setting and natural amenities, all may appeal to graduates when they decide whether or not to stay in their host country.

Retaining their population of foreign students is of interest to regional policy makers. Highly educated graduates with high human capital can contribute to local economic growth by increasing the productivity of innovative and skill-intensive industries, which are viewed as key components in current economic growth (Glaeser and Saiz 2003; Ottaviano and Peri 2006; Suedekum *et al.* 2009; Moretti 2012).

In this section we will provide several descriptive statistics about the location decisions of international graduates in the Netherlands and to what extent they stayed in the Netherlands. The analysis is based on several databases which were made available by Statistics Netherlands: (1) the Dutch population registry (GBA) and (2) Migration motives database, which combines social data with immigration motive information from the Dutch Immigration and Naturalisation Service (IND).

Although it is combined in a single uniform database, the information regarding migrants' immigration motives is gathered differently depending on the migrant's country of origin, and therefore may contain small discrepancies. Non-EU immigrants require a residence visa, and therefore have to register with the IND while applying for a specific visa. The specific visa type provides a clear indication for these migrants' motives for immigration. In contrast, EU citizens do not need a visa in order to stay in the Netherlands and therefore are not required to register with the IND. However, all foreigners who stay in the Netherlands for four months or longer have to register with their municipality of residence, hence all migrants in the Netherlands, including those from EU countries, are registered and included in the population registry database. Since registration with the municipality does not require the purpose of the stay to be stated, the migration motive for EU citizens (and of some non-EU citizens with a general visa type or 'unknown' motive) is derived by Statistics Netherlands using the Social Statistics Database (SSD), which contains information from other, separate databases regarding employment or student status.

An important advantage of the Dutch immigration and population registry policies is that they allows us to make a clearer distinction between exchange students ('Credit mobility') and international students enrolled in programmes at local HEIs ('Diploma mobility'). The first group is not the focus of this research, since these students' stay in the Netherlands is usually short-term and dependent on universities' mutual participation in exchange programmes, the largest of these being the EU's Erasmus Programme. Fortunately, since most participants are from EU countries and stay for a relatively short period, they are usually not registered in the Dutch immigration or population registries.

The necessity for all immigrants to register with a municipality also provides us with unique information regarding their first choice of residence – presumably in proximity to an HEI in the case of students – as well as subsequent location choices. Subsequent location choices reveal much about the preferences and occupational status of migrants, particularly since these choices are made when the immigrant has better information about neighbourhoods and municipalities in the destination country (Bartel 1989; Åslund 2005). Subsequent location choices of migrants are also assumed to be dependent on their municipality of first registration. For example, universities may be oriented towards a city's or a region's dominant industry, and encourage graduates to seek internships or employment opportunities in the same region. Also, immigrants may prefer to relocate within a region in which they have already begun to establish a network.

Number of international students per year, origin and municipality of first registration

The number of migrants arriving in the Netherlands for the purpose of studies increased dramatically between 1999 and 2011. This increase is apparent both in the volume and in the student proportion of the total group of migrants (Table 10.7). From 5,500 incoming students in 1999, which was equal to 8.7% of the migrant population that year, the number has increased to over 19,000 in 2011, or 21% of the incoming migrants.

Examining this growth by municipality of first registration, it appears that many Dutch cities experienced a significant increase in the number of migrants (Table 10.8). In Eindhoven, for example, the number of students grew from only 71 in 1999 (less than 5% of all immigrants to Eindhoven that year), to over 900 in 2011 (or 31% of total immigrants to Eindhoven). However, the strongest absolute growth in international student numbers occurred in the Amsterdam area (municipalities of Amsterdam and Amstelveen), where the number of international

Table 10.7 International migrants in the Netherlands by year

Year	Non-students	Students	Students/all migrants
1999	57,771	5,521	8.72%
2000	69,412	5,735	7.63%
2001	68,120	7,038	9.36%
2002	61,782	8,475	12.06%
2003	49,729	8,171	14.11%
2004	42,228	8,918	17.44%
2005	42,057	10,885	20.56%
2006	37,787	10,097	21.09%
2007	53,179	14,365	21.27%
2008	67,531	18,347	21.36%
2009	68,334	16,145	19.11%
2010	68,847	17,798	20.54%
2011	71,646	19,117	21.06%
Total	758,423	150,612	16.57%

Source: Statistics Netherlands (1999–2011).

students grew from 662 in 1999 to 4,100 in 2011. The proportion of international students out of the total migrants in the Amsterdam area also grew during this period, from 7.5% to 26.6%, implying that over a quarter of new immigrants in Amsterdam have arrived for purposes of study.

Although most municipalities have experienced growth in numbers of international students, particularly in their proportion of the total population of migrants, some municipalities have benefited more than others. For example, in 1999 approximately 10% of new international students in the Netherlands arrived in Rotterdam, as compared to 7.7% in 2011, despite an absolute growth in the number of international students during these years. In this period, the proportion of students that arrived in Eindhoven grew from 1.3% to 4.7%, and in Amsterdam from 12% to 21.4%, suggesting that these cities became relatively more attractive for international students. Rotterdam is an example of a city whose proportion dropped.

Migration period – the extent to which students stay, by year of arrival

The extent to which international graduates choose to stay in the Netherlands is particularly relevant for public policy. After graduation, the local economy can benefit most from highly skilled international workers who have already obtained some familiarity with the local markets and challenges. Table 10.9 describes the migration period of students and non-student immigrants who have stayed in the Netherlands, by year of immigration. Most bachelor's study programmes end after 3–4 years, and master's programmes after 1–2 years. Therefore, it is plausible to assume that student immigrants who have stayed in the Netherlands for

Table 10.8 International students in Dutch municipalities by year of arrival

	Amsterdam/Amstelveen			Rotterdam		
	Students	Students/all migrants	Students/all int. Students	Students	Students/all migrants	Students/all int. students
1999	662	7.5%	12.0%	547	12.6%	9.9%
2003	886	10.4%	10.8%	933	18.9%	11.4%
2007	2,946	24.1%	20.5%	1,117	23.8%	7.8%
2011	4,099	26.6%	21.4%	1,483	22.0%	7.8%
	Eindhoven			Groningen		
	Students	Students/all migrants	Students/all int. Students	Students	Students/all migrants	Students/all int. students
1999	71	4.9%	1.3%	275	27.4%	5.0%
2003	203	14.7%	2.5%	315	34.3%	3.9%
2007	703	31.7%	4.9%	698	42.3%	4.9%
2011	905	31.3%	4.7%	1,311	38.2%	6.9%

Source: Statistics Netherlands (1999–2011).

at least five years have already graduated or left their initial study programme.[12] Almost 55% of immigrants who arrived for purposes of study in 1999 have stayed in the Netherlands for at least five years (compared with 75% who arrived for other purposes). These rates have remained similar for immigrants who arrived in 2003, but a smaller proportion of immigrants who arrived in 2007 have remained after five years (45.5% of students, 62% of other immigrants).

Nevertheless, it is important to note that, due to the increase in the total number of immigrants (both students and non-students) to the Netherlands, the number of international students who arrived in 2007 and have stayed in the Netherlands for at least five years has more than doubled since 1999 (6,600, compared with 3,200). A possible explanation is that the increase in international mobility of both students and workers has resulted in better information about and accessibility to jobs abroad, which enables graduates to easily access other countries' labour markets. Additionally, the growing international orientation of Dutch study programmes in HEIs[13] (including the use of English for all courses offered) contributes to their attractiveness in the eyes of international students, and is also aimed at preparing graduates to integrate into global markets, and therefore reduces the dependence of graduates of the local labour market.

Examining the numbers and proportions of international students by their origin groups reveals another interesting finding (see Table 10.10 for origin groups). In 1999, the largest group among international students was from EU countries or of Western European origin (37.3%). In 2011, despite a growth of 66% in EU and Western European students, this group's proportion of the total number of international students dropped to 17.9%. In contrast, the largest origin group of

Table 10.9 Migration period, proportions of immigrants that stayed in the Netherlands by year of arrival and purpose of arrival

Year of arrival	1999		2003		2007	
	Non-students	Students	Non-students	Students	Non-students	Students
2000	93.0%	89.0%				
2001	86.4%	70.5%				
2002	80.8%	60.8%				
2003	75.9%	54.9%				
2004	71.9%	48.4%	92.2%	92.7%		
2005	68.4%	43.3%	84.3%	76.1%		
2006	64.9%	37.4%	76.8%	63.7%		
2007	61.9%	33.0%	71.3%	53.3%		
2008	59.4%	29.6%	67.1%	44.2%	86.8%	86.3%
2009	57.4%	27.0%	63.8%	37.8%	76.1%	67.3%
2010	55.6%	24.7%	61.1%	31.9%	68.2%	55.1%
2011	53.8%	22.8%	58.6%	27.8%	62.0%	45.5%

Source: Statistics Netherlands (1999–2011).

Notes: Years indicate the year of arrival of an immigrant into the Netherlands (1 January–31 December).
Percentages indicate the proportion of the immigrants that were registered in the Netherlands after 1 January of that year.

international students was Asia-Pacific, with 34.2% of all students (or 6,540 students). This was a sharp increase over 1999, when this group represented 14.6% (850 students) of the total number of international students.

Municipalities of registration

Among both student and non-student immigrants who arrived in the Netherlands and were registered in the population registry on 1 January 2012, the most popular municipalities of residence were Amsterdam, 's-Gravenhage (The Hague)[14] and Rotterdam. This is not particularly surprising, since these are the three largest cities in the Netherlands and are likely to attract migrant populations. However, examining the rest reveals the tendency of international students to cluster in towns with HEIs. Seventy-six per cent of international students live in 15 cities in the Netherlands (all having at least one HEI), compared with 47% of non-student immigrants who display dispersion patterns over Dutch cities (Table 10.11 and Figure 10.2).

Amsterdam metropolitan area analysis

The Amsterdam metropolitan area is the most popular region among both student and non-student immigrants in the Netherlands. As seen in Table 10.11 and Figure 10.2, approximately 20% of immigrants who have arrived in the

Table 10.10 Number of migrants year by year of arrival and origin group

Origin group	Asia-Pacific		EU and Western Europe		Eastern Europe and former Soviet Union countries		Middle East and Africa		Other	
Year of arrival	Students	Share of total intl. students	Students	Share of total intl. students	Students	Share of total intl. students	Students	Share of total intl. students	Students	Share of total intl. students
1999	805	14.6%	2059	37.3%	562	10.2%	576	12.2%	1419	25.7%
2003	3113	38.1%	1769	21.6%	850	10.4%	751	9.2%	1688	20.7%
2007	4609	32.1%	2777	19.3%	1684	11.7%	1636	11.4%	3659	25.5%
2011	6540	34.2%	3419	17.9%	2567	13.4%	1937	10.1%	4654	24.3%

Source: Statistics Netherlands (1999–2011).

Table 10.11 Municipalities of residence of immigrants in the Netherlands (both first and subsequent choices)

#	Non students	Number	% of total	#	Students	Number	% of total
1	Amsterdam	58,501	12.8%	1	Amsterdam	11,743	15.9%
2	's-Gravenhage	40,449	8.9%	2	's-Gravenhage	6,578	8.9%
3	Rotterdam	34,331	7.5%	3	Rotterdam	6,469	8.7%
4	Eindhoven	10,862	2.4%	4	Delft	4,283	5.8%
5	Utrecht	10,545	2.3%	5	Maastricht	3,777	5.1%
6	Groningen	7,318	1.6%	6	Groningen	3,719	5.0%
7	Delft	6,821	1.5%	7	Eindhoven	3,703	5.0%
8	Maastricht	6,427	1.4%	8	Utrecht	2,965	4.0%
9	Leiden	6,207	1.4%	9	Amstelveen	2,578	3.5%
10	Nijmegen	5,950	1.3%	10	Wageningen	2,361	3.2%
11	Almere	5,841	1.3%	11	Enschede	2,308	3.1%
12	Tilburg	5,765	1.3%	12	Leiden	1,990	2.7%
13	Amstelveen	5,507	1.2%	13	Nijmegen	1,501	2.0%
14	Enschede	5,458	1.2%	14	Tilburg	1,235	1.7%
15	Haarlem	5,294	1.2%	15	Leeuwarden	1,089	1.5%

Source: Statistics Netherlands (2012).

Note: Values in this table refer to immigrants who were registered in the Netherlands on 1 January 2012.
'Students' are defined as immigrants who initially arrived to the Netherlands for the purpose of studying.

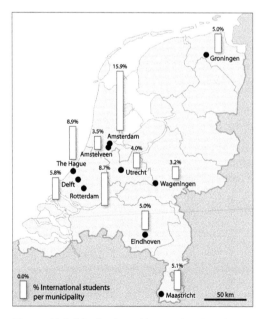

Figure 10.2 Distribution of international students in municipalities in the Netherlands (both international students and graduates – registered on 1 January 2012)

Netherlands for study purposes (both current students and graduates) are residing in Amsterdam or in nearby Amstelveen. Amsterdam has 21 HEIs (vocational education and universities), among them the University of Amsterdam (UvA), the Free University of Amsterdam (VU) and the Hogeschool van Amsterdam (HvA). Some 109,000 students are studying in Amsterdam, and 49,900 are also living in the city.[15] In 2012, international students and graduates accounted for 1.5% (11,743) of the city's 779,000 inhabitants, and immigrants who had arrived since 1999 formed 9% (70,244) of the city's population.

Similar to the trends in the rest of the country, immigrants from EU countries and Western Europe represent 19% of international students in Amsterdam, but 35% of total non-student immigrants in the city (Table 10.12). In contrast, immigrants from Asia-Pacific region represent 35% of international students in Amsterdam, but only 12% of the non-student immigrants in the city. Eighty-seven per cent of international students who were registered in the Amsterdam Metropolitan Area on their first registration in the Netherlands have chosen to relocate within Amsterdam and not move to a different municipality (compared with 74% and 77% of international students in Rotterdam and Groningen, respectively).

Upon arrival in the Amsterdam Metropolitan Area, most international students are registered in relatively few neighbourhoods in close proximity to the universities (Figure 10.3). These location decisions are partly predetermined, since a fixed amount of university-arranged student housing is available to them in specific

Table 10.12 Percentages of migrant origin groups by first or subsequent registration (Amsterdam Metropolitan Area)

		First registration	*Subsequent registration*
Students	Asia-Pacific	35.40%	35.00%
	EU and Western Europe	19.40%	18.10%
	Eastern Europe and former Soviet union countries	15.10%	16.80%
	Middle East and Africa	7.30%	8.30%
	Other	22.90%	21.80%
Non-students	Asia-Pacific	12.00%	11.80%
	EU and Western Europe	35.40%	32.00%
	Eastern Europe and former Soviet union countries	13.10%	14.80%
	Middle East and Africa	10.10%	18.70%
	Other	29.50%	22.70%

Source: Statistics Netherlands (2012).

Note: Values in this table refer to immigrants who were registered in the Netherlands on 1 January 2012.

'Students' are defined as immigrants who initially arrived to the Netherlands for the purpose of studying

locations. Two of the largest student housing complexes are located in Uilenstede en Kronenburg (municipality of Amstelveen, near the VU main campus) and in Weesperbuurt-Plantage (near the UvA main campus). Unlike privately arranged accommodation, student housing associations usually offer temporary contracts that expire at the end of the study period without any possibility of contract extension. Therefore, international students or graduates who wish to stay in the Netherlands must relocate from their initial residence. Thus, examining the subsequent location choices of students and graduates provides a relatively complete picture of their location preferences, since the majority must relocate by the end of their study programme.

As expected, subsequent location decisions exhibit a more dispersed pattern. The population of graduates and students who have chosen to relocate while still completing their studies appears to spread over many neighbourhoods in the Amsterdam area. The neighbourhoods with the largest population of students on subsequent registration are now *Buitenveldert-West* in the south, *Jordaan* and *Oude-Pijp* in the city centre and *Bijlmer-Centrum* in the south-east of Amsterdam. Although these neighbourhoods differ in several characteristics and are located in separate areas of the city, some of their shared characteristics can be used to explain their popularity among international students and graduates. For example, all neighbourhoods have features and amenities that appeal to international migrants, such as good accessibility to employment centres, historic amenities and cultural diversity (Glaeser *et al.* 2001; Jaeger 2006; Rodríguez-Pose and Ketterer 2012; Van Duijn and Rouwendal 2013).

Buitenveldert-West is where the main campus of the VU is located, and it is near to the large employment centre of Amsterdam WTC and to Amsterdam Zuid rail and its metro station. Unlike the Weesperbuurt-Plantage neighbourhood

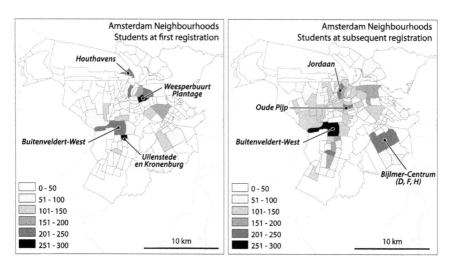

Figure 10.3 Number of international students in Amsterdam-area neighbourhoods: first registration (left) and subsequent registrations (right)

in the city centre, where the main campus of the UvA is located, the relatively non-central location makes the rents in this neighbourhood more affordable for students and recent graduates and enables them to enjoy good accessibility to employment centres. The Jordaan and Oude-Pijp are historic neighbourhoods in the city centre that offer relatively high rental prices and poorer accessibility to jobs, but also proximity to the city centre and a rich cultural heritage. Cultural heritage is valued highly by both locals and immigrants, and also because it usually attracts other cultural and leisure activities such as cafés, restaurants and nightlife (Rodríguez-Pose and Ketterer 2012; Van Duijn and Rouwendal 2013). Bijlmer-Centrum is located on the south-eastern outskirts of the city, but is likely to attract students and graduates due to its very low housing prices and a relatively large community of migrants (according to Statistics Netherlands data, approximately 15% of the neighbourhood's population are immigrants who have arrived since 1999). Additionally, the neighbourhood is very accessible, due to its main rail and metro station, and it also has a large shopping and leisure centre (ArenA Boulevard and Amsterdamse Poort), large music halls and sport venues (the Amsterdam ArenA stadium).

Conclusions

Since 1999 the Netherlands has experienced a sharp growth in the number of incoming international students. Using unique Dutch micro-data on international immigrants in the Netherlands and their motives for immigration, we have been able to study this group's distribution trends and location preferences in Dutch municipalities and particularly in the Amsterdam Metropolitan Area. We find that international students represent more than 20% of all incoming immigrants to the Netherlands. Approximately 45% of immigrants who have arrived in the Netherlands for study purposes stay in the Netherlands for at least five years, and most of them choose to relocate in the municipality in which they were registered on arrival in the country. International students and graduates tend to cluster in specific Dutch municipalities, and over three-quarters choose to live in 15 specific municipalities. Amsterdam is the most attractive Dutch city for international students, and almost 20% of international students and graduates in the Netherlands live in the Amsterdam Metropolitan Area. After completing their studies, they subsequently choose to locate in neighbourhoods which are generally characterized by good accessibility to employment, large community of immigrants and rich cultural heritage.

Conclusion

International students form approximately one-fifth of the total immigration to the Netherlands. Their large proportion and relatively high human capital levels emphasize the importance, for potential regional economic growth, of understanding what determines their location decision during their studies and after their graduation. This chapter has included an analysis of migration and location decisions of international students in the Netherlands. Our analysis has followed international students' location decisions at three main decision points – the decision whether to enrol for an international study programme in the Netherlands, the choice of HEI within the Netherlands, and location decisions after graduation. In order to investigate each of these different choices which international students face, we made use of several unique data sources including population registry and immigration data from the Dutch Statistical Office and enrolment of international students in Dutch HEIs from NUFFIC. Our findings shed light on the factors which determine the decision patterns of international students and graduates. As expected, we have found that international students are primarily attracted to countries with high academic quality, economic status and QOL indicators. Our findings also show that after choosing to come to the Netherlands students from different nationality groups generally choose to study in a municipality which has a relatively higher presence of foreigners and a concentration of ICT and financial industries. Finally, we have found that 45% of international graduates stay in the Netherlands for at least five years after their arrival, and most choose to stay in the municipality of their first registration.

Appendices

Appendix Table 10.A: list of countries included

Appendix Table 10.A List of countries included

#	Origin	Destination	#	Origin	Destination
1	Australia	Australia	21	Italy	Italy
2	Austria	Austria	22	Japan	Japan
3	Belgium	Belgium	23	Luxembourg	Luxembourg
4	Brazil	–	24	Mexico	–
5	Canada	Canada	25	Netherlands	Netherlands
6	Chile	Chile	26	New Zealand	New Zealand
7	China	–	27	Norway	Norway
8	Czech Republic	Czech Republic	28	Poland	Poland
9	Denmark	Denmark	29	Portugal	Portugal
10	Estonia	Estonia	30	Russia	Russia
11	Finland	Finland	31	Slovakia	Slovakia
12	France	France	32	Slovenia	Slovenia
13	Germany	Germany	33	South Africa	–
14	Greece	Greece	34	South Korea	South Korea
15	Hungary	Hungary	35	Spain	Spain
16	Iceland	Iceland	36	Sweden	Sweden
17	India	–	37	Switzerland	Switzerland
18	Indonesia	–	38	Turkey	Turkey
19	Ireland	Ireland	39	United Kingdom	United Kingdom
20	Israel	Israel	40	United States	United States

Source: OECD Statistics.

Note: Missing data resulted several destination countries being excluded from the analysis.

Appendix Table 10.B: destination countries' key characteristics used in the gravity model analysis

Appendix Table 10.B Destination countries key characteristics used in the gravity model analysis

	Country	Population ('000, 2010 levels)	GDP per capita (2010)	Number of top universities (QS top 200, 2011)	Life expectancy at birth (2011 levels)
1	Australia	22,297.52	40,790.00	5	81.9
2	Austria	8,389.77	40,064.84	1	80.9
3	Belgium	10,895.58	37,727.84	5	80
4	Canada	34,108.75	39,049.96	8	81

5	Chile	17,094.28	16,155.92	0	79.1
6	Czech Republic	10,519.79	25,257.84	0	77.7
7	Denmark	5,547.68	40,189.88	3	78.8
8	Estonia	1,340.16	20,393.29	0	74.8
9	Finland	5,363.35	36,307.00	1	80
10	France	62,959.39	34,256.27	5	81.5
11	Germany	81,777.00	37,430.09	12	80.4
12	Greece	11,307.50	28,443.77	0	79.9
13	Hungary	10,000.02	20,555.61	0	74.4
14	Iceland	318.01	35,592.56	0	81.8
15	Ireland	4,474.36	40,478.13	3	80.6
16	Israel	7,623.60	26,531.13	2	81.6
17	Italy	60,483.39	31,911.10	1	81.9
18	Japan	128,057.40	33,785.24	11	83.4
19	Luxembourg	506.95	86,269.35	0	80
20	Netherlands	16,615.39	42,195.57	11	80.7
21	New Zealand	4,368.00	29,710.88	2	80.7
22	Norway	4,889.25	57,259.45	2	81.1
23	Poland	38,186.86	19,908.16	0	76.1
24	Portugal	10,637.35	25,444.29	0	79.5
25	Russia	142,958.20	19,833.00	1	68.8
26	Slovakia	5,430.10	23,263.64	0	75.4
27	Slovenia	2,048.58	26,941.00	0	79.3
28	South Korea	49,410.37	28,797.31	0	80.6
29	Spain	46,070.97	31,903.80	2	81.4
30	Sweden	9,378.13	39,345.59	5	81.4
31	Switzerland	7,822.30	48,656.57	6	82.3
32	Turkey	72,698.00	15,603.71	0	74
33	United Kingdom	61,344.00	35,686.80	29	80.2
34	United States	309,330.20	46,587.62	54	78.5

Source: OECD country Factbook (2010), QS World University Ranking (2011).

Appendix C: the gravity model

We begin by specifying the production-constrained gravity equation:

$$T_{ij} = A_i O_i d_{ij}{}^{\beta} \left(\Pi_k w_{jk}^{\alpha_k} \right)$$
(C.1)

where:

$$A_i = \left(\Sigma_j d_{ij}{}^{\beta} \left(\Pi_k w_{jk}^{\alpha_k} \right) \right)^{-1}$$
(C.2)

Where T_{ij} is the international student flow from country i and country, A_i functions as a balancing factor for the model, O_i is the total number of international students from country of origin i, d_{ij} is the geographical distance between countries i and j, β is the distance decay parameter, w_{jk} is a vector of characteristics of the destination countries j and α_k is a vector of parameters that reflect the influence of the respective characteristics on international student flows. The distance between countries is included as a power function, since its properties are more suitable to describe the declining marginal effect on student flows of large distances between the countries in the sample.

Following Fotheringham and O'Kelly (1989), the model in (1) can be linearized and estimated by Ordinary Least Squares in the following form:

$$\ln\left(T_{ij}\right) - \frac{1}{n}\Sigma_j \ln\left(T_{ij}\right) = \beta\left[\ln\left(d_{ij}\right) - \frac{1}{n}\Sigma_j \ln\left(d_{ij}\right)\right] + \tag{C.3}$$

$$\Sigma_k \alpha_k\left(\ln\left(w_{jk}\right) - \frac{1}{n}\Sigma_j \ln\left(w_{jk}\right)\right) + \epsilon_{ij}$$

Rearranging equation (3) we get:

$$\ln\left(T_{ij}\right) = k_i + \beta \ln\left(d_{ij}\right) + \Sigma_k \alpha_k \ln\left(w_{jk}\right) + \epsilon_{ij} \tag{C.4}$$

where:

$$k_i = \frac{1}{n}\Sigma_j \ln\left(T_{ij}\right) - \beta\left(\frac{1}{n}\Sigma_j \ln\left(d_{ij}\right)\right) + \Sigma_k \alpha_k\left(\frac{1}{n}\Sigma_j \ln\left(w_{jk}\right)\right) \tag{C.5}$$

The term k_i performs as a vector of origin-specific constants, which reflects destination countries' propulsiveness, or propensity to generate outflows of international students.

The model in equation (4) will be estimated using two specifications which differ in the number of explanatory variables w_{jk} included.

Appendix D: interpretation of the Multinomial Logit (MNL) model coefficients

In order to interpret the estimated MNL coefficients we return to the model design and the estimated choice probabilities of each individual i to choose alternative HEI: $Pr_{i,j} = \dfrac{e^{V_{ij}}}{\Sigma_j e^{V_{ij}}}$. Since the reference group are local students of Dutch nationality, their indirect utility function is:

$$V_{Dutch,j} = \beta_{j,0} + \epsilon_{Dutch,j} \tag{D.1}$$

while the indirect utility of other origin groups i is:

$$V_{ij} = \beta_{j,0} + \Sigma_k \Sigma_l \beta_{k,l} X_{j,k} Z_{i,l} + \epsilon_{i,j} \tag{D.2}$$

Therefore, the probability that an individual from origin group i will choose alternative HEI j can be expressed in the following odds-ratio formulation:

$$\frac{Pr_{i,j}}{Pr_{Dutch,j}} = \frac{e^{V_{i,j}} / \Sigma_j e^{V_{i,j}}}{e^{V_{Dutch,j}} / \Sigma_j e^{V_{Dutch,j}}} = \frac{e^{V_{i,j}}}{e^{V_{Dutch,j}}} * \frac{\Sigma_j e^{V_{Dutch,j}}}{\Sigma_j e^{V_{i,j}}} \tag{D.3}$$

Assuming all properties are fixed except one attribute k, the expression in C.3 becomes:

$$\frac{Pr_{i,j}}{Pr_{Dutch,j}} = e^{\beta_{k,l} X_{j,k}} * \frac{\Sigma_j e^{V_{Dutch,j}}}{\Sigma_j e^{V_{i,j}}} \tag{D.4}$$

The probability that an individual from origin group i would choose an alternative j, as compared to other alternatives, is simpler to derive:

$$\frac{Pr_{i,j}}{Pr_{i,h}} = \frac{e^{V_{i,j}} / \Sigma_j e^{V_{i,j}}}{e^{V_{i,h}} / \Sigma_j e^{V_{i,j}}} = \frac{e^{V_{i,j}}}{e^{V_{i,h}}}, \forall h \neq j \tag{D.5}$$

Assuming all properties are fixed except one property k, the expression in C.5 becomes:

$$\frac{Pr_{i,j}}{Pr_{i,h}} = e^{\beta_{k,l} X_{j,k}} \tag{D.6}$$

The interpretation of $\beta_{k,l}$ is therefore the difference in odds ratio which results from a change of one unit of attribute k, or the difference in odds ratio if attribute k is present (in the case of dummy variables).

Notes

1 Since students' decisions are guided by expected labour outcomes, if their expected benefit exceeds the study and mobility costs they signal the students' potential productivity.
2 See King *et al.* (2010) for a meta-analysis on recent literature and statistics on student mobility into and out of the UK. They summarize the main results presented and discussed on the literature on the UK, including trends, international comparisons, determinants of mobility, mobile students profile and higher education institution policies and practices.

3 These two concepts are, of course, related but not necessarily identical.

4 There may, of course, be differences between amenity levels within countries, but since we are focusing here on flows between countries as a whole, they are not dealt with explicitly.

5 In most countries, exchange students are not enrolled at the university as foreign students are.

6 See at: http://www.topuniversities.com/university-rankings/world-university-rankings/2011

7 See at: http://www.happyplanetindex.org/data/

8 Dummy coefficients in the model are interpreted using the following equation: $ct = 100 * \left(e^{\beta} - 1\right)$. See Halvorsen and Palmquist (1980) for more information regarding the interpretation of dummy variables' coefficients in semi-logarithmic models.

9 The database is available online at http://www.studiekeuzeinformatie.nl/studiekeuzedatabase/.

10 Formally, $Pr_{i,j} = \dfrac{e^{V_{ij}}}{\Sigma_j e^{V_{ij}}}$, with $V_{ij} = \beta_{j,0} + \Sigma_k \Sigma_l \beta_{k,l} X_{j,k} Z_{i,l} + \epsilon_{i,j}$. $Pr_{i,j}$ is the probability for individual i to select HEI j, $V_{i,j}$ is the indirect utility that individual i derives from alternative j, $X_{j,k}$ is the K-th characteristics of alternative j, and $Z_{i,l}$ is a dummy variable which is equal to 1 when individual i belongs to nationality group l, and is equal to zero otherwise. $\beta_{j,0}$ is an alternative specific constant which captures unobserved features of alternatives j. The reference group is set to be Dutch nationality, and therefore the interpretation of the estimated coefficients is the preference of a particular group l compared to the preferences of Dutch students.

11 That is, the number of programmes taught in English may be the result of the presence of many foreign students, rather than a cause.

12 Note that students may come to the Netherlands after finishing a bachelor's programme in their native country. The fact that most bachelor's programmes in the Netherlands are taught in Dutch can be expected to contribute to this phenomenon.

13 This was stimulated by the so-called Bologna agreement.

14 Note that these figures refer to where students *and graduates* live. Although The Hague has fewer university campuses (although several HBOs), it is popular among graduates because they can find more employment there.

15 Source: Studiekeuze Informatie, http://www.studiekeuzeinformatie.nl/studiekeuze database/.

References

Adsera, A and Pytlikova, M 2012, *The role of language in shaping international migration.* IZA Discussion Paper No. 6333.

Agarwal, VB and Winkler, DR 1985, Foreign demand for United States higher education: a study of developing countries in the eastern hemisphere. *Economic Development and Cultural Change* 33, 623–644.

Aslanbeigui, N and Montecinos, V 1998, Foreign students in US doctoral programs. *Journal of Economic Perspectives* 12, 171–182.

Åslund, O 2005, Now and forever? Initial and subsequent location choices of immigrants. *Regional Science and Urban Economics* 35(2), 141–165.

Bartel, AP 1989, Where do the new US immigrants live? *Journal of Labor Economics* 7(4), 371–391.

Beine, M, Noel, R and Ragot, L 2013, *The determinants of international mobility of students*. CEPII Working Paper No. 2013-30.

Bertrand-Cloodt, D, Corvers, F and Heijke, H 2012, Are the Netherlands losing their highly able graduates by going abroad for work or PhD? Paper presented at the 1st CEMIR Conference on International Migration: Competition for Talent and Brain Circulation.

Bessey, D 2012, International student migration to Germany. *Empirical Economics* 42(1), 345–361.

Bijwaard, G and Wang, Q 2013, Return migration of foreign students. IZA Discussion Paper No. 7185.

Bourke, A 2000, A model of the determinants of international trade in higher education. *The Service Industries Journal* 20, 110–138.

Brown, WM and Scott, DM 2012, Human capital location choice: accounting for amenities and thick labor markets. *Journal of Regional Science* 52(5), 787–808.

Comay, Y 1970, The benefits and costs of study abroad and migration. *Canadian Journal of Economics* 3, 300–308.

Dreher, A and Poutvaara, P 2011, Foreign students and migration to the United States. *World Development* 39(8), 1294–1307.

Felbermayr, GJ and Reczkowski, I 2012, *International student mobility and high-skilled migration: the evidence*. Ifo Working Paper No. 132.

Findlay, AM, King, R, Smith, FM, Geddes, A and Skeldon, R 2011, *World class? An Investigation of globalization, difference and international student mobility*. Transactions of the Institute of British Geographers.

Fotheringham, AS and O'Kelly, ME 1989, *Spatial interaction models: formulations and Applications*. Dordrecht: Kluwer Academic.

Glaeser, EL and Saiz, A 2003, *The rise of the skilled city*. National Bureau of Economic Research, Working Paper No. w10191.

Glaeser, E, Kolko, J and Saiz, A 2001, Consumer city. *Journal of Economic Geography* 1(1), 27–50.

González, CR, Mesanza, RB and Mariel, P 2011, The determinants of international student mobility flows: an empirical study on the Erasmus programme. *Higher Education* 62(4), 413–430.

Gottlieb, PD and Joseph, G 2006, College-to-work migration of technology graduates and holders of doctorates within the United States. *Journal of Regional Science* 46(4), 627–659.

Gungor, ND and Tansel, A 2012, Brain drain from Turkey: an investigation of students return intentions. *Applied Economics* 40, 3069–3087.

Gupta, V, Hanges, PJ and Dorfman, P 2002, Cultural clusters: methodology and findings. *Journal of World Business* 37(1), 11–15.

Halvorsen, R and Palmquist, R 1980, The interpretation of dummy variables in semilogarithmic equations. *American economic review* 70(3), 474–475.

Hercog, M and van de Laar, M 2013, *Determinants of international mobility decision: the case-study of India*. UNU-MERIT Working Paper Series 2013-067.

Jaeger, DA 2006, *Green Cards and the location choices of immigrants in the United States, 1971–2000*. Institute for the Study of Labor (IZA), (IZA Discussion Papers, No. 2145).

Jena, F and Reilly, B 2013, The determinants of United Kingdom student visa demand from developing countries. *IZA Journal of Labor and Development* 2(6), 1–22.

Karemera, D, Oguledo, VI and Davis, B 2000, A gravity model analysis of international migration to North America. *Applied Economics* 32(13), 1745–1755.

King, R, Findlay, A and Ahrens, J 2010, *International student mobility literature review.* Report to Higher Education Funding Council for England.

Lee, KH and Tan, P 1984, The international flow of third level lesser developed country students to developed countries: determinants and implications. *Higher Education* 13, 687–707.

Letouzé, E, Purser, M, Rodríguez, F and Cummins, M 2009, Revisiting the migration–development nexus: a gravity model approach. UNDP Human Development Reports, Research Paper no. 2009/44.

Mazzarol, T and Soutar, GN 2002, Push-pull factors influencing international student destination choice. *International Journal of Educational Management* 16, 82–90.

Moretti, E 2012, *The new geography of jobs.* New York: Houghton Mifflin Harcourt.

Musumbaa, M, Jinb, YH and Mjeldea, JW 2011, Factors influencing career location preferences of international graduate students in the United States. *Education Economics* 19(5), 501–517

Naidoo, V 2007, Research on the flow of international students to UK universities: determinants and implications. *Journal of Research in International Education* 6(3), 287–307.

Oosterbeek, H and Webbink, D 2011, Does studying abroad induce a brain drain? *Economica* 78, 347–366.

Ottaviano, G and Peri, G 2006, The economic value of cultural diversity: evidence from US cities. *Journal of Economic Geography* 6(1), 9–44.

Parey, M and Waldinger, F 2011, Studying abroad and the effect on international labour market mobility: evidence from the introduction of ERASMUS. *Economic Journal* 121, 194–222.

Perkins, R and Neumayer, E 2014, Geographies of educational motilities: exploring the uneven flows of international students. *Geographical Journal*, 180(3), 246–259.

Pimpa, N 2003, The influence of family on Thai students' choices of international education. *International journal of Educational Management* 17(5), 211–219. Scientific and Technical Report JRC 70059 EN.

Rodrigues, M 2012, *Determinants and impacts of student mobility: A literature review.* Scientific and technical reports, European Commission, Luxembourg: Publications Office of the European Union, Joint Research Centre-Institute for the Protection and Security of the Citizen.

Rodrigues, M 2013, *Does students' mobility during higher education pay? Evidence from 16 European countries.* European Commission: JRC Scientific and Policy Reports.

Rodríguez-Pose, A and Ketterer, TD 2012, Do local amenities affect the appeal of regions in Europe for migrants? *Journal of Regional Science* 52(4), 535–561.

Sá, C, Florax, R and Rietveld, P 2004, Determinants of the regional demand for higher education in the Netherlands: A gravity model approach. *Regional Studies* 38(4), 375–392.

Salisbury, MH, Umbach, PD, Paulsen, MB and Pascarella, ET 2009, Going global: understanding the choice process of the intent to study abroad. *Research in Higher Education* 50, 119–143.

Shanka, T, Quintal, V and Taylor, R 2006, Factors influencing international students' choice of an education destination – a correspondence analysis. *Journal of Marketing for Higher Education* 15, 31–46.

Soo, KT and Elliott, C 2010, Does price matter? Overseas students in UK higher education. *Economics of Education Review* 29(4), 553–565.

Soon, JJ 2010, The determinants of students' return intentions: A partial proportional odds model. *Journal of Choice Modelling* 3(2), 89–112.

Suedekum, J, Wolf, K and Blien, U 2009, *Cultural diversity and local labour markets.* IZA Discussion Papers, No. 4619.

Szelényi, K 2006, Students without borders? Migratory decision-making among international graduate students in the US. *Knowledge, Technology and Policy* 19(3), 64–86.

Van Bouwel, LAC and Veugelers, R 2010, Does university quality drive international student flows? Center for Economic Policy Research Discussion Paper 7657.

Van Duijn, M and Rouwendal, J 2013, Cultural heritage and the location choice of Dutch households in a residential sorting model. *Journal of Economic Geography* 13(3), 473–500.

Veenhoven, R 1996, Happy life expectancy. *Social Indicators Research* 39(1), 1–58.

Wiers-Jenssen, J and Try, S 2005, Labour market outcomes of higher education undertaken abroad. *Studies in Higher Education* 30, 681–705.

11 Location choices of highly educated foreign workers

The importance of urban amenities

Or Levkovich and Jan Rouwendal

Introduction

Skills are generally thought to be one of the drivers of economic growth. Human capital is an important determinant of productivity and 'the race between education and technology' (Goldin and Katz 2009) is an important driver of income distribution. Globalization has resulted in a decline of manufacturing in the Western world and a shift of core activities towards innovative and skills-intensive industries, for which human capital is one of the key resources. The increasing mobility, particularly of highly educated workers, underlines the need to make cities attractive places for such people to work and live. The ability of cities to attract international migrants, particularly those with higher levels of human capital, is therefore increasingly seen as an important indicator of their growth potential (Glaeser and Resseger 2010; Glaeser and Saiz 2003; Moretti 2012).

The effect of immigration on economic growth has been studied extensively in the recent literature, including, in particular, examination of the effects of different compositions of groups of migrants, mostly based on skills and nationality diversification. Positive effects on productivity may result from diversity in ideas and skills, which may improve innovation (Hunt and Gauthier-Loiselle 2008; Niebuhr 2010; Ottaviano and Peri 2006; Suedekum, Wolf and Blien 2009). Also, immigration flows of human capital have been found to encourage local employment levels through a multiplier effect (Moretti 2010; Moretti and Thulin 2013). Moreover, the presence of migrants may positively affect the utility of residing in a region by creating a multicultural environment which is positively perceived by a tolerant native population (Moretti 2004; Niebuhr 2010; Ottaviano and Peri 2006; Suedekum *et al.* 2009). In contrast, negative impacts on productivity may arise from communication and cultural barriers, and a relatively high proportion of migrants may also crowd out natives from jobs, particularly those with medium skills levels (Eeckhout, Pinheiro and Schmidheiny 2010). Migration flows may also result in social tensions between groups, and may generate fear of foreign infiltration among natives (Bellini, Ottaviano, Pinelli and Prarolo 2008; Ottaviano and Peri 2006; Ozgen, Nijkamp and Poot 2011; Suedekum *et al.* 2009).

Since the presence of migrants is so essential for urban and regional growth, it is important to know what makes a city an attractive place for highly skilled migrants. This chapter aims to shed light on the issue by considering the location choices of highly educated foreign workers, and how their valuation of urban amenities differs from that of domestic workers. To do so, we apply a residential location-choice model to estimate the attractiveness of residential locations to low- and high-skilled, domestic and foreign workers, and calculate and compare their willingness to pay for each of these amenities. Our location-choice model is based on earlier work by Bayer and his co-authors (Bayer, McMillan and Rueben 2004), and is estimated on data about the location choices of households in the Netherlands.

The text is organized as follows. In the next section we will describe relevant and recent research on the valuation of urban amenities and their role as attraction factors, and studies that have investigated the location choices of individuals, particularly skilled and migrant workers. In the then following section we discuss the residential sorting model and explain the design of the estimation model. After an introduction to the data that was used and the variables that were included, a section will follow that describes the results of the estimation. Finally, a discussion and concluding remarks are presented.

The importance of urban amenities as attraction factors for foreign skilled workers

Since the beginning of the twenty-first century, increasing attention has been given to the role of cities as centres of consumption and production. This perspective suggests that urban amenities and urban attraction factors are important for the growth of cities (Adamson, Clark and Partridge 2004; Brueckner 2000; Glaeser, Kolko and Saiz 2001). The perception of cities as centres of consumption focuses the analysis of residential location choices on the provision of urban amenities, as these determine the unique characteristics of a city and the utility which individuals derive from them.

Much research is still being conducted around the question of what determines valuation patterns of urban amenities. Valuation of urban amenities differs between population groups, based on their specific characteristics such as origin, skills and income levels. These differences influence the location decisions of individual households between these groups. The implication is that households are sorted into different cities, or into neighbourhoods within a city, based on their individual willingness to pay for the provision of certain urban amenities (Bayer, Ferreira, and McMillan 2007; Brueckner 2000; Van Duijn and Rouwendal 2013). Assertions that urban amenities are not valued equally by heterogeneous households, and that urban amenities can develop endogenously for social and economic conditions, are emphasized in studies that refer to the preferences of migrants. Rodríguez-Pose and Ketterer (2012) examine the role of urban amenities in the location choice processes of of migrants in Europe, and find that historic as well as natural amenities are important in determining the attractiveness of regions. They also find that factors such as the presence of a large migrant community, regional wealth and favourable local labour market conditions are relevant in determining the geographical appeal to migrants of different EU regions. Åslund (2005), Damm (2012) and Jaeger (2006) studied the location choices of international migrants. They do not base the set of alternatives directly on urban amenities but on the effects of social interaction – the existing population demographics – and of the local labour market. Their findings emphasize the importance of existing communities and networks of migrants, and the expected labour outcome, in the choice of a migration destination. A local migrants' network is viewed as an attractive amenity for migrants, since it provides information about the local labour market at the destination and it assists new migrants in finding jobs (Åslund 2005; Bauer, Epstein, Gang and Al 2007; Borjas 1994; Jaeger 2006; Munshi 2003).

However, an existing community of migrants should also be considered as an endogenously determined amenity. Namely, a concentration of migrants in a city or neighbourhood may be the result, as well as the cause, of migrants' location decisions. This concern was addressed by instrumental variable techniques[1] by Ottaviano and Peri (2006) and Mocetti and Porello (2010), which used the distance to an immigration gateway as an instrument for the current concentration of migrants. Damm (2012) deals with the endogenous concentration of migrants by exploiting a natural experiment in which refugees in Denmark were assigned quasi randomly to municipalities. Hunt and Gauthier-Loiselle (2008) and Niebuhr (2010) instrumented the existing proportion of skilled migrants by the lagged proportion of low-skilled migrants, as the proportions of both groups are likely to be correlated (some urban amenities appeal to both), but the presence of unskilled migrants is unlikely to be correlated with skilled migrants' effects on innovation and productivity.

Migrants' location decisions are also largely determined by their individual skill levels. Bartel (1989) focuses particularly on the subpopulation of highly educated migrants and finds that their location decisions may be opposite to those of the rest of the migrant population. For example, she finds that highly skilled migrants from Europe or Asia to the US tend to locate away from areas with a large community from the same ethnic origin. This finding shows that neglecting heterogeneity in personal characteristics within groups of migrants, particularly in skill levels, may lead to biased estimates of their choice of residential locations and their valuation of urban amenities.

Comparing the location choices of migrant workers of different skill levels, Gottlieb and Joseph (2006) find that holders of doctoral degree have a much higher valuation of regional amenities, even in comparison with other highly skilled migrants. The authors explain this by arguing that doctorate holders have more bargaining power in employment negotiations, enabling them to demand and secure a high level of amenities. In addition, they also find that educated migrants tend to value areas with higher percentages of university graduates, or better-educated cities. Contrary to Gottlieb and Joseph's findings, Brown and Scott (2012) find that higher-educated workers (measured as academic degree holders) value recreational and destination labour market amenities similarly to the rest of the migrant population. They also find that, compared with less-skilled workers, highly skilled migrants place a higher value on the benefits of thick labour markets. Highly educated workers thus appear to be more likely to seek larger labour markets in which they can specialize in their industry and occupation. This may result in higher productivity and wages, which may favour further concentration of human capital from other specialized industry peers.

Despite the extensive research which was conducted in the field of valuation of urban amenities, and their attraction effect on skilled migrants, it is evident that the complexity of the issue leaves much room for further research. Researchers generally agree that residential decisions depend closely on several urban amenities, such as a large labour market, an existing community of migrants, urban scale, accessibility, natural factors and historic amenities. However, most studies do not provide estimations of the willingness to pay (either positive or negative) for amenities. This chapter aims to contribute to the literature by focusing on this issue. The valuation of marginal willingness to pay (MWTP) for urban amenities has a direct use in urban policy, but it may also help in making a comparison of the preferences and location decisions of groups of domestic and foreign, skilled and low-skilled workers. Understanding whether the decisions of highly educated migrants have more resemblance to those of low-skilled migrants, or to those of skilled native workers, would further help to focus urban or regional policy that aims to attract skilled migrants.

The residential sorting model

Methodology

The most prevalent method of estimating location choices in the literature is by using the multinomial logit (MNL) model. Allowing for a sufficient amount of heterogeneity among the consumers allows aggregate substitution elasticities to be determined by the data, which makes the presence of the independence of irrelevant alternative property at the level of the individual decision maker – which has long been regarded as an important drawback – less of a problem.[2] The MNL-based sorting model is used below to estimate the probabilities for each household *i* to choose each location *n*, based on the assumption of households' maximization of utility. The estimated parameters reveal the valuation of the alternative locations' characteristics. In this respect the sorting model is similar to hedonic regression models, which are most commonly used in literature for this purpose.[3] However, in addition to the average MWTP for amenities, which is also revealed by hedonic analysis, the residential sorting model provides the MWTP of specific groups of households.

The residential sorting model – design of the model

The logit-based residential sorting model was introduced in Chapter 6. The model used here has the same structure. To deal with the endogeneity of the housing price variable, we construct an instrument using the procedure employed in

Chapter 6. A similar endogeneity concern now occurs in relation to endogenous amenities like the proportion of migrants located in a city, which is also determined in part by the unobserved amenities. As mentioned, the concentration of migrants was previously instrumented by exogenous variables such as a historical immigrant 'gateway', through which historical immigration flows have entered the country (Mocetti and Porello 2010; Ottaviano and Peri 2006). Although this variable might be suitable to explain location choices over a large geographical area like the United States, it is practically inapplicable in a small country like the Netherlands. Therefore, we construct an instrument for the proportion of migrants in municipalities by using the same procedure as in the construction of the price instrument. Namely, we construct the counterfactual proportion of migrants as it would have been if there were no unobserved municipal characteristics.

Therefore, the second step of the estimation includes instrumental variables for both prices and the proportion of migrants. As was done by Bayer *et al.* (2004) and Van Duijn and Rouwendal (2013), we construct the instruments based on the sorting model and existing data. We do so by assuming no unobserved neighbourhood characteristics ($\xi_n = 0$). Following this, we simultaneously compute the price and proportion of migrants' vectors which would clear the market under this restriction. Intuitively, the price instrument is the set of prices that would prevail in equilibrium if the only amenities relevant to location decisions are those observed in the model, and the instrument for the proportion of migrants is the proportion that would be observed in this situation. The computed instruments are valid, since they are correlated with the original price and proportion of migrants variables, respectively, and they are defined such that they would have zero correlation with unobserved characteristics.

Spatial extensions

The Randstad study area is an urban cluster characterized by high population density and continuity in the urban landscape. Municipal borders are irregular and do not represent a barrier (they are hardly noticeable), which raises the issue of spatial interdependence between the different municipalities. Households can reside in one municipality and enjoy the amenities of the neighbouring municipalities, without experiencing high travel costs. To address this issue we add a spatially weighted average of amenity levels in the neighbouring municipalities, a so-called spatial lag, to the set of explanatory variables.[4] Additionally, we also consider the possibility that the unobserved amenities may be spatially correlated, and therefore, following Anselin (1988) and Anselin *et al.* (1996), we test for spatial correlation in the residuals of the model using Moran's I and Lagrange-multiplier test (see results in Table 11.1).

The statistical values obtained for Moran's I and the Lagrange-multiplier test for residual spatial correlation show little evidence that such correlation exists. Although these values suggest that we can estimate the model without considering spatial correlation in the model's residuals, we include an additional estimation of the model using Drukker *et al.*'s (Drukker, Egger, and Prucha 2013;

Table 11.1 Test statistics for spatial dependence

	Statistic	p-value
Moran's I	−0.051	0.419
Lagrange multiplier	0.033	0.855
Lagrange multiplier (Robust)	0.076	0.783

Note: The statistics are computed using GAUSS, following Anselin (1988).

Drukker and Prucha 2011) GMM/IV estimation method for the purpose of checking robustness.[5]

Calculations of the MWTP for urban attributes

Estimation of the sorting model produces a set of coefficients that determine the valuation of each of the observed attributes by the average household in the sample as well as for specific types of households. We use these estimated coefficients to compute the MWTP for the observed location attributes. The MWTP for a characteristic is the change in the housing price that keeps utility constant after a small change in the value of that characteristic. Below we report average values of the MWTP, which refer to the whole population, as well as deviations from that average that are related to household characteristics. By computing these MWTPs, we get insight into the monetary value placed on various urban amenities by each group in the population, based on skill level and origin. This facilitates measuring which amenities are perceived to be more valuable and attractive to each of the groups, explanation of their location patterns and comparison of the differences between groups in preferences for urban amenities.

Data and study areas

Databases

For residential location choices data we use the Netherlands housing research survey (WoON) 2012, which was conducted jointly by the Ministry of the Interior and Kingdom Relations and Statistics Netherlands. Data about municipality characteristics is also taken from Statistics Netherlands.

Randstad municipalities analysis

The western area of the Netherlands is characterized by high levels of urbanization, and it is in fact a set of cities located relatively close to each other, with a central part that is still mainly agricultural in use (the Randstad). Among the cities which are included in the Randstad are the four largest cities in the Netherlands – Amsterdam, Rotterdam, Den-Haag (The Hague, also known as 's-Gravenhage) and Utrecht. The region also includes other municipalities with a relatively large population, such as Almere, Zaanstad, Amersfoort, Leiden, Zoetermeer and Dordrecht. Despite its high overall population density, the centre of the Randstad remains relatively rural ('Het Groene Hart' – The Green Heart) and its municipalities maintain an agricultural character. The borders of the Randstad are not officially specified, and in this analysis we include 135 different municipalities (see Appendix Table 11.A for the full list), all within a short commuting distance of the main population centres in the four largest cities (Figure 11.1).

Since the Randstad is relatively small and urbanized, commuting is common and individuals may live in one municipality but work and enjoy amenities in another nearby municipality. To address the issue of spatial interdependence we introduce spatial data into the model, using spatial matrixes which were constructed based on contiguity of neighbouring municipality as well as on inverse distance between municipality centroids.

Variables included – household characteristics

Households are identified based on several characteristics, as indicated by each respondent in the WoON 2012 survey. We use the respondent's age, a dummy

Figure 11.1 The Randstad study area within the Netherlands

variable indicating whether the household includes children, and the logarithm of household income. We also add additional dummy variables indicating whether the respondent is a high-skilled domestic worker, a low-skilled migrant or a high-skilled migrant. Since these variables play a key role in our analysis, we discuss them in some detail.

The identification of a respondent's migration status or skill level is somewhat uncertain. While skill level is more clearly determined, as we define a person as 'skilled' by whether he or she indicates having obtained at least a professional or university degree, inaccuracies may still exist, as some may be more inclined to indicate a different skill level. For instance, students at an advanced of stage in their degree studies may identify themselves as degree holders.

We identify respondents as 'migrants' if they have indicated themselves to be not of Dutch descent. The question in the WoON survey on which this information is based is wide open for interpretation by respondents and researchers alike. This definition can be criticized, but it has the clear advantage of enabling selection of those who do not regard themselves as of Dutch descent. It may also be argued that the self-identification of migrants is more suitable for our research because we want to distinguish between the preferences of the Dutch and the others.[6] According to WoON 2012 survey data, approximately 24% of the survey respondents who live in the Randstad area are of foreign origin (6,322 respondents). NUTS3 (Nomenclature of Units for Territorial Statistics) areas (*COROP* – Coordination Commission Regional Research Programme) with the highest concentration of migrants are the Amsterdam metropolitan area (Groot Amsterdam) and The Hague metropolitan area (Agglomeratie 's-Gravenhage), each with approximately 31% of respondents identifying themselves as migrants. Areas with the lowest concentration of migrants are Delft-Westland and East Zuid-Holland *(Oost Zuid-Holland)*, with 11% and 13% of migrants, respectively. The Randstad area also has a large proportion of skilled respondents; approximately 45% of the skilled respondents in WoON 2012 report that they live in one of the Randstad municipalities. Of the skilled population in the Randstad, approximately 21% (or 1,832) respondents are skilled migrants. Skilled migrants also form 29% of the total migrant respondents in the Randstad.

Variables included – urban amenities

In order to explain the location choice of different population groups in the Randstad area, we included several amenities as explanatory variables. Following the findings of previous researches, we included recreational, cultural and natural amenities, as well as amenities which stress labour possibilities, accessibility and urban scale. As a proxy for the existence of migrant networks, we also included the proportion of migrants in each municipality as an explanatory variable. Average municipality housing prices are also included in our analysis. Both prices and the proportion of migrants are instrumented as explained before.

Housing prices are calculated using hedonic regressions, which were based on data gathered from NVM, the Dutch real estate association. Data on the proportion of migrants in each municipality is taken from Statistics Netherlands. A migrant is defined as a person with at least one parent not born in the Netherlands. This broad definition is quite different from the WoON data definition of a foreigner, according to which respondents are required to indicate whether they consider themselves to belong to a non-Dutch ethnic group. Although the differences between definitions may create problems, they are not critically restrictive, since the Statistics Netherlands definition is used to characterize a location in terms of the size of its migrant community, while the WoON definition is used to characterize individuals' preferences.

Consistent with the discussion presented in the literature review regarding the possible positive and negative effects of an existing foreign community, we introduce the proportion of migrants into the model both directly and as a square term. The purpose of this specification is to identify whether the marginal effect of an increase in the proportion of migrants differs between lower and higher levels of proportion. In accordance with the literature, we expect that the positive effects of an existing community of migrants will be dominant when the proportion of migrants is relatively low, and the negative effects will be dominant where the proportion of migrants is higher (Bellini *et al.* 2008; Ottaviano and Peri 2006; Ozgen *et al.* 2011; Suedekum *et al.* 2009).

To represent culture and recreation we use the number of national monuments in the municipalities (see Appendix Table 11.A), which have been shown by Van Duijn and Rouwendal (2013) to be a good proxy for historical and cultural heritage, as well as other recreational and commercial activities which are attracted by historical scenery, like cafés and restaurants. The data is taken from the Dutch Cultural Heritage Agency. We also use the area of nature coverage in a municipality as an indicator for the natural scenery amenity in a municipality, which is assumed to have a positive valuation, due its recreational and aesthetic attributes.

Since previous research found that labour market conditions matter for the location choices of migrants, particularly those with a high level of education, we added the number of jobs in a municipality, and its level of accessibility (see Appendix Table 11.A). We also included a rail-accessibility variable, which is measured by the average distance of all residents in an area from the nearest train station (available from Statistics Netherlands). Much like the number of jobs variable, which represents the 'thickness' of the labour market, we also add the location-quotient of employment in information and communication (ICT) industries, an employment sector which includes computer and software development, as well as the media industry. A relatively high concentration of these knowledge-intensive industries (approximately 60% of employees in this sector have a university or professional degree) in a specific municipality is assumed to be particularly appealing for skilled workers of foreign origin. The ICT sector is over-represented (location quotient (LQ) of 3.47) in the Den Haag metropolitan area, Het Gooi (north-eastern Randstad), Utrecht, Amsterdam and Haarlem areas. In the rest of the sub-regions of the Randstad, notably in Groot-Rijnmond where Rotterdam is located, the ICT industry is quite under-represented (see Appendix Table 11.A).

In addition, we also attempt to proxy the urban scale of a municipality using the number of households as a variable. As was previously noted by Gottlieb and Joseph (2006), who include city size as a similar variable to reflect urban scale, this inclusion creates a problem, as urban scale is correlated both with the provision of recreational amenities (such as theatres, restaurants and major sport leagues) and with a thick labour market. Therefore, its coefficient is likely to have a positive bias. Examining the variables' correlation table (Table 11.2), we find that the number of households is too correlated with most variables to be included in the estimation.

Moreover, due to the number of households' high correlation with the number of jobs (99%), both variables may serve as a proxy for urban scale. The fact that urban scale may be embodied in many variables further emphasizes the problem of endogeneity in urban amenities variables, and the concern that it is difficult to identify amenities which are independent of other urban attraction factors.

Results

First-step estimation results

Table 11.3 describes the variables which were used in the estimation of the sorting model.

The results of the first step include the coefficients of the cross-effects between individual and location characteristics, as well as the vector of location-specific constants, which indicate the indirect utility of the mean household from each of the alternatives. The estimation shows that the coefficients of the households–amenities cross-effects are different from each other (Table 11.4). This serves as a preliminary demonstration that the valuation of urban amenities differs between different sub-groups of the population.

Examining the results of the first-step estimation, we first observe that skilled respondents have a positive and significant cross-effect with prices, as compared

Table 11.2 Correlation between urban amenities variables

	ln(price)	Perc. Migr	Accessibility	Jobs	Monuments	Nature	LQ (ICT)	Number of households
ln(price)	1							
Perc. Migr.	0.06	1						
Accessibility	−0.31	−0.47	1					
Jobs	0.02	0.68	−0.19	1				
Monuments	0.19	0.45	−0.11	0.79	1			
Nature	0.44	0.1	−0.1	−0.07	−0.05	1		
LQ (ICT)	0.42	0.26	−0.22	0.13	0.1	0.21	1	
Number of households	0	0.7	−0.2	0.99	0.8	−0.06	0.12	1

Source: Statistics Netherlands (wijk en buurtkaart, 2011), NVM (1985–2011), RCE (2011).

Table 11.3 Specification description

Individual characteristics (Z_l)	Alternative characteristics (X_k)	Spatial lags in the explanatory variables (PX_k)
• Age of respondent • Dummy if has kids • Income • Skilled native dummy • Low-skilled migrant dummy • Skilled migrant dummy	• ln (price) • Proportion of migrants • Proportion of migrants (square) • Accessibility (distance from intercity train station) • Number of jobs ('000) • Monuments • LQ (ICT) • Percentage of nature coverage	Included for all alternative characteristics variables except for prices.

Source: Statistics Netherlands (Population registry microdata, wijk en buurtkaart, 2011), NVM (1985-2011), RCE (2011).

with the other groups. This does not necessarily suggest that these groups value higher housing prices as a location attribute but, rather, that these groups are less sensitive to housing prices. The results also show positive and significant cross-coefficients of the existing community of migrants among both skilled native and migrant respondents of both skill levels, where the migrants' cross-coefficient is higher. The square terms of the migrant community proportion are, however, negative and significant coefficient among migrants. The net effect is that small proportions of migrants are more appreciated by migrants than by the average household, whereas the difference becomes smaller for larger proportions of migrants, and may even become negative.

Examining the cross-coefficients of the number of jobs in the municipality, values seem to be relatively low, particularly among skilled natives, who have a negative cross-coefficient, indicating a lower sensitivity to the number of jobs or to the urban scale of the municipality. These results can be explained by the cross-coefficients of the spatial lag, or the number of jobs in neighbouring municipalities. As expected, the values of these coefficients are generally higher, especially for the skilled groups of both local and migrant respondents. This corresponds with the higher preferences of skilled workers to reside in proximity to a large labour market and enjoyment of its urban-scale related amenities without actually residing there.

Regarding the valuation of a concentration of ICT employment, the results show positive and significant coefficients among migrants of both skill-level groups, with a much stronger valuation among skilled migrants. The results also show a negative and significant coefficient among skilled respondents and a positive coefficient among respondents with higher income levels. Since the

Table 11.4 First step results

	Age	Kids dummy	ln (income)	Skilled native	Migrant low-skilled	Migrant skilled
ln (Price)	-0.00191	-0.92884***	-0.52301***	2.064872***	-0.25085	1.532261***
	(0.0038)	(0.1482)	(0.0898)	(0.1616)	(0.1814)	(0.2256)
P.migr	-0.00140***	-0.04581***	-0.02218***	0.059102***	0.103589***	0.119127***
	(0.0001)	(0.0055)	(0.0031)	(0.0060)	(0.0074)	(0.0098)
P.migr (square)	0.000020***	0.000618***	-0.00001	-0.00049***	-0.00097***	-0.00127***
	(0.0000)	(0.0001)	(0.0000)	(0.0001)	(0.0001)	(0.0002)
Accessibility	-0.00066***	-0.01568***	0.003155	-0.01007*	0.001465	-0.05792***
	(0.0001)	(0.0049)	(0.0034)	(0.0055)	(0.0072)	(0.0095)
Jobs	-0.00005***	-0.00114***	0.000080	-0.00031	0.000290	-0.00183***
	(0.0000)	(0.0003)	(0.0001)	(0.0003)	(0.0003)	(0.0004)
Monuments	0.000002***	0.000059***	0.000072***	-0.00008***	0.000059***	0.000104***
	(0.0000)	(0.0000)	(0.0000)	(0.0000)	(0.0000)	(0.0000)
Nature	0.000181***	-0.00634***	0.006819***	-0.00741***	0.004789***	-0.00542***
	(0.0000)	(0.0011)	(0.0006)	(0.0011)	(0.0014)	(0.0018)
LQ (ICT)	0.002917***	-0.02809	0.095225***	-0.00471	0.051951**	0.107249***
	(0.0005)	(0.0196)	(0.0118)	(0.0223)	(0.0225)	(0.0288)
P.migr (spatial lag)	0.009090***	0.328049***	0.190527**	0.405741***	-0.18393	0.944389***
	(0.0030)	(0.1173)	(0.0803)	(0.1356)	(0.1501)	(0.2347)

(continued)

Table 11.4 (continued)

	Age	Kids dummy	ln (income)	Skilled native	Migrant low-skilled	Migrant skilled
P.migr (sq) (spatial lag)	-0.00016**	-0.00772**	-0.00375*	-0.01144***	0.004802	-0.01860***
	(0.0000)	(0.0031)	(0.0021)	(0.0035)	(0.0040)	(0.0059)
Accessibility (spatial lag)	0.002431**	0.033195	0.054198**	0.115608***	-0.07339	0.335551***
	(0.0010)	(0.0377)	(0.0259)	(0.0421)	(0.0521)	(0.0676)
Jobs (spatial lag)	-0.00009	0.008361	-0.00295	0.030109***	-0.01474	0.002236
	(0.0002)	(0.0089)	(0.0056)	(0.0098)	(0.0110)	(0.0145)
Monuments (spatial lag)	0.000089***	0.001479***	0.002323***	-0.00481***	0.003272***	0.002601***
	(0.0000)	(0.0005)	(0.0003)	(0.0006)	(0.0006)	(0.0008)
Nature (spatial lag)	0.000596**	-0.01740*	0.002991	-0.00208	0.010198	0.009520
	(0.0002)	(0.0093)	(0.0063)	(0.0102)	(0.0120)	(0.0163)
LQ (ICT) (spatial lag)	-0.02917***	0.299723***	-0.53668***	0.600603***	-0.80722***	-0.22486
	(0.0027)	(0.1067)	(0.0669)	(0.1184)	(0.1302)	(0.1545)

N=27163
Robust standard errors in parentheses

*** p<0.01, ** p<0.05, * p<0.1

<Estimation results>

ICT industry is skill intensive, this result is somewhat surprising. One possible explanation is that the LQ variable refers to a COROP area (NUTS3) which incorporates several municipalities. This means the industry may be concentrated in only one municipality within the COROP area, which would make the rest of the municipalities in the COROP area less attractive for skilled workers.

Cross-coefficients of monuments show that all groups are sensitive to these amenities. Somewhat surprisingly, the indicator for monuments in neighbouring municipalities has even larger coefficients than do those for the number of monuments in the municipality of residence. These results are also repeated in the preference for natural and recreational amenities, where, among all groups, preferences for natural amenities in neighbouring municipalities are found to be stronger.

Second-step estimation results

Table 11.5 describes the results of three model specifications – the OLS model, the 2SLS model where prices and proportion of migrants are instrumented, and the GMM/IV model for spatial autocorrelation in the residual, in the presence of endogenous regressors.

As expected, the results of the OLS model (column 1) show lower statistical significance levels of the estimated coefficients, and their values differ markedly from those of the other specification. Moreover, in examining the results of the GMM/IV specification we see that, as predicted by the spatial statistics indicators, the spatial correlation in the error term is indeed relatively weak (Spatial rho = 0.07). These two findings lead us to the decision to focus the analysis on the 2SLS model (column 2), which still considers spatial dependence in the explanatory variables.

The 2SLS model results, which are reported in column 2, show several important findings. First, as expected, price and distance from train stations coefficients were found to be negative, while coefficients for number of jobs, monuments and nature coverage were found to be positive. This indicates that the corresponding amenities were found to be negative and positive, respectively. As for the percentage of migrants, the linear term was found to be positive, while the square term was found to have a small but significant negative coefficient. The interpretation of this finding is that the percentage of migrants is valued positively by the average household, but that the effect of an additional percentage of migrants is smaller when the proportion of migrants is high, and may ultimately become negative. We return to this finding below.

The results of the spatially lagged amenities are found to be statistically insignificant for most amenities. Among the spatial-lag variables, the percentage of migrants' variables stands out. It appears that these coefficients are both statistically significant, as well as being estimated with much higher values as compared with the non-lagged variables. The interpretation of this finding is that having a large percentage of migrants in nearby municipalities is valued very positively, and it increases the expected attractiveness of a municipality much more, as

Table 11.5 Second step results

variable	(1)	(2)	(3)
	OLS (se)	2SLS (se)	GMM/IV (se)
ln (price)	−1.3412	−5.2204	−5.2055
	(0.473553)***	(0.592238)***	(1.195986)***
P.migr	0.163	0.172	0.1711
	(0.02166)***	(0.027089)***	(0.027197)***
P.migr (square)	−0.0032	−0.0039	−0.0039
	(0.000575)***	(0.000719)***	(0.000748)***
Accessibility	−0.0086	−0.0184	−0.0185
	(0.013818)	(0.017281)	(0.017646)
Jobs	0.0127	0.011	0.0109
	(0.001923)***	(0.002405)***	(0.002445)***
Monuments	−0.0001	0.0004	0.0004
	(0.000123)	(0.000154)**	(0.000195)*
Nature	0.0038	0.0168	0.0167
	(0.003834)	(0.004795)***	(0.005925)***
LQ (ICT)	−0.0473	0.0212	0.0097
	(0.07795)	(0.097486)	(0.099386)
P.migr (spatial lag)	0.6215	1.3812	1.3378
	(0.363302)*	(0.454356)***	(0.502419)***
P.migr (sq) (spatial lag)	−0.0149	−0.0274	−0.0264
	(0.009951)	(0.012445)**	(0.013068)**
Accessibility (spatial lag)	0.0705	0.0853	0.0832
	(0.105852)	(0.132382)	(0.13471)
Jobs (spatial lag)	0.0318	0.0161	0.0147
	(0.026278)	(0.032865)	(0.033811)
monuments (spatial lag)	−0.0025	−0.0001	−0.000025
	(0.001699)	(0.002125)	(0.002288)
nature (spatial lag)	−0.051	−0.1143	−0.1111
	(0.035821)	(0.044798)**	(0.048484)**
LQ (ICT industries) (spatial lag)	0.361	0.7951	0.8264
	(0.424465)	(0.530848)	(0.554267)
Constant	6.0811	45.8762	46.0308
	(5.795729)	(7.248299)***	(12.976206)***
Price level instrument	No	Yes	Yes
Proportion of migrants instrument	No	Yes	Yes
			Spatial Rho = 0.0538

Notes: n = 135.

Robust standard errors in parentheses
*** p<0.01, ** p<0.05, * p<0.1
<Estimation results>

compared to having large percentage of migrants in the municipality of choice itself. The spatially lagged variable of the percentage of migrants squared also has a higher coefficient value, as compared to the non-lagged variable. This suggests that also under spatial lags the positive effect of a large community of migrants declines at higher levels.

MWTP for urban amenities

Having estimated the two steps of the residential sorting model, we are able to use the coefficients in order to calculate the MWTP for each of the amenities included (as specified before). The calculation is based on the coefficients obtained by the estimation of the 2SLS, as specified in column 2 of Table 11.5. In the process of calculation we distinguish the valuation of each of the amenities by dividing the sample into four groups based on skill and origin: low-skilled natives, high-skilled natives, low-skilled migrants and high-skilled migrants (Table 11.6).

Since we are not able to distinguish migrants' origin, we cannot determine whether decision patterns differ between migrants from different countries of origins. Nevertheless, our finding partially contradicts Bartel (1989), who found that skilled migrants of certain origins to the US tend to relocate away from large concentrations of migrants, while low-skilled migrants tend to remain in areas where there is a concentration of migrants. We find evidence that suggests that the tendency of migrants to concentrate in certain locations depends on their skill level, as well as on the existing concentration of migrants in each location.

Moreover, the WTP for concentration of migrants is not necessarily always highest among groups of foreigners. For instance, where the proportion of migrants is low (below approximately 15–20%) the WTP for the presence of migrants is higher among skilled natives, as compared to that among low-skilled

Table 11.6 WTP for a 1 per cent increase of migrants in the municipal population (in euros)

P.migr	AWTP	Native – low education	Native – high education	Migrant – low education	Migrants– high education
0	7,561.7	5,205.9	11,709.0	8,913.2	13,470.8
5	5,837.5	3,804.2	9,230.7	7,198.6	10,878.8
10	4,113.4	2,402.5	6,752.3	5,484.0	8,286.8
15	2,389.2	1,000.7	4,274.0	3,769.4	5,694.8
20	665.0	−401.0	1,795.6	2,054.8	3,102.8
25	−1,059.1	−1,802.8	−682.7	340.2	510.8
30	−2,783.3	−3,204.5	−3,161.1	−1,374.4	−2,081.3
35	−4,507.5	−4,606.2	−5,639.4	−3,088.9	−4,673.3
40	−6,231.6	−6,008.0	−8,117.8	−4,803.5	−7,265.3
45	−7,955.8	−7,409.7	−10,596.1	−6,518.1	−9,857.3
50	−9,680.0	−8,811.4	−13,074.5	−8,232.7	−12,449.3

Note: <Estimation results – MWTP>

migrants. Figure 11.2 shows the MWTP for an additional percentage of migrants. For all groups its value is initially positive, indicating that the presence of some migrants is appreciated. However, when the proportion of migrants is higher, the appreciation for further growth decreases and becomes negative for all groups. The low-educated natives appreciate the presence of migrants least; the highly educated migrants appreciate it most, unless the percentage is larger than 20.

Investigating the average and marginal WTP for the rest of the examined urban attributes, we find several additional differences in valuation between the various groups (Table 11.7).

While skilled domestic workers have a relatively high MWTP for jobs (€667 for an additional 1000 work places), the rest of the groups have relatively similar MWTP values, around €430–500, for an additional 1000 jobs. Although skilled migrants have a higher valuation for number of jobs (or urban scale), compared with both groups of low-skilled workers, their MWTP is not sufficiently higher to conclude that there is a skill bias in the valuation of this amenity. On the other hand, the valuation of natural and recreational amenities supports the assertion that a skill bias exists in the valuation pattern of urban amenities. Educated workers of both origin groups present similar MWTP for nature coverage (€661 and €686 for every additional square kilometre, for local and foreign workers, respectively).

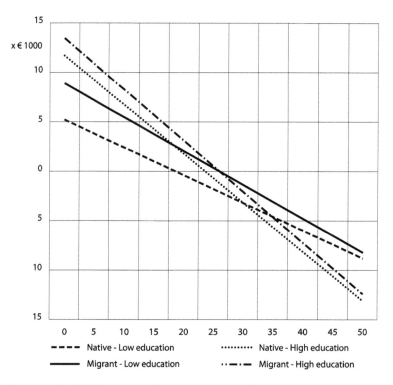

Figure 11.2 MWTP for an additional percentage of migrants in Randstad municipalities (by groups of skill and origin)

Table 11.7 MWTP for urban amenities (in euros)

	AWTP	Native – low education	Native – high education	Migrant – low education	Migrant – high education
Jobs	485.1	442.1	666.9	434.8	502.0
Monuments	15.7	14.4	16.8	16.0	25.1
Nature	735.8	719.1	661.5	870.7	686.1
Accessibility *	–808.3	–480.2	–1,363.4	–404.8	–3,763.1
LQ (ICT industries) *	924.5	252.8	104.1	2,210.8	6,103.7

Note: <Estimation results – MWTP>

* The figures in these rows are based on coefficients that are not all statistically significant from zero at the 10% level.

This is while lower-educated workers show a much higher MWTP of €719 and €870, for locals and migrants, respectively.

The MWTP for monuments or historic buildings presents a similar pattern. Consistent with the findings of Van Duijn and Rouwendal (2013), the highest values of MWTP are among highly educated respondents. However, the gaps between the values are relatively large. The highest MWTP is among skilled migrants (€25 for every additional monument), while the second-highest is €17, among educated natives. Lower-educated native and migrant workers have similar valuations of €14.4 and €16.0, respectively, values which are only slightly lower than that of the skilled natives' group. The results show that highly educated households generally still have a higher MWTP for historic buildings, as compared to low-educated households, but mainly that skilled migrants have a clearly distinct preference for historic cities. Despite the fact that these WTP values for monuments appear to be relatively low at first sight, they are particularly high when we are reminded of the number of monuments in Dutch municipalities (described in Appendix Table 11.A). Twenty-one municipalities in the sample have more than 200 monuments each, and the municipalities of Utrecht, Leiden, Haarlem and Den-Haag each have over 1,000 monuments. This implies that the average household is willing to pay around €20,000 to reside in one of these municipalities due to their provision of monuments and historic buildings alone. The WTP for monuments increases considerably in the case of Amsterdam, which has 7,442 listed monuments – between €106,000 and €186,000. Arguably, this number seems particularly high when compared to initial expectations. A possible explanation can be attributed to the indirect effects of cultural heritage. As mentioned before, monuments and historic centres are also correlated with other unobserved urban amenities, such as commercial and leisure consumption activities. These factors have an indirect contribution to the positive effect of monuments, and are reflected in the high WTP values that are measured here. Given the number of monuments in the sample, the differences in WTP values between population groups are sharpened. For example, a skilled migrant is willing to pay approximately €36,000 in order to reside in the city of Utrecht, due to its 1,460 monuments. In contrast, a low-skilled native is willing to pay €21,000 for Utrecht's historical heritage, a difference of €15,000 in valuation.

Average MWTP values of other labour-related amenities, such as accessibility level and concentration of ICT industries, are harder to interpret, due to the fact that they are based on statistically insignificant coefficients and therefore the values are susceptible to bias. However, the statistically significant coefficients which were obtained in the first stage of the estimation still allow us to determine group-relative valuation of these amenities by examining deviations from the mean. Highly educated migrants also have a higher WTP for residing where a concentration of knowledge-intensive ICT industries exists. This is particularly interesting when compared to the WTP of other groups – contrary to expectations, highly educated natives have a below-average valuation of this amenity (statistically insignificant), while low-educated migrants have a positive valuation. This discrepancy can be partially explained by the fact the LQ measures were available only at a COROP area level (NUTS3), which may have resulted in a bias in the estimated values.

Discussion and conclusion

The results of our estimation of the sorting model support the findings of previous research, as we find evidence that residential location choices in Dutch municipalities depend much on the provision of (broadly defined) urban amenities. Moreover, our results also provide further evidence that valuation patterns of urban amenities differ between individuals, based on their household characteristics, particularly origin and skill level. We find that job opportunities, as well as accessibility, natural amenities and, particularly, historic city centres, play a significant role in raising the attraction power of municipalities. Additionally, the role of social amenities, such as the proportion of migrants in a municipality, is also found to be an important explanatory variable. The implication is that cultural diversity and social interaction between inhabitants have a strong impact on households' location decisions and on the attractiveness of municipalities, at least as much as other consumer- or labour-related urban amenities. This positive effect on municipality attractiveness is found to be even stronger in municipalities neighbouring large communities of migrants, as reflected by the higher value of the spatially lagged variable's coefficient. Consistent with the findings of previous research, our results also show that both positive and negative effects may result from an existing community of migrants. We observe this because the MWTP for an additional proportion of migrants in a municipality changes with the proportion of migrants in the municipality – it is found to be high among all skill and origin groups where proportions of migrants are low, but decreases where the proportion and presence of foreigners is relatively high.

We also find that, with respect to most urban amenities, the location preferences of skilled migrants are generally more similar to those of the highly educated natives rather than to those of low-skilled migrants, assuming that other household characteristics are identical. This is visible both in the MWTP values of work-related amenities, such as the number of jobs or accessibility, and in preferences for other urban amenities, such as historic buildings and nature. In this sense, and also somewhat expectedly, preference for an existing community of migrants is an exception in the skill-based pattern of preference for urban amenities. Skilled migrants are found to be more similar to low-skilled migrants in their preferences for proportions of migrants in a municipality. Their MWTP values for an existing community of migrants even exceed those of the low-skilled migrants, assuming that all other characteristics are identical. This may be explained as: migrants of all skill levels are assumed to derive utility from cultural goods, but skilled migrants may also enjoy the network benefits of a large community of migrants, which may increase their expected labour outcomes. Furthermore, our results point to highly educated migrants having the highest MWTP among all groups for historic city centres and buildings. This valuation is highly significant for municipalities that are rich in historic districts.

These findings may be useful for urban policy that aims to attract educated migrant workers. First, municipalities can attract skilled and highly educated foreign workers by preserving their historic districts and developing them in order to maintain their historic and leisure value. Moreover, since the proportion of migrants is also found to be an important factor in location decisions, urban policy can aim to stress the positive effects and minimize the possible negative effects which may result this. Although an existing community of migrants is not an amenity which can be developed artificially as part of an urban policy, municipalities can still aim to preserve the positive effects of an existing community. One possible example of such policy might be to encourage language-proficiency courses, which may reduce communication barriers.

The findings from our research contribute to the literature by identifying the housing preferences and valuation of urban amenities of skilled and migrant workers based on their individual characteristics. We have addressed challenges such as model endogeneity and spatial dependence and have omitted variable bias by estimating a two-step residential sorting model and by instrumenting for housing prices and the existing proportion of migrants. We find that social interaction and labour market amenities are important determinants of location decisions, and that the location preferences of skilled migrants show more similarities to those of skilled native workers. If data availability permits, further research on the valuation of urban amenities by population groups should also focus on the country-of-origin composition of the group of migrants. This would be useful for identifying individual characteristics and would allow inclusion of the level of cultural diversity within municipalities into the model by using a diversity measure.

Acknowledgement

We would like to thank Mark Van Duijn and Jan Möhlmann for their useful comments and technical assistance with the estimation of the sorting model.

Appendix

Appendix Table 11.A: Randstad municipalities: full characteristics

Appendix Table 11.A Randstad municipalities: full characteristics

#	Municipality	COROP (NUTS3)*	Housing prices	P.migrants	Accessibility (av. Dist to train station)	Jobs	Monuments	Nature	LQ (ICT industries)
1	's-Gravenhage	1	200,282	47.3	3	268.86	1154	11.7	3.47
2	Aalsmeer	4	239,541	14.6	8.1	16.82	36	3.4	1.79
3	Alblasserdam	10	193,780	12.7	9.8	8.42	22	2.1	0.48
4	Albrandswaard	11	201,689	16.1	8.7	7.95	29	10.4	0.45
5	Almere	6	162,833	36.4	1.8	67.23	4	24	0.93
6	Alphen aan den Rijn	7	211,606	19.8	2.6	32.89	74	0.1	0.93
7	Amersfoort	3	219,143	22.4	2.4	85.5	424	7.8	2.1
8	Amstelveen	4	283,645	32.8	6.2	43.39	44	9.3	1.79
9	Amsterdam	4	312,538	49.5	2.5	513.18	7442	2.2	1.79
10	Baarn	3	263,941	15.5	1.5	11.81	151	50.7	2.1
11	Barendrecht	11	201,890	18.6	3.1	21.52	20	2.9	0.45
12	Beemster	4	223,123	8.2	6.5	3.04	90	0.2	1.79
13	Bergambacht	7	216,746	7.1	12.5	3.68	33	1.5	0.93
14	Bernisse	11	193,200	8	16.4	2.6	95	1.4	0.45
15	Beverwijk	13	187,115	21.4	1.7	20.72	35	11.7	0.22
16	Binnenmaas	11	199,482	8.1	9.9	7.25	73	2.5	0.45
17	Blaricum	2	321,091	16.5	7.6	1.87	69	22.4	2.43
18	Bloemendaal	5	366,400	17	1.8	4.16	237	66	1.44
19	Bodegraven	7	219,362	11.9	1.5	8.94	27	0.6	0.93
20	Boskoop	7	210,972	13.3	1.9	4.01	12	0.1	0.93
21	Brielle	11	214,160	11.6	11.6	4.73	374	2	0.45
22	Bunnik	3	255,884	10.9	2.5	7.05	56	4.7	2.1

23	Bunschoten	3	214,160	7.1	8.9	9.81	14	0.4	2.1
24	Bussum	2	268,466	19.4	1.4	11.9	49	12.5	2.43
25	Capelle aan den IJssel	11	199,285	29.5	3.2	45.54	17	0.4	0.45
26	Castricum	13	237,395	9.6	2.5	8.8	48	28.3	0.22
27	Cromstrijen	11	196,120	6.4	18.6	4.05	14	2.1	0.45
28	De Bilt	3	270,622	14.9	2.4	15.88	160	23.4	2.1
29	De Ronde Venen	3	248,570	12.6	10.6	11.86	35	0.3	2.1
30	Delft	8	230,609	29.7	1.5	52.49	689	4.9	0.65
31	Diemen	4	255,118	37	1.1	33.32	16	22.7	1.79
32	Dirksland	11	171,182	3.9	34.1	2.78	31	18.9	0.45
33	Dordrecht	10	179,240	27.2	1.7	57.43	891	14	0.48
34	Edam-Volendam	4	239,541	7	9	11.11	179	0	1.79
35	Eemnes	3	253,338	12.2	6.8	2.09	43	3.3	2.1
36	Giessenlanden	10	218,050	5.7	4.1	3.81	65	0.6	0.48
37	Goedereede	11	213,092	4	29.2	4.21	137	34.5	0.45
38	Gorinchem	10	204,532	23.3	1.8	23.77	218	1.9	0.48
39	Gouda	7	198,091	22.1	1.6	37.74	354	0.9	0.93
40	Graafstroom	10	190,133	3.6	7.5	3.5	91	1.7	0.48
41	Graft-De Rijp	4	198,289	7.2	11.2	1.47	137	1.9	1.79
42	Haarlem	5	251,319	24.5	2	70.58	1182	1.4	1.44
43	Haarlemmerliede en Spaarnwoude	5	238,346	12.3	5.2	1.4	16	13.4	1.44
44	Haarlemmermeer	4	225,819	22.3	4.3	149.43	20	0.5	1.79
45	Hardinxveld-Giessendam	10	211,396	4.6	2	8.42	11	3.5	0.48
46	Heemskerk	13	208,664	17.5	2.9	8.17	22	38.4	0.22
47	Heemstede	5	328,890	17.2	2.3	7.6	97	15.1	1.44
48	Hellevoetsluis	11	183,045	16.7	16.8	9.93	52	6	0.45

(continued)

Appendix Table 11.A (continued)

#	Municipality	COROP (NUTS3)*	Housing prices	P.migrants	Accessibility (av. Dist to train station)	Jobs	Monuments	Nature	LQ (ICT industries)
49	Hendrik-Ido-Ambacht	10	201,487	11.6	4.1	7.37	9	1.1	0.48
50	Hillegom	9	226,495	13.9	2.7	7.2	7	1.5	0.55
51	Hilversum	2	242,433	22	1.6	53.81	211	42.5	2.43
52	Houten	3	219,582	12.9	2.2	19.84	134	1.3	2.1
53	Huizen	2	260,532	18.6	7.5	12.86	39	29.3	2.43
54	IJsselstein	3	204,532	19.1	11.3	11.26	68	1.5	2.1
55	Kaag En Braassem	9	311,001	7.1	7.7	6.88	60	0	0.55
56	Katwijk	9	251,319	8.5	6.5	24.62	51	17.4	0.55
57	Korendijk	11	196,316	5.5	22.8	1.77	46	6	0.45
58	Krimpen aan den IJssel	11	215,665	12.3	7.4	8.8	14	2.9	0.45
59	Landsmeer	4	267,930	12.5	8	1.91	7	12.8	1.79
60	Lansingerland	11	216,313	13.7	6.7	18.57	17	3	0.45
61	Laren	2	361,667	20.9	5.1	5.48	98	50.3	2.43
62	Leerdam	10	204,737	21	1.6	8.75	54	3.5	0.48
63	Leiden	9	251,571	27.2	1.5	67.88	1243	1	0.55
64	Leiderdorp	9	244,136	19	3.8	10.01	32	1.4	0.55
65	Leidschendam-Voorburg	1	220,903	26.9	2.2	28.53	113	4.1	3.47
66	Leusden	3	230,840	12.8	6.1	14.22	53	34.2	2.1
67	Liesveld	10	211,817	4.9	13.4	4.37	90	1.9	0.48
68	Lisse	9	231,765	11.5	6.8	9.8	41	9.4	0.55
69	Lopik	3	208,457	6.4	15	4.2	127	2.1	2.1
70	Maassluis	11	215,019	23.3	1.3	7.53	41	3.2	0.45
71	Middelharnis	11	190,895	5.4	37.1	7.4	159	1.7	0.45
72	Midden-Delfland	8	254,353	8.2	3.4	5.53	99	1.8	0.65

73	Montfoort	3	227,176	8.2	6.8	4.85	98	1.6	2.1
74	Muiden	2	276,642	15.7	5.2	1.54	75	7.9	2.43
75	Naarden	2	296,998	18.4	2	10.67	163	29.3	2.43
76	Nederlek	11	207,208	7.7	11.6	3.92	24	5.8	0.45
77	Nieuw-Lekkerland	10	200,883	5.9	12.8	2.2	26	10	0.48
78	Nieuwegein	3	206,175	22.4	7.5	51.22	80	3.3	2.1
79	Nieuwkoop	7	227,403	7.8	10.3	7.89	27	7.6	0.93
80	Noordwijk	9	278,307	14.8	5	11.35	74	52.6	0.55
81	Noordwijkerhout	9	238,823	12	5.5	6.48	12	8.3	0.55
82	Oegstgeest	9	275,813	21.4	3.1	6.34	44	3.7	0.55
83	Oostflakkee	11	156,136	5.1	31	2.02	28	7	0.45
84	Oostzaan	4	251,071	10.8	5.4	2.67	7	11	1.79
85	Oud-Beijerland	11	212,879	9.2	14.9	12.13	28	0.5	0.45
86	Ouder-Amstel	4	287,932	20.2	3.2	9.3	36	0.9	1.79
87	Ouderkerk	11	206,381	6	8.9	2.62	38	1.1	0.45
88	Oudewater	3	245,605	6.3	9.4	3.1	159	0.1	2.1
89	Papendrecht	10	197,300	15	6.5	11.94	2	4.1	0.48
90	Pijnacker-Nootdorp	1	224,244	15.5	4	12.21	22	7.3	3.47
91	Purmerend	4	196,709	23.2	1.9	26.44	30	12.1	1.79
92	Renswoude	3	224,915	4.6	4.6	1.82	34	5.5	2.1
93	Rhenen	3	216,963	9.7	2.6	5.03	53	32.9	2.1
94	Ridderkerk	11	200,482	14.4	5.6	20.87	57	2.1	0.45
95	Rijnwoude	7	218,705	7.8	5.8	6.53	81	0.7	0.93
96	Rijswijk	1	197,300	27.8	1.8	35.24	76	0.4	3.47
97	Rotterdam	11	182,313	46.9	2.8	370.03	466	2.9	0.45
98	Schiedam	11	164,141	33.5	1.7	35.26	238	1.7	0.45
99	Schoonhoven	7	217,832	15	12.9	4.82	148	1.2	0.93

(continued)

Appendix Table 11.A (continued)

#	Municipality	COROP (NUTS3)*	Housing prices	P.migrants	Accessibility (av. Dist to train station)	Jobs	Monuments	Nature	LQ (ICT industries)
100	Sliedrecht	10	205,147	11.3	1.9	13.57	8	0.6	0.48
101	Soest	3	243,161	19.1	2.2	19.83	43	38.3	2.1
102	Spijkenisse	11	172,384	22.7	13.7	21.36	5	5.2	0.45
103	Stichtse Vecht	3	248,570	11.9	2.9	6	196	1.5	2.1
104	Strijen	11	211,183	7.5	13.3	2.23	14	3.5	0.45
105	Teylingen	9	245,851	12.7	2.7	12.53	107	2.3	0.55
106	Uitgeest	13	204,123	10.3	1.5	3.76	20	1.7	0.22
107	Uithoorn	4	228,086	18.4	11.5	12.56	12	0.4	1.79
108	Utrecht	3	250,316	31.5	1.9	229.85	1459	2	2.1
109	Utrechtse Heuvelrug	3	259,232	13.5	4.4	20.98	421	45	2.1
110	Veenendaal	3	217,397	15.8	1.4	30.25	16	3.4	2.1
111	Velsen	13	227,858	15.2	2.5	31.46	138	27.6	0.22
112	Vianen	3	205,557	14.3	10.4	12.07	181	8.1	2.1
113	Vlaardingen	11	184,514	24.4	1.9	23.3	56	11	0.45
114	Vlist	7	231,997	5.7	6.1	3.14	91	0.1	0.93
115	Voorschoten	9	263,413	20.5	1.5	5	103	6.4	0.55
116	Waddinxveen	7	208,875	12.8	1.2	12.14	6	0.9	0.93
117	Wassenaar	1	329,220	29.8	3.9	7.49	272	49.3	3.47
118	Waterland	4	254,353	10.3	10.3	3.15	317	2.3	1.79
119	Weesp	2	260,532	23.7	1.3	10.25	221	0.5	2.43
120	Westland	8	230,840	9.5	6.5	57.14	76	4.8	0.65
121	Westvoorne	11	246,836	9.1	17.6	3.62	29	28.3	0.45
122	Wijdemeren	2	282,513	11.4	6	6.34	249	14.7	2.43
123	Wijk bij Duurstede	3	233,160	10.5	10.5	5.09	166	8.5	2.1

124	Woerden	3	230,379	12.5	2.9	25.58	103	0.7	2.1
125	Wormerland	12	207,831	11	2.5	4.09	33	1.1	0.25
126	Woudenberg	3	240,021	7.7	5	4.05	30	24.5	2.1
127	Zaanstad	12	192,621	25.7	2.1	56.62	258	5.6	0.25
128	Zandvoort	5	277,473	18.7	1	4.66	11	77.9	1.44
129	Zederik	10	220,024	4	8.4	4.47	106	3.6	0.48
130	Zeevang	4	205,969	9.5	8.2	1.25	23	1	1.79
131	Zeist	3	264,999	21.4	3.9	36.21	155	44.9	2.1
132	Zoetermeer	1	200,482	27.7	3.5	48.9	16	1.3	3.47
133	Zoeterwoude	9	245,605	9.3	4	7	40	0.7	0.55
134	Zuidplas	11	210,130	13.2	1.2	6.5	14	4.8	0.45
135	Zwijndrecht	10	192,236	18.4	2.3	19.52	13	1.5	0.48

COROP area (NUTS3)	Number
Agglomeratie S-Gravenhage	1
Het Gooi En Vechtstreek	2
Utrecht	3
Groot-Amsterdam	4
Agglomeratie Haarlem	5
Flevoland	6
Oost-Zuid-Holland	7
Delft En Westland	8
Agglomeratie Leiden En Bollenstreek	9
Zuidoost-Zuid-Holland	10
Groot-Rijnmond	11
Zaanstreek	12
IJmond	13

Source: Statistics Netherlands (wijk en buurtkaart, 2011), NVM (1985–2011), RCE (2011).

Appendix Figure 11.B: map of Randstad municipalities: alternative specific constants

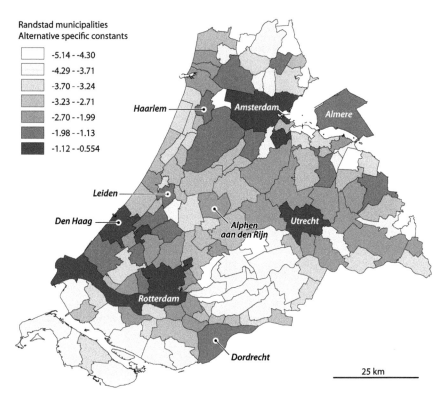

Figure 11.B Map of Randstad municipalities: alternative specific constants

Notes

1 See any econometrics textbook for a discussion of this technique. Briefly, the instrument allows the researchers to use a part of the variation of the endogenous variable that does not suffer from the endogeneity.
2 This was shown by McFadden and Train (2000) for the mixed (or random coefficient) logit models, in which unobserved heterogeneity is included, but similar arguments can be put forward for an MNL model that refers to a heterogeneous group of decision makers. See Bayer *et al.* (2004). See Gottlieb and Joseph (2006) for an application of the mixed logit model to migration choices.
3 See Bayer *et al.* (2007) for a comparison of the sorting model and hedonic price analysis.
4 Denote the new variable by $PX_{i,k}$, where i refers to the municipality and k to the explanatory variable whose spatial lag is determined. Then $PX_{i,k} = \Sigma_{j=1, j \neq i}^{n} \dfrac{\dfrac{1}{d_{i,j}}}{\Sigma_j \dfrac{1}{d_{i,j}}} * X_{j,k}$. In

words, this states that $PX_{i,k}$ is the weighted average of the values of $X_{j,k}$ in all other municipalities $j=1 \ldots n, j \neq i$. The weights are standardized so that they add up to 1.

5 The GMM/IV is a two-step estimation of the spatial autoregressive disturbances model that is able to deal with endogenous regressors. Its formulation can be found in Drukker *et al.* (2011, 2013).

6 Note that the definition of a migrant as a non-native may also be inaccurate because second-generation migrants do not all consider themselves to be (only or predominantly) Dutch.

References

Adamson, DW, Clark, DE and Partridge, MD 2004, Do urban agglomeration effects and household amenities have a skill bias? *Journal of Regional Science*, 44(2), 201–224.

Anselin, L 1988, *Spatial econometrics: Methods and models*. Operational Regional Science Series.

Anselin, L, Bera, A, Florax, R and Yoon, M 1996, Simple diagnostic tests for spatial dependence. *Regional Science and Urban Economics* 26(1), 77–104.

Åslund, O 2005, Now and forever? Initial and subsequent location choices of immigrants. *Regional Science and Urban Economics*, 35(2), 141–165.

Bartel, AP 1989, Where do the new US immigrants live? *Journal of Labor Economics*, 7(4), 371–391.

Bauer, T, Epstein, GS, Gang, IN and Al, ET 2007, The influence of stocks and flows on migrants' location choices. *Research in Labor Economics*, 26(6), 199–229.

Bayer, P, Ferreira, F and McMillan, R 2007, A unified framework for measuring preferences for schools and neighborhoods. *Journal of Political Economy*, 115(4), 588–638.

Bayer, P, McMillan, R and Rueben, K 2004, *An equilibrium sorting model of sorting in an urban housing market*. National Bureau of Economic Research working paper 10865.

Bellini, E, Ottaviano, G, Pinelli, D and Prarolo, G 2008, *Cultural diversity and economic performance: evidence from European regions*. Hamburg Institute of International Economics (HWWI), (3–14).

Borjas, GJ 1994, *Ethnicity, neighborhoods, and human capital externalities*. National Bureau of Economic Research working paper 4912.

Brown, WM and Scott, DM 2012, Human capital location choice: accounting for amenities and thick labor markets. *Journal of Regional Science*, 52(5), 787–808.

Brueckner, J 2000, Urban sprawl: diagnosis and remedies. *International Regional Science Review*, 23(2), 160–171.

Damm, AP 2012, *Neighborhood quality and labor market outcomes: evidence from quasi-random neighborhood assignment of immigrants*. Centre for Research and Analysis of Migration Discussion Paper, 35.

Drukker, DM and Prucha, IR 2011, A command for estimating spatial-autoregressive models with spatial-autoregressive disturbances and additional endogenous variables. *The Stata Journal*, (1), 1–13.

Drukker, DM, Egger, P and Prucha, IR 2013, On two-step estimation of a spatial autoregressive model with autoregressive disturbances and endogenous regressors. *Econometric Reviews*, 32(5–6), 686–733.

Eeckhout, J, Pinheiro, R and Schmidheiny, K 2010, *Spatial sorting: why New York, Los Angeles and Detroit attract the greatest minds as well as the unskilled*. CESifo working paper 3274.

Glaeser, E and Resseger, MG 2010, The complementarity between cities and skills. *Journal of Regional Science*, 50(1), 221–244.

Glaeser, E and Saiz, A 2003, *The rise of the skilled city*. National Bureau of Economic Research working paper 10191.

Glaeser, E, Kolko, J and Saiz, A 2001, Consumer city. *Journal of Economic Geography*, 1(1), 27–50.

Goldin, C and Katz, L 2009, *The race between education and technology*. Cambridge, MA: Harvard University Press.

Gottlieb, PD and Joseph, G 2006, College-to-work migration of technology graduates and holders of doctorates within the United States. *Journal of Regional Science*, 46(4), 627–659.

Hunt, J and Gauthier-Loiselle, M 2008, *How much does immigration boost innovation?* National Bureau of Economic Research working paper 14312.

Jaeger, DA 2006, Green Cards and the location choices of immigrants in the United States, 1971–2000. *Institute for the Study of Labor (IZA)*, (IZA Discussion Papers, No. 2145).

McFadden, D and Train, K 2000, Mixed MNL models for discrete response. *Journal of Applied Econometrics*, 15(5), 447–470.

Mocetti, S and Porello, C 2010, How does immigration affect native internal mobility? New evidence from Italy. *Regional Science and Urban Economics*, 40(6), 427–439.

Moretti, E 2004 Human capital externalities in cities. In: J. Vernon Henderson and Jacques-François Thisse (eds) *Handbook of regional and urban economics* 4, 2243–2291.

Moretti, E 2010, Local multipliers. *American Economic Review*, 100(2), 373–377.

Moretti, E 2012, *The new geography of jobs*. New York: Houghton Mifflin Harcourt.

Moretti, E and Thulin, P 2013, Local multipliers and human capital in the United States and Sweden. *Industrial and Corporate Change*, 22(1), 339–362.

Munshi, K 2003, Networks in the modern economy: Mexican migrants in the US labor market. *Quarterly Journal of Economics*, (May), 549–598.

Niebuhr, A 2010, Migration and innovation: does cultural diversity matter for regional R and D activity? *Papers in Regional Science*, 89(3), 563–585.

Ottaviano, G and Peri, G 2006, The economic value of cultural diversity: evidence from US cities. *Journal of Economic Geography*, 6(1), 9–44.

Ozgen, C, Nijkamp, P and Poot, J 2011, *Immigration and innovation in European regions*. Discussion paper series // Forschungsinstitut zur Zukunft der Arbeit, No. 5676.

Rodríguez-Pose, A and Ketterer, TD 2012, Do local amenities affect the appeal of regions in Europe for migrants? *Journal of Regional Science*, 52(4), 535–561.

Suedekum, J, Wolf, K and Blien, U 2009, *Cultural diversity and local labour markets*. IZA Discussion Paper, No. 4619.

Van Duijn, M and Rouwendal, J 2013, Cultural heritage and the location choice of Dutch households in a residential sorting model. *Journal of Economic Geography*, 13(3), 473–500.

12 Revealed residential preferences of international migrants working in creative and knowledge intensive industries

The settlement process

Bart Sleutjes and Sako Musterd

Introduction

The creative and knowledge-intensive sectors have become more and more important in both national and regional economies, and increasingly urban economies have become internationalized. International migration of well-skilled, often well-paid, people serves different purposes in the economy. It can fill short-term labour gaps or be used to address long-term skills shortages and help with the gradual development of the labour force. This has spurred policy and scientific interest in transnational migrants and their preferences and wishes. It is said that cities have to strengthen their links to global pools of creative-knowledge talent in order to remain competitive and that cities must pay attention to the conditions that attract and retain top layers of international migrants. One policy response has been that immigration policies in many European countries and at the EU level have shifted from restrictive policies to policies that actively aim at attracting higher strata of foreign workers. This development was spurred by labour shortages in the information technology sector and in parts of the service industries such as banking and the health sector. In 1999, EU countries formulated a common framework to manage migration and an important role was ascribed to legal migration for the enhancement of the knowledge-based economy in Europe in 'The Hague Programme' of 2004. Also a 'blue card' was introduced in 2009 which enabled employees with a sufficiently high income to smoothly enter EU countries. Consequently, many urban economies, and particularly those with a strong international orientation, have acknowledged a growing inflow of international 'knowledge' workers. This includes the two regional case studies in this research project. The Amsterdam Metropolitan Area and the Eindhoven Metropolitan Region have a growing international population, in which 'better-off' migrants account for a large proportion of population growth. In the Amsterdam Metropolitan Area, already 13 per cent of residents are of 'Western migrant' origin; in the municipality of Amsterdam the proportion is 16 per cent (Regiomonitor 2014). The Eindhoven region offers more high-tech employment than regional technical graduates can fill in, which makes the region heavily dependent on talent from elsewhere, at least in the short term

(Van der Zee 2013). The (specific) number of international knowledge workers in the region quadrupled between 2007 and 2012 and is expected to further double before 2020. Around 80 per cent of the population growth is expected to consist of single-person households. It is a great challenge for both the city and the region to accommodate these workers and to offer housing that matches their demands (Municipality of Eindhoven 2014). Therefore, it is important to know more about their preferences and residential behaviour.

In Chapter 5 we focused on the stated preferences of highly skilled workers in the Amsterdam and Eindhoven regions and in Chapter 9 we zoomed in on the stated preferences of highly educated international migrants. In Chapter 11 the *revealed* preference of international migrants was put under the microscope, as will also be the case in this chapter. We pay specific attention to the higher socio-economic strata (*better-off* international migrants). The core issue that is dealt with in this chapter regards the first steps in their settlement process. We follow the migrants from the moment they enter the country and see what their next steps are. The analyses focus on the better-off because information on the level of education was too limited for a direct focus on the highly skilled. We elaborate on the residential milieus and types of dwelling where they settle when entering the regions of Amsterdam or Eindhoven; we will investigate the different housing orientations of different household categories, and the differences between the two metropolitan areas. We are particularly interested in residential trajectories and therefore also investigate the relocation behaviour of better-off international migrants. In the next section we start with a discussion of a selection of the literature relating to the role of housing in the settlement process of migrants and the potential specificities of the residential behaviour of (better-off) international migrants. This leads to the formulation of more precise research questions, which we answer in the empirical part of this chapter. We begin that part with a data section, followed by a descriptive section and an analytical section, and we end by presenting some conclusions.

Framing the debate in the literature

Although an extensive literature exists on the residential preferences of skilled workers in general (see Chapter 2 for an overview), there is still a lack of knowledge regarding specific preferences and behaviour with respect to the dwelling choices and orientations towards certain residential milieus of better-off international migrants. Urban policy makers across Europe have adopted the view that, for internationally oriented workers, residential preferences and lifestyles deviate from those of other categories of workers. However, the empirical and theoretical basis of such opinions is still rather weak (see for example Scott 2006; Storper and Manville 2006; Hansen and Niedomysl 2009). Are international (creative) knowledge workers really that different from 'domestic' (creative) knowledge workers with regard to their residential orientations? To what extent are there differences between spatial contexts? A key outcome of a large-scale comparative research project carried out in 13 European metropolitan areas was that historically grown and different contexts should be taken into account (Musterd and Murie 2010). In that project the collective of researchers also found that international creative knowledge workers were, above all, attracted to the city because of employment opportunities (also see Storper and Scott 2009) and existing personal networks (also see Hansen and Niedomysl 2009). These, in turn, were highly dependent on local or regional institutional, social, economic and spatial contexts. Another key finding was that residential conditions hardly played a role in attracting them to the labour market region. However, it has been suggested that residential factors, and with them a preference for specific residential milieus, such as highly urban quarters, or highly suburban neighbourhoods, may play a role after the job condition has been fulfilled, and may also play an important role in *retaining* the so-called creative-knowledge workers (Lawton, Męczyński and Barber 2013). This is also suggested in the revealed preference studies in this volume, where in addition to the availability of jobs other amenities also turned out to be important for location decisions (Chapters, 6, 7 and 11).

One way of testing key elements of such assumptions is to follow the better-off international migrants when they move to another place after they have settled in the metropolitan region – supposedly for employment reasons. The resettlement process may reveal whether or not there are indeed differences between international migrants and non-migrants. These processes also provide more information on the types of dwellings and residential milieus that these better-off international migrants focus on. The distinction between reasons for first settling and for subsequent settling may seem nuanced, but in fact it is not. Urban economic policies should not confuse the reasons for economic development with reasons for finding a nice place to live. We therefore have to know more about the residential behaviour of the better-off international migrants upon arrival as well as a bit later, when they resettle. In this regard it is very important to take the great variety of such migrants into consideration. Whereas some stay only for a short term, many others will not leave. It is also interesting to see whether there is a difference between experiences in the two metropolitan areas examined, which have different professional structures.

Regarding the residential orientation of those who are employed in creative industries and in knowledge-intensive industries, in the first place we must, think of similar considerations that play a role for other households. On the basis of classic social spatial literature (see, for example, Robson 1975), we may assume that households express preferences and behaviour that are partly a function of their own characteristics. Young and small households will more frequently favour central-city accommodation, whereas family households are known for their need of space, in and outside of the dwelling. The elderly will favour apartment buildings, but also places with a good supply of services, which again makes cities attractive to them. Apart from demographic factors, there are also economic dimensions in play. Those who can afford the most generally have most choice and will be better able to realize their preferences, whereas for others all kinds of constraints may affect their actual behaviour. The institutional context is very important as well, because this may seriously affect the supply side and impacts on matching demand with supply.

Recent literature has added a range of nuances to the classic knowledge of residential behaviour and pointed to the need to include cultural considerations in the choice of place to settle. This is reflected, for example, in the residential behaviour of family households, who more often than before seem to express a preference for living in more urbanized environments (Boterman 2012). This seems to relate to an increase of cultural capital, which is in turn related to an increasing number of households with higher education. That said, the majority of family households are still oriented toward more spacious residential neighbourhoods.

When we study the subsequent residential behaviour of international migrants we have to take these housing market processes into account. However, the question is whether there will be a component on top of this that is specifically related to the fact that we are dealing with *better-off* international migrants. We have already referred to the possibility that some migrants will stay for only a short period of time. This will hold true especially for the migrants who are attached to multinational companies, also known as 'expats'. Some migrants can best be called 'transnational migrants'. They do not seem to settle in one place; rather, they are part of an international community that proportions social spaces that are less bounded to one specific national context. The concept of 'brain circulation' may be appropriate to such segments, especially when they are highly skilled (Pethe and Hafner 2013). For these categories one might assume that they are especially in need of rental housing with rent contracts that are easy to terminate; they will also require to have many services around them, which would suggest an urban location. Another category of international migrants includes those who arrive not with a specific firm, but because of the availability of a job in one or another firm. Some may be globally oriented and come and go, but some may stay for a very long time. The initial place of settlement may not be representative of what they really are looking for in terms of residential space; but for those who stay longer, the next step in their housing career will tell us more. Mobility rates in Europe are not as high as they appear to be in a country like the US, so the stayers may dominate the scene (Martin-Brelot *et al.* 2010). There is also a large group of international exchange students, who are there for study; some stay a short time, others stay longer, even after finishing their studies, because they have found a job or a partner (see Chapter 10). Finally, there is a category of international migrants who arrive without a specific attachment to a course of study or a job. For them, existing personal networks play an important role.

As stated, we assume that international migrants, especially those who will stay for a longer period of time, do not always make the most ideal housing decision immediately upon arrival. Nevertheless, such first addresses do have to be there and they have to be readily available. Therefore it is also important to know more about what these first milieus and dwellings actually are. People need some time to become acquainted with the local and regional housing market; their next dwelling and location will be much more 'tuned' to the requirements of household than the first. If we want to know more about their residential behaviour it is therefore wise to consider the first *and* second and possibly following addresses as well, and see what their characteristics are. All in all, knowledge about the residential orientations of the higher socio-economic strata of international migrants is still rather limited. This brings us to a more precise formulation and operationalization of the research questions that drive this chapter.

> 1. In which types of residential milieu and which types of housing do better-off international migrants from different countries settle upon arrival in the Amsterdam or Eindhoven regions? And what differences are there between the two regions?

Here, the main focus will be on the 'port of entry'. The definition of location is first based on the urban/suburban dichotomy. We consider a port of entry 'urban' if the migrant started their housing career in one of the urban centres in the two regions: Amsterdam or Haarlem in the Amsterdam Metropolitan Area and Eindhoven or Helmond in the Eindhoven Metropolitan Region. The port of entry is 'suburban' when the migrant's first known address in the Netherlands was outside these four urban centres. Neighbourhood status is based on the following characteristics, which can be subdivided into housing characteristics (proportion of owner-occupied dwellings; average net housing value (in Dutch: WOZ)); socio-economic characteristics (proportion of high-income households; proportion of low-income households); and socio-cultural characteristics (proportion of Western migrants).

> 2. Which residential patterns, in terms of housing type and residential milieu, can be distinguished in the subsequent relocation behaviour of better-off international migrants? And what differences are there between the two regions?

This question deals with the mobility patterns of better-off international migrants after settling at the port of entry. First, we want to know how many migrants relocate. Second, if relocation has taken place, we are interested in the differences between the first and the final address with regard to location and status. Following our assumptions, the address where they eventually settle will likely have a higher status than the port of entry and better reflect the migrant's preference for urban or suburban locations. Again, different groups of migrants, with respect to age categories, household situation and income groups, are distinguished.

Data

The basis for the analysis is a set of micro data from Statistics Netherlands, the Social Statistical Database. This longitudinal dataset is based on micro-level register and income tax data for the entire population, using data for the period 2003–12. It contains detailed information, derived from various data sources, on individual backgrounds (such as address, age, country of birth, household and personal income at different points in time), residential mobility (migration type, migration date, motives) and residential milieus (municipality, neighbourhood status, urban or suburban). The files contain changes in personal situations through time and can be linked to each other through a unique identification code.

This way it was possible to study address changes over time and link them to changes in the personal or household situation. The datafiles for each year list all changes for each person since his or her first entry into the Netherlands, dating back to 1994. This made it possible to see whether changes in address coincided with changes in demographic details in the same year.

In order to get information on the dwelling type, the location and the neighbourhood status of the addresses at different points in time, the data were linked to the Housing Register Plus data base (WRG+). Neighbourhood data include detailed information on the housing market, the socio-economic status and the socio-cultural neighbourhood composition. This enabled us to study the neighbourhood status at the port of entry, as well as changes in status after relocation.

Insufficient adequate data on the level of education of migrants was available in the data, making it necessary to set strict selection criteria in order to distinguish labour migrants with higher socio-economic status from the large group of former guest workers and colonial migrants and their descendants in the Netherlands. The selected population includes only those migrants who moved to the metropolitan regions of Amsterdam and Eindhoven during 1994–2012. Moreover, they had to be 18 years or older at the time of immigration, and had to have moved for work- or study-related reasons or for an internship. Also, those known as knowledge migrants (under the 'knowledge worker rule', only applicable to persons from outside the EU) were included. Only people who were born outside the Netherlands and do not have a Dutch parent were selected. A final selection criterion was the region in which the first known address is located: only migrants whose 'port of entry' is within the Amsterdam Metropolitan Area or the Eindhoven Metropolitan Region were included. The various selections produced a return of 1,254 international migrants, 1,040 of whom lived in the Amsterdam region immediately after entering the country.

In order to compensate for the lack of data on education, we used income-level information to distinguish those working in higher socio-economic strata (the top four income deciles of the labour market) from others. We also distinguished between four nationality categories:

- from countries with advanced economies (Western Europe, USA, Canada, Australia, New Zealand, Japan, South Korea, Taiwan, Singapore, Israel)
- from countries in Central and Eastern Europe (excluding Russia)
- from countries with growing economies: Brazil, Russia, India, China, South Africa ('BRICS')
- from other, predominantly developing, countries

In order to answer the second research question, we measured the housing conditions of better-off international migrants at two point in time: at t1, when the migrant first settled; and at t2. The situation at t2 refers to the last known address of the migrant worker; it can be the same address as at t1. The attributes of the migrant worker at t2 were measured at the time of occupation of the last known address. If they had not moved, the attributes for t2 were measured for 2012. There was no minimum number of years between t1 and t2.

Who are the migrants; what is their residential orientation at t1 and t2; what kind of residential environment are they relocating to?

Migrants' characteristics

In both city regions, the majority of the better-off international migrants are from countries with advanced economies, but the proportion is much higher in the Amsterdam region (72 per cent) than in the Eindhoven region (53 per cent); in the latter region the proportion of migrants from Central and Eastern Europe is relatively high (Table 12.1[1]). The group of migrants from the BRIC countries is relatively small in both regions. This may be due to the relatively recent rise in the number of migrants from these countries, which may not be reflected in the data used for this study. Migrant workers in both regions tend to be young when

Table 12.1 Nationality and household situation of the better-off international migrant population at t1 and t2

	Total	*Amsterdam Metropolitan Area*	*Eindhoven Metropolitan Region*
Country of origin			
Advanced economies	69%	72%	53%
Central and Eastern Europe	11%	8%	30%
BRICS	6%	5%	8%
Less developed countries	14%	15%	9%
Age at t1 and t2			
Under 30 at t1	46%	45%	50.5%
Under 30 at t2	21%	21%	24%
Household situation at t1			
Single-person household	52%	53%	50%
Two-person household	36%	36%	35%
More than two persons in household	12%	11%	14%
Household situation at t2			
Single-person household	31%	31%	32%
Two-person household without children	30%	30%	26.5%
Household with children	39%	39%	41.5%
Remains single-person household	22%	22%	23%
Household growth	30%	30%	27%
From no children to children	33%	33%	32%
Duration of residence at t1 > 3 years	47%	48.5%	40%
Owner occupier at t1	42%	40%	49%
Owner occupier at t2	54%	56%	48%

Source: See note 1.

they first settle there on arrival from abroad (t1). Almost half were below 30 years of age. This dropped at t2 to around 22 per cent. Upon first entry (t1) about half of the migrant population under study were single-person households, 36 per cent were couples, and 12 per cent had a household of more than two persons. There was little difference between the two regions. At t2, the situation had changed significantly and showed many transformations from single-person households or couples without children to family households.

We also investigated the changing income distribution of the population between t1 and t2 and found that the proportions in the lowest three income deciles had decreased sharply in both city regions, whereas (logically) the four highest deciles had all increased. Around 35 per cent of the international workers had experienced an increase in income. These changes in the household sphere obviously have an impact on where international migrant workers tend to settle.

Residential orientations of better-off international labour migrants

The 'port of entry' of better-off international migrants in the Amsterdam and Eindhoven metropolitan regions is most often directed to urban areas (Table 12.2). In the Amsterdam Metropolitan Area, nearly all migrants (91 per cent) started their housing career in one of the region's urban centres (Amsterdam or Haarlem). In the Eindhoven region (Eindhoven or Helmond) the proportion of urban starters was much smaller (56 per cent); the other 44 per cent started their housing career in one of the region's suburban municipalities, such as Veldhoven, Best and Waalre. This difference is remarkable, since the proportion of urban centres in the total regional population is equal (41 per cent) in both regions. Thus, although in both regions recently arrived better-off international migrants had a stronger tendency toward urban centres than the population in general, this trend was much stronger in the Amsterdam region than in the Eindhoven region. At t2, 88 per cent of the migrants in the Amsterdam Metropolitan Area were still living in Amsterdam or Haarlem. In the Eindhoven region, at t2 a small majority of 51 per cent were living in a suburban area. Thus, whereas the better-off international migrants in the Amsterdam Metropolitan Area are predominantly urban oriented, the migrants who entered the Eindhoven region show much more diversity in their urban–suburban orientation. This finding is in line with the generally more suburban housing preferences of workers in the Eindhoven region that emerged in Chapters 5 and 9.

Although we had expected that many better-off international migrants would prefer rental housing because of the flexibility it gives to them, surprisingly, a high proportion had already opted for an owner-occupied dwelling at their first address upon entry into the two regions. In the Eindhoven region, the proportion of owner-occupiers was 49 per cent; and in the Amsterdam region, 40 per cent. At t2, the proportion of owner-occupiers was much higher in the Amsterdam region, and it had hardly changed in the Eindhoven region. This is, especially for the Amsterdam region, a remarkable finding, since the urban parts of the region in particular have only a limited stock of owner-occupied housing. It shows that the

Table 12.2 Characteristics of the address at t1 and t2

	Total	Amsterdam Metropolitan Area	Eindhoven Metropolitan Region
Location: urban or suburban			
Urban area t1	85%	91%	56%
Suburban area t1	15%	9%	44%
Urban area t2	80%	88%	49%
Suburban area t2	20%	12%	51%
Ownership status			
Owner-occupier at t1	42%	40%	49%
Owner-occupier at t2	54%	56%	48%
Neighbourhood status at t1: with . . .			
Above-average share of low incomes (>37%)	66.5%	67%	64%
Above-average share of high incomes (>25%)	31%	33%	24%
Above-average share of owner-occupied dwellings (>38%)	41.5%	35%	71%
Above-average share of Western migrants (>16%)	46%	53%	9%
Above-average net housing value (>€273,000)	38%	40%	29%

Source: See note 1.

better-off international migrants in that environment have a much stronger orientation to homeownership, as compared to the rest of the population. This may indicate that many better-off international migrants come to the Netherlands with the intention of staying for a long time. However, it may also illustrate that the rental market is not meeting their housing demands.

Regarding the neighbourhood status of the port of entry, around two-thirds of all better-off international migrants appear to start in a neighbourhood with an above-average proportion of low-income households (higher than 37 per cent), with only minor differences between the two regions. These neighbourhoods will likely be among the most accessible. One third begin their housing career in a neighbourhood with an above-average proportion of higher-income households (higher than 25 per cent). In Eindhoven, the proportion starting in a high-income neighbourhood is somewhat smaller.

In the Amsterdam region 35 per cent start in a port of entry with an above-average proportion of owner-occupied dwellings. In the Eindhoven region 71 per cent start in such neighbourhoods. In terms of housing values, in the Amsterdam region 40 per cent start in a neighbourhood with an average net value of over €273,000. In the Eindhoven region, this is only 29 per cent. In terms of socio-cultural status, in the Amsterdam region more than half of the better-off international migrants have their first address in a neighbourhood with an above-average proportion of Western migrants. This goes for only 9 per cent of the better-off internationals in the Eindhoven region.

Relocation or staying put by better-off international migrants

A clear majority (almost three-quarters) of the population that immigrated after January 1994 have relocated at least once during their stay in the Netherlands (Table 12.3). Thus, the final address (t2) is usually different from the port-of-entry address (t1). Only 9 per cent of all better-off international migrants who relocated at least once had left the Netherlands by the beginning of 2013. Of those immigrants who had only one address while staying in the Netherlands, 11 per cent had left the country. However, since the denominators differ, the relative differences between these two percentages are much larger. Of those who relocated at least once, 13 per cent (9/72) left the country; yet, of those who did not relocate 39 per cent (11/28) left the country. This suggests that those who did not resettle were in the Netherlands only temporarily. Differences between the two city regions are small. Of the relocating migrants in the Amsterdam region, 88 per cent stayed within the same region as the port of entry. In the Eindhoven region this was 66 per cent.

Changes in location and neighbourhood status after relocation

Of all those who relocated from a dwelling in the Eindhoven, region 19 per cent moved from an urban to a suburban setting, as against 11.5 per cent in the Amsterdam Metropolitan Area (Table 12.4). This once more suggests that people settling in the Eindhoven region are somewhat more suburban oriented than those settling in the Amsterdam region. The vast majority of all other

Table 12.3 Movers and non-movers within the better-off international migrant population

	Total	Amsterdam Metropolitan Area	Eindhoven Metropolitan Region
Had one address in the Netherlands	28%	27%	30%
. . . and still lives in the Netherlands	17%	16%	19%
. . . and now left the Netherlands	11%	11%	11%
Relocated at least once within the Netherlands	72%	73%	70%
. . . within region	84%	88%	66%
. . . outside region	16%	12%	34%
. . . and still lives in the Netherlands	63%	63%	64.5%
. . . and now left the Netherlands	9%	10%	5.5%

Source: See note 1.

moves were between different urban or different suburban residential milieus, whereas few relocations occurred from suburban to urban areas. These findings also show that better-off international migrants in general stick with their first choice.

With respect to changes in status after relocation, one out of four relocated migrants in the Amsterdam region traded a rented *dwelling* for an owner-occupied dwelling; in the Eindhoven region slightly fewer did so (18 per cent). Most, however, moved within the rented or the owner-occupied sectors. A similar picture emerges when looking at relocations to *neighbourhoods* with a higher proportion of owner-occupied dwellings, as compared to the situation at t1. At t1 more migrants in the Eindhoven region (71 per cent) than in the Amsterdam region (35 per cent) lived in a neighbourhood with relatively many owner-occupied dwellings. However, between t1 and t2, a relocation to a district with relatively more owner-occupied dwellings occurred somewhat more in the Amsterdam region (27 per cent) than in the Eindhoven region (22 per cent). We also looked specifically at relocations to a district with a higher net housing value (WOZ in Dutch), compared to the situation at t1. In the Amsterdam region 25 per cent of all movers experienced this type of upward mobility, which is comparable to movers in the Eindhoven region (21 per cent). Furthermore, we compared the proportion of Western migrants in the total neighbourhood populations at t1 to the neighbourhood at t2 for each relocated migrant. We found that 18 per cent of the better-off international migrants had relocated to a neighbourhood with a higher proportion of Western migrants, with only minor differences between the two regions. The final indicator of upward mobility among movers is relocation to a neighbourhood with a higher proportion of high-income households, as compared to the situation at t1. This was the case for 24 per cent of all relocating better-off

Table 12.4 Changes in location and neighbourhood status after relocation

	Total	*Amsterdam Metropolitan Area*	*Eindhoven Metropolitan Region*
Relocated from urban to suburban	13%	11.5%	19%
Relocated from rental to owner-occupied dwelling	25%	26%	18%
Relocated to neighbourhood with higher share owner-occupied housing	26%	27%	22%
Relocated to neighbourhood with higher net housing value (WOZ)	24%	25%	21%
Relocated to area with higher share of Western migrants	18%	17%	19%
Relocated to neighbourhood with higher share high incomes	24%	21%	30%

Source: See note 1.

international migrants, and occurred somewhat more in Eindhoven (30 per cent) than in Amsterdam (21 per cent). Still, an overall conclusion is that most better-off international migrants did not change their living environment drastically after relocation, either in terms of urban or suburban orientation or in terms of socio-economic status.

Understanding the relocation process

In order to obtain a better understanding of the relocation process, in this section we first elaborate on the changing demographic and socio-economic conditions – at household and at neighbourhood level – that drive relocation in general and then will go into some of the more specific types of relocation (from urban to suburban; towards more affluent neighbourhoods).

Relocating or staying put: which factors drive mobility?

The first (logistic regression) analysis shows which characteristics of better-off international migrants correlate with a higher probability of relocation (Table 12.5). Not surprisingly, young migrant workers at t1 have a higher probability of having relocated at t2. Also, having children between t1 and t2 raises the likelihood of relocating, which is again not a surprise, because more space and child-related services (such as schools and playgrounds) will be required. A long residence at the first address correlates negatively with the chances of relocation; this may point to satisfaction with the first location, but may also be caused by barriers to relocation. A variable for change in income was not included in the model, since a cross-tabulation showed that all respondents who experienced an increase in income had relocated between t1 and t2, which would bias the results strongly. Households without an increase in income are more equally dispersed over the mover and non-mover categories. Still, this finding indicates that income change is a strong predictor for relocation behaviour: a higher income often results in relocation. We did, however, include an indicator for income increase in the analyses on relocations to specific types of districts.

Characteristics of the residential environment at t1 also have an influence on the probability of relocation. Mobility seems to be higher in the Amsterdam Metropolitan Area than in the Eindhoven Metropolitan Region. This may be related to the more urban character of the Amsterdam region. Secondly, living in a neighbourhood with an above-average proportion of high-income households (>25 per cent) is positively and significantly related to the chance of relocation. In the Amsterdam sub-model, better-off international migrants were less likely to relocate if they lived in a neighbourhood with an above-average proportion of Western migrants at t1, suggesting that they might feel at home where there are many other Western migrants. The existence of (expat) communities may play a role here. The non-significance of this factor in the Eindhoven region might be explained by the generally lower concentration of international people within the region.

Table 12.5 Characteristics of better-off international migrants who relocated during their stay in the Netherlands

Dependent variable: relocated between t1 and t2 (or not)	Model a: All Exp(B)	Model b: Amsterdam Exp(B)	Model c: Eindhoven Exp(B)
Migrant from advanced economy (ref: other migrants)	.794	.802	.819
Age at t1 below 30 (ref: age = above 30)	3.256***	3.312***	3.379*
Household change from no children to household with children (ref: rest)	1.926*	2.280*	1.623
Household change from single-person to multiple-person household (ref: rest)	1.192	1.028	1.481
Household change from multiple-person to single-person household (ref: rest)	2.187	1.681	4.399
Owner-occupier at t1 (ref: renter at t1)	.859	.393	.508
Length of residence at t1 > 3 years (ref: < 3 years)	.053***	.043***	.061***
Address at t1 in Eindhoven region (ref: Amsterdam region)	.490*	X	X
Address at t1 is in city (ref: suburban area)	1.224	1.043	1.401
Address at t1 is in neighbourhood with above average % of low incomes	1.619	1.857	.922
Address at t1 is in neighbourhood with above average % of high incomes	2.526*	3.056*	.952
Address at t1 is in neighbourhood with above average % of Western migrants	.575	.439*	9.520
Address at t1 is in neighbourhood with above average net housing value (WOZ)	.903	1.168	.649
Address at t1 is in neighbourhood with above average % of owner-occupied dwellings	.816	.871	.783
Constant	10.000	12.449	1.449
R-square	.467	.496	.520

Source: See note 1.

Note: *** $p < 0.001$; ** $p < 0.01$; * $p < 0.05$

Determinants of relocation from urban to suburban settings

For all better-off international migrants who had moved to another address at t2, we also studied the underlying factors that might help to explain relocation behaviour resulting in changes in their residential milieu. When zooming in on just those households that did (or did not) move from an urban to a suburban area, we see that better-off international migrants in the Amsterdam area whose household changed from one without one with children have a relatively very high likelihood of relocating (Table 12.6). Compared with other households they have an almost eight times higher probability of moving from an urban to a suburban area. Surprisingly, in the Eindhoven model this variable's effect is not significant. This may be related to the, in general, more suburban character of the city of Eindhoven. Also, within the city limits of Eindhoven, many neighbourhoods with single-family dwellings can be found. This contrasts with the more densely built city of Amsterdam, where the urban housing market is dominated by apartments. It is also interesting to see that an increase in household income does not have a significant effect on the move from an urban to a suburban area.

Determinants of relocation towards more affluent areas

We also performed an analysis of the factors that may help in understanding the move to neighbourhoods with a higher net housing value; and separately we also developed models for understanding who is moving to neighbourhoods with more owner-occupied housing; and for moving to neighbourhoods with a higher proportion of high-income households. In the Amsterdam region we see some expected

Table 12.6 Characteristics of better-off international migrants relocating from urban to suburban areas

Dependent variable: relocation from an urban to a suburban area (or not)	Model a: All Exp(B)	Model b: Amsterdam Exp(B)	Model c: Eindhoven Exp(B)
Migrant from advanced economy (ref: rest)	.916	.537	2.329
Age at t2 below 30 (ref: age = above 30)	2.093	3.826*	.000
Household change from no children to household with children (ref: rest)	3.560*	7.858**	.265
Household change from single-person to multiple-person household (ref: rest)	.895	.595	9.796
Household change from multiple-person to single-person household (ref: rest)	3.973	3.228	11.367
Household income (in deciles) increased (ref: income has not increased)	1.028	.602	3.079
Length of residence at t1 > 3 years (ref: < 3 years)	1.294	1.360	.858
Constant	.037***	.036***	.021**
R-square	.083	.178	.271

Source: See note 1.

Note: *** p <0.001; ** p<0.01; * p<0.05

outcomes. Young people have a significantly lower likelihood of moving to such places than older people; households that see their situation change from without children to with children have a three to seven times higher probability of moving to such places than others, and household income increase also has a significant impact on the probability of moving to such neighbourhoods. Age and having children did not emerge as significant factors in the Eindhoven region. However, rising income had much stronger effects in the Eindhoven region than in the Amsterdam region. When the household income increases, people in the Eindhoven area seem to feel a stronger urge to move to more affluent neighbourhoods; to neighbourhoods with a higher proportion of owner-occupied dwellings; and to neighbourhoods with a higher proportion of high-income households than in the Amsterdam region. When household income increases, there is also a significantly larger likelihood that households will move to neighbourhoods with a higher proportion of so-called Western migrants. This effect was significant in both regions, but stronger in the Eindhoven region. It could also be shown that being a migrant from a country with an advanced economy is not relevant, which indicates that Western migrants do not have a stronger tendency than others to locate amongst other migrants – certainly not in the later stages of their housing career in the Netherlands.

Conclusions

This chapter has aimed to find answers to two research questions. In this section, these questions will be answered, before we turn to some overall conclusions and policy recommendations.

Answers to research questions

1. In which types of residential milieu and which types of housing do betteroff international migrants from different countries settle upon arrival in the Amsterdam or Eindhoven regions? And which differences are there between the two regions?

The results of the study show that a large majority of the better-off international migrants in the Amsterdam Metropolitan Area start their residential career in the Netherlands in an urban residential environment, in the cities of Amsterdam or Haarlem. In the Eindhoven region, urban and suburban dwellers are more equally dispersed. Surprisingly, almost half of the dwellings in the ports of entry are owner occupied; and not surprisingly, more in the Eindhoven region (where there are more) than in the Amsterdam region.

In terms of neighbourhood status of the port of entry, the majority of internationals start in a neighbourhood with an above-average proportion of low incomes, but for one third, the port of entry is a high-income neighbourhood. Easy access to such neighbourhoods is likely to explain these beginnings. In terms of housing values, 38 per cent start in a neighbourhood with an above-average net value, but in the Eindhoven region this proportion is somewhat smaller (29 per cent). Finally, a notable difference between Amsterdam and Eindhoven was found to be related to the socio-cultural status of the port of entry. Whereas in Amsterdam more than half of the better-off international migrants start in a neighbourhood with a relatively large concentration of Western migrants, this goes for only 9 per cent of internationals in Eindhoven.

> 2. Which residential patterns, in terms of housing type and residential milieu, can be distinguished in the subsequent relocation behaviour of better-off international migrants? And what differences are there between the two regions?

For 28 per cent of the sample of better-off international labour or study migrants, the port of entry is or was their only address in the Netherlands. This implies that a large majority (72 per cent) have relocated at least once. It was interesting to see that the probability of leaving the country dropped from almost 40 per cent when a household did not relocate, to about 13 per cent after a household had relocated at least once. In terms of location choice, 13 per cent relocated from an urban to a suburban area, and more often in the Eindhoven region (19 per cent). By and large, however, the proportion of urban dwellers at t2 largely resembles that at t1, in both regions, indicating that most relocation take place either within or between cities, or within or between suburban areas. About one quarter moved from a rented to an owner-occupied dwelling, and more in the Amsterdam region than in the Eindhoven region. Also in terms of neighbourhood status, for a majority no great changes in status are experienced after relocation. The chances of upward mobility are larger for those migrants whose household has changed into a household with children or received an increase in income. There are also differences between the two regions. In the Amsterdam region, upward mobility is reflected in a tendency to move to areas with a higher proportion of owner-occupied dwellings. In the Eindhoven region, better-off international migrants more often relocate to districts with a higher proportion of high-income households. These differences can be explained by the fact that the Eindhoven region had a better starting position regarding the proportion of owner-occupied dwellings, while in the Amsterdam region more people lived in higher-income neighbourhoods at t1 than in the Eindhoven region.

Overall conclusions and recommendations

A number of overall conclusions can be drawn based on the analysis of the higher socio-economic strata of labour migrants' ports of entry and relocation patterns. Foremost, in line with the studies on stated preferences, we see large differences between the Amsterdam and Eindhoven regions with regard to the settlement and relocation behaviour of better-off international migrants. Whereas a large majority of workers in the Amsterdam region are urban oriented, the workers in the Eindhoven region are more mixed and settle just as often in suburban as in urban areas. The residential orientation of knowledge workers thus seems to be highly diverse, both between and within regions. In line with the previous studies outlined in Chapters 2 and 3, knowledge workers should therefore not be seen as a homogenous group (e.g. Andersen et al. 2010), and policies targeted at attracting them should take these differences into consideration. There is no 'one size fits all' policy for attracting or retaining knowledge workers, in line with Servillo, Atkinson and Russo (2011). Yet it is interesting that less than two-thirds of all the better-off international migrants we considered had entered the two regions in relatively inexpensive neighbourhoods, while one third had arrived in more expensive neighbourhoods. So there seems to be a function for many cheaper places as well as for some more affluent places.

Another main finding is that although a large majority of better-off international migrants in the two regions (72 per cent) relocated at least once during their stay in the Netherlands, a large majority remained with their first choice in terms of preference for urban or suburban locations. The proportion of suburban dwellers was only slightly higher at the second point of measurement. Of all those who relocated, a minority (13 per cent) moved from an urban to a suburban area, while the number of movements in the opposite direction was very marginal. Most relocations took place from urban to urban areas or from suburban to suburban areas. An interesting finding is that in the Eindhoven region, a larger proportion of better-off international migrants than in the Amsterdam region left the region after relocation.

These findings indicate, on the one hand – and most importantly – that not all international knowledge workers prefer urban settings. On the other hand, the results illustrate that a different type of worker, in terms of residential preferences, settles in the Amsterdam and the Eindhoven regions. In the Amsterdam region, people not only start off in urban areas, but also continue living there after relocation. If we assume that the final address more closely resembles people's actual preferences than the port of entry, workers in Amsterdam are clearly more strongly urban oriented. In the Eindhoven region, both the ports of entry and the second addresses are equally distributed across the region, which indicates more diverse residential preferences among the better-off international migrants in this region. This may be related to the relative dominance of technical sectors in the regional economy.

Relocation is more likely in relation to changes in the household situation, especially when the change is from a household without children to a household with children. Relocation is also, unsurprisingly, more likely at relatively young age. We also found that respondents more often move out of neighbourhoods with an above-average proportion of high-income households. Further research is needed to find whether this implies that they are searching for an even more expensive place to live or that the household is adapting its situation to the neighbourhood situation in another direction as well.

Another main conclusion is that for the majority of internationals no great changes were experienced in terms of homeownership or neighbourhood status after relocation. Each indicator of upward mobility was experienced by at most one quarter of all better-off international migrants. In general, we found that relocation to neighbourhoods with a higher socio-economic status is more likely after an increase in household income, but also happens more often after changes in household size, especially after the birth of children.

The large differences between Amsterdam and Eindhoven regarding both preferences for urban and suburban milieus and the valuation of amenities suggest that different types of policies are needed in each region. Eindhoven, as a tech pole with many suburban residential environments in a green setting, should, based on our results, be highly attractive to the dominant types of workers there. Independent research projects have established the relationship between technical workers and a suburban orientation, irrespective of origin. Kotkin (2000) referred to the green and suburban milieus that would be highly attractive to the more suburban-oriented technical workers and families with children. Musterd (2004) found in empirical research in the Amsterdam region that 'those who represent the financial sector (accountants, bank employees), and those who are active in information, communication and technology, tend to be oriented on [*sic*] suburban locations' (p. 231). If we assume that such types of regularities also hold for the Eindhoven region, the technical profile of the region has a splendid residential environment, at least for the socio-economically better-off. The suburban character seems to be a strength, certainly at the regional level. An explicit focus on the realization of highly urban residential milieus might be a good strategy for those who are employed in sectors that associate more with urban environments, such as the creative industries sector, and also for younger segments of the population. Different cities will have different volumes of employees who will appreciate such milieus. The finding that 34 per cent of all better-off international migrants in Eindhoven leave the region after relocation is somewhat concerning and may be associated with a lack of residential environments for exactly these types of households. More research is needed to find out which types of workers choose to leave the region.

In Amsterdam there is clearly more demand for urban milieus: not only do internationals predominantly start in urban milieus, but also most of them stick to these types of areas after relocation. However, the higher likelihood of relocation to a suburban area after the birth of children indicates that, at least at the regional level, there should be a sufficient diversity in terms of residential milieus. Recently, policies have been developed and are being planned to make the city more attractive to middle-income groups, including family gentrifiers, for example through the sale of social rented dwellings. Although these policies might help to retain families with children in the city, they may in fact exacerbate another problem that emerged in the stated preferences studies (Chapter 9 of this volume): the affordability of housing. In the longer run, such developments may make the city less accessible for mainly younger (international) workers who are (as yet) outside the highest income ranges, but who do – as we have seen – have a strong urban preference and likely must be viewed as 'fresh blood' for innovative urban economies. Our project's finding that two-thirds of all better-off international migrants first settle in relatively inexpensive neighbourhoods,tells a similar story.

Note

1 For all tables in this chapter the source is: Own calculation University of Amsterdam on the basis of micro data provided by Statistics Netherlands, which obtained these from the Municipal Base Administration (demographic data, household and person data, addresses), and from the Housing Register, which contains data originating from the Dutch municipalities.

References

Andersen, KV, Bugge, MM, Hansen, HK, Isaksen, A and Raunio, M 2010, One size fits all? Applying the creative class thesis onto a Nordic context, *European Planning Studies* 18(10), 1591–1609.

Boterman, WR 2012, *Residential practices of middle classes in the field of parenthood.* Amsterdam: Universiteit van Amsterdam.

Hansen, HK and Niedomysl, T 2009, Migration of the creative class: evidence from Sweden. *Journal of Economic Geography* 9(2), 191–206.

Kotkin, J 2000, *The new geography: how the digital revolution is reshaping the American Landscape.* New York: Random House.

Lawton, P, Męczyński, M and Barber, A 2013, Policies towards place attraction and policies for place retention. In: Musterd, S and Kovacs, Z (eds), *Place making and policies for competitive cities*, 105–125. Oxford: Wiley-Blackwell.

Martin-Brelot, H, Grossetti, M, Eckert, D, Gritsai, O and Kovács, Z 2010, The spatial mobility of the 'creative class': a European perspective. *International Journal of Urban and Regional Research* 34(4), 854–870.

Municipality of Eindhoven 2014, *Manifest nieuwe Woonvisie Eindhoven*, Eindhoven: Municipality of Eindhoven,.

Musterd, S 2004, Amsterdam as a creative cultural knowledge city; some conditions. *Built Environment* 30(3), 225–234.

Musterd, S and Murie, A (eds) 2010, *Making competitive cities.* Chichester: Wiley-Blackwell.

Pethe, H and Hafner, S 2013, Internationalisation and policies towards transnational migration. In: Musterd, S and Kovacs, Z (eds), *Place making and policies for competitive cities*, 239–261. Oxford: Wiley-Blackwell.

Regiomonitor Amsterdam 2014, http://regiomonitor.nl, Urban Geography, University of Amsterdam and Department of Research and Statistics, Amsterdam: Municipality of Amsterdam.

Robson, B 1975, *Urban social areas.* Oxford: Oxford University Press.

Scott, AJ 2006, Creative cities: conceptual issues and policy questions. *Journal of Urban Affairs* 28(1), 1–17.

Servillo, L, Atkinson, R and Russo, AP 2011, Territorial attractiveness in EU urban and spatial policy: A critical review and future research agenda. *European Urban and Regional Studies.* Published online 21 December 2011, DOI: 10.1177/0969776411430289.

Storper, M and Manville, M 2006, Behaviour, preferences and cities: urban theory and urban resurgence. *Urban Studies* 43 (8), 1247–1274.

Storper, M and Scott, AJ 2009, Rethinking human capital, creativity and urban growth. *Journal of Economic Geography* 9(2), 147–167.

Van der Zee, FA 2013, Netherlands, Brainport Eindhoven: top technology region spreading its wings. In: OECD (ed.) *Innovation-driven growth in regions: the role of smart specialisation*, 72–78. Preliminary version, Paris: OECD.

Part IV

13 Skills and cities

Jobs and amenities

*Sako Musterd, Marco Bontje
and Jan Rouwendal*

Debates

What helps to stimulate urban economic development? This is a simple yet difficult to answer question that triggers much debate. At present there seem to be two lines of thought, each with its own 'supporters'. On the one hand, there are advocates of 'soft conditions theory', who state that amenities, open social climates, and diversity are the key factors for success. On the other hand, there are scholars who underline the importance of the availability of employment, path-dependent developments, existing personal networks, and so-called 'hard conditions', such as tax incentives, infrastructures, and the like. The opposing views have sometimes resulted in fierce discussion. Clearly, the debates have helped to develop a better understanding of the dimensions and the necessary and sufficient conditions that may be relevant for the development of policies aimed at making cities stronger in economic terms. In this volume we have tried to bring these debates together, while focusing on the residential preferences of high-skilled workers and those employed in creative and knowledge-intensive industries. The aim has been to form a deeper understanding of the stated and revealed preferences of these workers and employees, both for those coming from within the Netherlands and for those coming from abroad (migrants and students).

It is widely known that in the academic literature there was particularly tough comment on the writings of Richard Florida (such as his 2002 book). This may have been tougher than is usual in academic discussion, perhaps because the main frame of reference was North American cities, while other places on the globe, such as European cities, offer very different sets of conditions. In comparison, Europe is more characterised by its fragmented institutional landscape, by multiple languages and national regimes, lower levels of residential mobility, more and deeply embedded historic cities, often with highly attractive inner-city living conditions, very significant cultural differences, and so on. What also played a role was that Florida was seen more as a glamorous marketer than as a serious academic. Moreover, Florida followed a neo-liberal approach and suggested interventions that were predominantly attractive to middle-class and upper-class residents. This quickly resulted in opposite reactions. Florida's suggestion that local policy makers could easily create the creative city, while many established scholars knew from wide experience that this was very unlikely, resulted in clear reactions too. It produced Peter Hall's (2004) response that 'creative cities cannot be created out of thin air'. Others stated that urban (economic) development depends on a complex interplay of agendas dealing with residential space, employment, and recreational domains (Kooijman and Romein 2007). The 'one size fits all' suggestion and the idea that 'best practices' could be copied easily and applied to other situations have been heavily criticised. This went along with a rejection of the idea that cities would be able to attract highly skilled workers by other means than jobs offered by firms. Storper and Scott (2009) argued that lack of growth results from a lack of jobs, rather than from a lack of inflow of people. They also noticed that highly educated people are less mobile than is often presumed (confirmed in an extensive European study by Martin-Brelot *et al.* 2010). The key point is that highly skilled people have invested significantly in their own profiles. Why, then, would they want to move to places with limited employment opportunities? Scott (2006) added to the argument by saying that economic networks and the economic character of a region are much more important for attracting of highly skilled workers than are social and cultural atmospheres. At the same time, almost all those who are involved in the debate still emphasise that the quality of the living environment is also one of the drivers of location choice for skilled individuals (e.g. Storper and Scott 2009).

Jobs and amenities

The contributions in this volume have clarified that jobs *and* amenities play a role in residential decision-making processes. In all cases, work-related amenities and job availability are key factors. However, the historically developed context, with its amenities, is important too, as well as the insight that urban economic success is a process, not a state. The particularities and historically developed special characteristics of cities may actually offer unique competitive advantages; distinctiveness between one city and another can have an impact in the economic competition to attract firms and, with them, employees (Pratt 2008; Musterd and Kovács 2013). In fact, if each city-region were to adopt the same policy measures and focus on the same features and amenities, this would ultimately lead to greater uniformity, and the risk of loss of unique characteristics and competitive advantage (Peck 2012). Specific urban profiles may act as an attracting or repulsing force. Strong urban economies offer employment, which attracts people in search for a job. When the employees, managers and other workers arrive, they start to demand facilities as well. These include, depending on which city you are in, matters such as housing facilities, residential environments, public space of a certain kind, all manner of opportunities to interact with others, educational institutions, and so on. These facilities are not disconnected from economic development, yet nor should they be regarded as a sufficient condition for economic success.

At the regional level, other factors may play a role as well. A certain competition may develop which has an impact on sorting the population across metropolitan space. In Europe, central cities that offer amenities such as well-maintained historic inner cities, or districts with a wide range of urban services, have shown themselves to be attractive to a wide range of households, lately even households with children (Boterman and Karsten 2014). Such a sorting process is not driven by specifically economic factors (which are key to understanding the attraction of individuals and their households to the urban region), but mainly by housing consumption reasons. Even though job availability may come first as a factor in moving to the region, the residential options play an important role as well. This may also be a consideration, at some point, for firms that have to make the decision to locate somewhere. Also, if such provision is not properly taken care of, workers may start looking for another job elsewhere sooner than they otherwise would have done.

In short, both economic opportunities – job availability in particular – and basic social and residential conditions are important for the economic, demographic, and cultural development of metropolitan areas. In this volume we have tried to show what households actually said they preferred in these spheres, while also looking at their actual residential behaviour. The combination of these two approaches has provided insights which may play a role in policy debates on creating conditions for urban economic development. Here we briefly present some of the highlights that we have derived from the various contributions to this volume.

Starting with the results of the first empirical analysis on stated preferences (Chapter 5), we can argue that first of all these support some of the other international comparative research projects carried out in Europe. Both have demonstrated the importance of so-called 'classic' conditions for residential behaviour. These conditions include the presence of jobs that fit the educational level and skills, the stage in the life course, the level of education, and the existence of social networks (i.e. partner, family) that may already have a long history (Grabher 2004; Musterd and Murie 2010; Lawton *et al.* 2013). However, other than work-related factors, amenities also play a role. It was shown that employees or workers in various economic domains prefer different residential environments. Here, in particular the distinction between creative industry workers and those who are involved in high-tech and other knowledge-intensive sectors was investigated. The stated preferences of these two main categories are clearly different, with the former (creative industry workers) being more urban oriented, as compared to the latter (more suburban oriented). Further-refined analysis of those operating in these sectors might result in even more spatial nuances. This is policy-relevant information, because the population structure and the division of workers between different economic sectors may change over time, with repercussions for the types of (urban) environments people ask for.

The question may be raised whether these outcomes are found only in stated preference research, or whether we also find evidence in revealed preference research. The analysis performed in Chapter 6 provides some answers to this question. Here, so-called sorting models have been addressed. An essential element in sorting models, and in those that were presented in Chapter 6, is the potential trade-off between the characteristics of a location. Supporting Roback's (1982) theory, the authors found that indeed there appeared to be trade-off relationships between the level of wages people receive, the housing prices they have to pay, and the urban amenities they might enjoy. If urban amenities in a certain location become better, the house prices may go up, and wages might perhaps go down a bit, because there is compensation through the provision of more interesting places to live.

However, a relevant question is whether there could be a similar trade-off relationship between urban amenities and the availability (or accessibility) of a large volume of (the right) jobs. More concretely, one may wonder whether consumers would still attach a high value to cultural heritage and related endogenous amenities (such as urban atmosphere) if a city were located in an area with a smaller density of jobs. If there were such a trade-off, Florida's suggestions for stimulating urban growth by investing in urban amenities alone would be supported, even when applied in a city like Detroit, where only a limited quantity of jobs are available (which he did!). And if such a trade-off were found to exist, the findings from the stated preference study presented in this volume would be challenged as well. Van Duijn and Rouwendal, in an extension of their 2013 paper, investigated this specific trade-off. Job accessibility was used as an indicator for the local labour market. They put the interaction between an indicator for cultural heritage and a proxy for employment opportunities – the distance to the nearest 100,000 jobs – as a new variable into the model they had already developed. The conclusion was that protected historic areas are especially valued *in combination with* good accessibility of jobs. In other words, investing in urban amenities is especially beneficial in areas where the labour market is already dense. We interpret this as supporting our view that there is primacy of jobs in the preferences of households, stated or revealed. It also implies that strategies for fighting urban decline with investment in urban amenities are risky. As Van Duijn and Rouwendal conclude, 'Urban amenities are especially important in combination with and as a complement to a strong labour market.'

Spatial choice differences: urban and suburban

Large and smaller cities, urban and suburban or rural centres all attract people. They arrive for a new job in the region, or because they want to follow a course of study in one of the educational institutions. The exceptional few just take the risk and arrive without any such objectives, often using existing personal networks to settle somewhere. However, the internal spatial distribution of the type of persons or type of households or type of professions differs for all who settle in the region. That is, in the suburbs we see different professions than in the inner cities, while household types also differ between one place and another within the urban region. This provides information for local policy makers. They have to make sure that there are sufficient supplies of various kinds to respond to the differentiated demand that comes into the region. Ultimately, policies that succeed in combining investment in job availability (firms), in creating a varied set of residential milieus in the right locations, and in providing the amenities that the population asks for, seem potentially to be the most successful.

Creative workers often express housing preferences that reflect their urban orientations. Highly educated professional workers in business services or in technical spheres more frequently prefer suburban locations. From the analysis of existing local studies, and on the basis of the literature review, it was not immediately clear whether the difference in the location preferences of people working in the creative sector and of those in the technical sector should be ascribed to the differing orientations of people in these sectors (creatives might need 'buzz', and technical workers perhaps less so) or simply to their (changing) demographic characteristics. The analysis of stated and revealed preference, as shown in Chapters 5 and 6 and in following chapters, suggested that, indeed, a substantial part of that difference must be ascribed to demographic factors such as raising a family. However, there also appeared to be an independent effect of the sector in which people are employed. This is evident from multivariate analysis, after controls for the demographic situation, in both the research based on stated and on revealed preferences. It was confirmed that those who are oriented toward technical jobs appreciate the typical urban environment less than do those who are oriented toward creative jobs. This difference in tastes contributes to the over-representation of skilled workers belonging to the latter group in the inner cities of metropolitan areas and in those metropolitan areas that have a particular lively central city, such as Amsterdam. People employed in creative industries do seem to have a stronger preference for urban living, as compared to those employed in technical or other knowledge-intensive spheres.

What if?

The modelling exercises in this volume, where sorting models are used in combination with economic scenarios and future population and housing projections, provide even more input for policy makers, as well as information on possibly changing preferences (such as a stronger urban orientation of households that formerly had a weaker urban orientation). The simulation models dealt with in Chapter 7, in which such information is combined, produce interesting results, here often translated into effects on the willingness to pay for certain dwellings in certain locations. Among other things, the chapter predicted large price effects between regions, assuming a change in the housing supply between regions, or a change in other regional characteristics, such as the proportion of nature, based on scenarios produced by independent institutions. Changing preferences may also have a large effect. For example, if the urban orientation of households increases substantially, strong price effects will be noticeable, especially in historic city districts. Predictions also considered changes in the regional distribution of specific household types due to changing prices and differences in household types in terms of their willingness to pay for housing in certain locations. Finally, the models also facilitate calculating the impact of changes in local conditions. In general, the models can answer a range of 'what if' questions, such as: what will be the price effects if the proportion of apartment buildings is doubled in municipality X? Or what will be the effects if all other municipalities in the province do the same?

International migrants

International migrants' stated and revealed preferences were focused on in Part III. Starting in Chapter 9 with an analysis of the stated preferences of this category, it was found that the often-temporary stay of international migrants is reflected in less car ownership (and thus greater use of public transport); in greater demand for all-in housing and for apartments; in more urban housing in the vicinity of workplaces and more rented accommodation; in general, more urban spaces with ample facilities; and good access to airports. Internationals from advanced economies are somewhat more urban oriented than those from other countries. As with the native Dutch, the differences between workers in the creative industries and in the technical spheres, in terms of stated preferences, are very clear, the former being more urban oriented, as compared to the latter, who in general prefer suburban housing. The lack of available and affordable housing was mentioned as a significant problem by both natives and international migrants, but was seen as a bigger problem by the latter. It is true that they have no access to social housing, and in a local market like that of Amsterdam where half of the stock is social housing this will have accessibility effects in general. However, as already noted, the empirical studies in this volume show that, due to the specific set of characteristics of international workers, they also have more specific residential orientations, and dwelling needs that deviate somewhat from the 'native' demand. The quality and location of the dwelling near to their work, as well as the service levels in and around the dwelling appear to be of major importance and, due to the fact they often stay for a limited period of time, they also need to be able to rent.

Dutch and international knowledge workers showed a fair degree of agreement on a range of aspects of their housing situation. For example, they saw a quiet residential environment as a key condition for attractive living. They saw housing attributes such as price, space and ownership as more important than neighbourhood attributes. However, with reference to the neighbourhood, native Dutch more often mentioned the composition of the population, while internationals mentioned the proximity of facilities for daily shopping and proximity to work and to the city centre as decisive location factors.

These findings too have important policy implications. We observed that policy makers are biased toward meeting the demands of the most urban among the international migrants and focus on urban amenities and cultural services. They therefore direct their interventions toward young, predominantly childless migrants in creative industries, from advanced economies. Knowledge workers in technical professions, often living in family households and from a broader range of origins, often express a preference for single-family suburban housing, but even though they are a majority, they receive less policy attention. The plans in Amsterdam and Eindhoven to enlarge the central urban residential milieu and to continuously building on their 'urban' profile' (high density, cultural events) may be 'good plans'. However, local policy needs also to respond to suburban demand and keep an eye on the balance that is needed to facilitate the entire, heterogeneous group of international knowledge workers. Investments in urban residential milieus should go side by side with investments in suburban milieus.

International students

An important category of international migrants with significant potential impact on the urban creative knowledge economies is students. In this volume (Chapter 10), three questions specifically aimed at students' preferences were addressed: why are students selecting the Netherlands as a place to study? What are their choices with regard to HEIs in the Netherlands, as compared to local students' choices? And what are the location preferences (choice of residential municipalities) of international students in the Netherlands, during studies and after graduation, and their tendency to stay in the Netherlands after graduation? Crucial findings were that countries with a high level of GDP per capita, many top-ranked universities and a high score on the quality of life indicators (as reflected by life expectancies) are all features of the most attractive destinations for international students. As to the choice for a certain institution for higher education, the study showed that all international students prefer to study in a municipality with a high percentage of foreigners. They also seem to prefer places where knowledge spill-over between HEIs and industry can be found and where employment opportunities are best. This likely is also at the basis of the spatial orientation of immigrant students. Some three-quarters of the international students in the study live in only 15 municipalities. Over 20 per cent of all international students coming to the Netherlands settled in the Amsterdam area. A little under half of the students who arrive in the Netherlands for study purposes remain in the country for at least five years, and most of them stay in the municipality where they registered upon their arrival. Their residential orientation after finishing their study is characterised by accessibility to employment, the presence of a significant community of immigrants and places that are rich in terms of cultural heritage. For policy, this implies that international students are indeed a potential source of highly skilled labour which can be absorbed by the local economy, provided that the local economy has the right assets. Their willingness to remain in a certain location is determined not just by the presence of a university. Other conditions are crucial as well.

Work-related and consumption-related amenities for international migrants

Detailed analysis of how individuals value work-related and consumption-related amenities (Chapter 11) has produced several interesting findings. For example, the location preferences of skilled migrants appear to be rather similar to those of the highly educated natives and more dissimilar to those of otherwise 'identical' low-skilled migrants. This was found for work-related amenities (number of jobs or accessibility) and for preferences for other urban amenities, such as historical monuments and nature. Compared to all other groups, highly educated migrants show the highest willingness to pay extra for historic city centres and buildings.

In particular, they pay large amounts of money in municipalities with large historic centres. This finding may be useful for urban policy makers who wish to attract and retain foreign-educated workers. They would be well advised to create opportunities for job growth, but they would also benefit from the preservation of historic districts. The proportion of migrants in the municipality is an attraction factor as well (if it is not too large). Policy makers could stress that value; and at the same time reduce the negative effects by encouraging language-proficiency courses. This may reduce communication barriers.

Settling and resettling

Regarding the settlement and resettlement process, international migrants show a diversified picture, as was shown in Chapter 12. The majority of internationals' 'port of entry' neighbourhoods appear to be low-income, affordable and accessible neighbourhoods; such inexpensive neighbourhoods clearly have an important function. Yet, more than one third of internationals make a high income neighbourhood their port of entry, indicating that there is also demand for such environments. A large majority (around 70 per cent) left their first place of settlement in the following years. If they relocated, the probability that they would stay in the Netherlands was much higher (about 87 per cent) than that of those who did not relocate, where only 60 per cent remained.

The differences between Amsterdam and Eindhoven are substantial. In Amsterdam, better-off migrants turn out to be more urban oriented than in Eindhoven, where they settle more in suburban environments. International knowledge workers are not a homogeneous group. Therefore there is no one-size-fits-all policy for this group. A very important finding is that not all international migrants prefer an urban residential milieu, even if they arrive for a job in the Amsterdam and Eindhoven metropolitan areas. Housing needs should be investigated per context. In tech poles, like Eindhoven, there may be a stronger preference for suburban residential milieus than in cities which have a strong creative industries sector, where the urban dimension stands out. Yet, even in the metropolitan area of Amsterdam there is a sustained need for suburban milieus as well, not just because many households will sooner or later form a family but also because of the different spatial orientations of different professional categories.

Ongoing debate and additional research

International migrants in general have become part of the current urban environments around the globe. The internationalization of economic processes and increased opportunities to migrate from A to B have resulted in significant flows of migrants searching for life chances in places with prospects. Nowadays, the prospects of places are not only connected to larger cities because of their agglomeration advantages. It is recognised that on top of that, local amenities may make a difference as well. However, additional research is required to investigate to what extent amenities are connected to economies of agglomeration. Work-related amenities, such as the number of jobs available or the accessibility of workplaces or accessibility to production- and consumption-related services may all have some relationship to the agglomeration of certain economic activity. Moreover, where large agglomeration advantages are present, there will also be more services and more cultural amenities, such as theatres, restaurants and interesting public spaces. The potential interrelation between economies of agglomeration and urban amenities and the conditional development of each of these fields requires further, longitudinal, research.

Another area for future research is the position of the less-affluent. Policies currently focus on large-scale investments and development in highly-urban residential milieus, and on stimulating urban amenities in particular. This not only prioritises the provision of more expensive accommodation for affluent sections of the population, but also neglects the needs in less-urban areas. In addition, the policies seem to have negative consequences for young and starting creative knowledge workers. These starters are often young and urban oriented, yet they are increasingly unable to compete with the policy makers' target groups. Consequently, they face increasing difficulty in finding accessible and affordable housing in the parts of the city that are most attractive to them. Nevertheless, they are essential for the continuation of the cycle of urban economic development. Much innovation comes from newcomers and the just-graduated. They require attention too.

References

Boterman, WR and Karsten, L 2014, On the spatial dimension of the gender division of paid work in two-parent families: the case of Amsterdam, the Netherlands. *Tijdschrift voor Economische en Sociale Geografie* 105(1), 107–116.

Florida, R 2002, *The rise of the creative class and how it's transforming work, leisure, community and everyday life*. New York: Basic Books.

Grabher, G 2004, Learning in projects, remembering in networks? Communality, sociality, and connectivity in project ecologies. *European Urban and Regional Studies* 11(2), 103–123.

Hall, P 2004, Creativity, culture, knowledge and the city. *Built Environment* 30(3), 256–258.

Kooijman, D and Romein, A 2007, The limited potential of the creative city concept: policy practices in four Dutch cities. Draft based on a presentation and paper at the 'Regions in focus' conference in Lisbon.

Lawton, P, Murphy, E and Redmond, D 2013, Residential preferences of the 'creative class'? *Cities* 31(2), 47–56.

Martin-Brelot, H, Grossetti, M, Eckert, D, Gritsai, O and Kovács, Z 2010, The spatial mobility of the 'creative class': a European perspective. *International Journal of Urban and Regional Research* 34(4), 854–870.

Musterd, S and Kovács, Z (eds) 2013, *Place-making and policies for competitive cities*. Chichester: Wiley-Blackwell.

Musterd, S and Murie, A 2010 (eds) *Making competitive cities*. Oxford: Wiley Blackwell.

Peck, J 2012, Recreative city: Amsterdam, vehicular ideas and the adaptive spaces of creativity policy. *International Journal of Urban and Regional Research* 36(3), 462–485.

Pratt, AC 2008, Creative cities: the cultural industries and the creative class. *Geografiska Annaler B* 90(2), 107–117.

Roback, J 1982, Wages, rents and the quality of life. *Journal of Political Economy* 90, 1257–1278.

Scott, AJ 2006, Creative cities: conceptual issues and policy questions. *Journal of Urban Affairs* 28(1), 1–17.

Storper, M and Scott, AJ 2009, Rethinking human capital, creativity and urban growth. *Journal of Economic Geography* (9), 147–167.

Van Duijn, M and Rouwendal, J 2013, Cultural heritage and the location choice of Dutch households in a residential sorting model. *Journal of Economic Geography* 13, 473–500.

Index

For Product Safety Concerns and Information please contact our EU
representative GPSR@taylorandfrancis.com
Taylor & Francis Verlag GmbH, Kaufingerstraße 24, 80331 München, Germany

www.ingramcontent.com/pod-product-compliance
Ingram Content Group UK Ltd.
Pitfield, Milton Keynes, MK11 3LW, UK
UKHW021013180425
457613UK00020B/932

* 9 7 8 0 3 6 7 8 7 0 9 0 4 *